高职高专"十二五"规划教材

新编外贸英语函电
New English Correspondence for Business

- 伊辉春 主　编
- 张　蓓　朱娇燕 副主编
- [英] Leslie Taylor 主　审

U0419178

化学工业出版社
·北京·

全书共有 1 个简介和 10 个按照谈判主题划分的单元。每个单元包括 9 部分，大致可分为写作技巧指导、常用词语与语句、信函范例与套写、案例与写作任务、练习等几类。单元设计以"模拟套写"为指导，以电子邮件、站内信为载体，以真实交易过程为案例，全面培养学生阅读和撰写外贸英语信函的能力，并注重职业素质养成。书中所选的常用语句高频通用，划分细致清楚，查找方便快捷，结合写作指导使得信函撰写过程真正实现了"模拟套写"。书中案例背景清晰，谈判环节步步递进，往来信件连贯，把工作任务和写作任务融为一体，写作任务明确，写作指导具体，让函电教学真正形成了"教学做合一"的模式。

本书是国际贸易及相近专业的外贸英语函电教材，可供相关专业的师生和从事相关专业工作的人员学习参考。

图书在版编目 (CIP) 数据

新编外贸英语函电/伊辉春主编. —北京：化学工业出版社, 2016.3（2021.1重印）
ISBN 978-7-122-26064-2

Ⅰ.①新… Ⅱ.①伊… Ⅲ.①对外贸易-英语-电报信函-写作 Ⅳ.①H315

中国版本图书馆 CIP 数据核字(2016)第 011562 号

责任编辑：蔡洪伟　于　卉　王　可　　　　　　　文字编辑：龙　婧
责任校对：王素芹　　　　　　　　　　　　　　　　装帧设计：刘丽华

出版发行：化学工业出版社（北京市东城区青年湖南街 13 号　邮政编码 100011）
印　　装：三河市延风印装有限公司
710mm×1000mm　1/16　印张 16　字数 321 千字　2021 年 1 月北京第 1 版第 5 次印刷

购书咨询：010-64518888　　　　　　　　　　　　售后服务：010-64518899
网　　址：http://www.cip.com.cn
凡购买本书，如有缺损质量问题，本社销售中心负责调换。

定　　价：32.00 元　　　　　　　　　　　　　　　　　版权所有　违者必究

编写人员名单

主　　编　伊辉春

副 主 编　张　蓓　朱娇燕

编写人员　伊辉春　张　蓓　朱娇燕
　　　　　　蔡文芳　谢文琴　朱岱霖

前言

外贸英语函电，传统意义上是指纸质信函、电报、电传等，而如今是指电子邮件、网站站内信、微信、短信等。通讯方式的转变带来了信函格式、信函语言的转变，这对教材改革提出了新的要求。

一、本书的特点

1. **新颖** 本书信函以电子邮件、站内信为载体，格式新。语句与时俱进，符合即时通讯语言。"模拟套写"的单元设计令人耳目一新，别具一格。

2. **真实** 案例真实，交易背景清晰，把工作任务和写作任务融为一体。外贸谈判环节具体明了，辅以相关单证，真实展现了外贸交易过程。

3. **实用** "模拟套写"是教育部对本课程的教学指导原则。本书摆脱了传统教材大篇幅讲解词句的通识语言教学模式，转而采用了模拟套写的职业英语教学模式。单元内的各部分都是围绕"模拟套写"设计而成的。各部分之间互相补充，互相支撑，把信函撰写过程从传统的翻译改变成了"词块"组装。经过教学实践验证，"模拟套写"的教学模式高效实用。学生通过反复地研读、加工和抄写，对常用语句掌握更加牢固，所套写出来的语句准确度高，信函质量高，用时短。

二、教学建议

本书内容看起来难度大，但只要实施正确，则教学过程轻松愉快，可以收到事半功倍的效果。

1. **我该怎么说** 单元内"我该怎么说"部分是为了模拟套写常用语句而设计的。这部分在形式上与传统的"汉译英"相似，但教学中切不可当成翻译来操作。建议按以下步骤实施：

（1）按照"谁""做""什么""事"的顺序，引导学生理清句子的功能和结构。例如，"请务必尽早开立相关信用证"，应归类为"出口商""催促""信用证""开立"；

（2）依据以上类别，在"信用证"单元的"常用语句集"里查找到对应的语句，选择最相近的一个；

（3）对所选语句进行截取、替换、拼接、填补、删减等简单必要的加工，就可以得到所需要的语句。

2. **信函撰写任务** "案例"部分中的邮件撰写任务是模拟套写的综合练习，撰写时要防止学生逐句翻译案例背景。教学中应当首先确定信文的撰写要点，然后按要点理清句子功能结构,再按照结构类别在"常用语句集"里查找最相近的语句,按需要加工,最后一句放到信文中去。

3. **跟我写** 这部分是通过填补的办法来练习如何套写信函,教学中建议首先熟悉其"贸易背景",然后再看"电子邮件模板"。

4. **仿照例句补全句子** 这是"实训写作"部分中套写语句的练习题,旨在训练学生熟悉、应用加工语句的方法,如截取、替换、拼接、填补、删减等。教学中必要时要引导学生查阅更多参考语句,以扩大可参考的示范例句范围。

本书由伊辉春任主编,张蓓、朱娇燕任副主编。伊辉春编写了"简介""报盘与还盘""订单"和"支付"四单元和各单元中的"跟我写""常用语句集"两部分;张蓓编写了"信用证""装运"和"投诉与索赔"三单元;朱娇燕编写了"询价与回复"和"保险"两单元;蔡文芳编写了"建立外贸关系"单元;谢文琴编写了"包装"单元;朱岱霖参与了编写。

本书由英国国际贸易专家 Leslie Taylor 博士任主审,业界马永红女士参与了审稿。

本书"模拟套写"的教学思路是本课程教材改革的一次大胆尝试,加之编者水平有限,书中难免有疏漏和错误,敬请专家、广大师生、外贸专业人士批评指正。

本书配有电子课件和参考答案,授课教师可通过 Email(53624002@qq.com)免费索取。

本书配套教材《外贸常用语句汇编》提供完整全面的外贸常用语句,有意向者可向出版社订购。

编者
2015 年 11 月

Contents

Introduction (简介) ·· 1

Part Ⅰ. International Business Correspondence（外贸书面通信的方式）················ 1
   1. 电子邮件 ··· 1
   2. 传真 ··· 5
   3. 站内信 ··· 5
   4. Skype ··· 7
Part Ⅱ. Business Correspondence Writing （信件的撰写）······························ 8
   1. 传统外贸书信的撰写原则 ··· 8
   2. 当下外贸信件的特点 ··· 8
   3. 外贸信件的撰写技巧 ··· 8
Part Ⅲ. Practical Writing（实训写作）··· 9
Part Ⅳ. Glossary of Common Sentences （常用语句集）····························· 11

Unit 1　Establishing Business Relations (建立外贸关系) ············ 14

Part Ⅰ. Objectives（目标）·· 14
Part Ⅱ. How to Express（我该怎么说）··· 14
   1. Making Self-Introduction（出口商自我介绍）···························· 14
   2. Requesting for Establishing Business Relations（进口商寻求建交）···· 15
   3. Asking for Information and Samples（进口商索要资料与样品）········ 15
Part Ⅲ. Case（案例）·· 16
   1. Requesting for Product Information（进口商索要产品资料）············ 16
   2. Replying to the Request for Product Information（出口商回复索要产品资料）··· 17
   3. Requesting for Credit Status（出口商要求提供资信证明）·············· 18
   4. Replying to the Request for Credit Status （进口商回复请求提供资信证明）··· 19
   5. Asking for Agency（进口商请求充当代理）······························ 20

6. Offering an Agency（出口商任命代理）······ 21
Part Ⅳ. Writing Directions（写作指导）······ 22
Part Ⅴ. Terms and Sentence Frames （术语与句型）······ 25
  1. Terms（术语）······ 25
  2. Sentence Frames（句型）······ 26
Part Ⅵ. Follow Me （跟我写）······ 29
Part Ⅶ. Practical Writing （实训写作）······ 30
Part Ⅷ. Linkage（知识链接）······ 32
Part Ⅸ. Glossary of Common Sentences （常用语句集）······ 34

Unit 2　Enquiry and Reply（询价与报价）······ 39

Part Ⅰ. Objectives（目标）······ 39
Part Ⅱ. How to Express（我该怎么说）······ 39
  1. Wishing to Buy（进口商寻购）······ 39
  2. Specific Enquiry （进口商具体询价）······ 40
  3. Responding Enquiries （出口商回复询价）······ 40
Part Ⅲ. Case（案例）······ 41
  1. Establishing Business Relations（出口商寻求建立贸易关系）······ 41
  2. Enquiry（进口商询价）······ 42
  3. Replying to Enquiry（出口商回复询价）······ 43
Part Ⅳ. Writing Directions（写作指导）······ 44
Part Ⅴ. Terms and Sentence Frames （术语与句型）······ 45
  1. Terms（术语）······ 45
  2. Sentence Frames（句型）······ 47
Part Ⅵ. Follow Me （跟我写）······ 49
Part Ⅶ. Practical Writing （实训写作）······ 50
Part Ⅷ. Linkage（知识链接）······ 52
Part Ⅸ. Glossary of Common Sentences （常用语句集）······ 54

Unit 3　Offer and Counteroffer（报盘与还盘）······ 58

Part Ⅰ. Objectives（目标）······ 58
Part Ⅱ. How to Express（我该怎么说）······ 58

  1. Offer（出口商报盘） ·· 58

  2. Counteroffer（进口商还盘） ·· 59

  3. Asking for a Reduction in Price（进口商要求降价） ······················ 59

 Part Ⅲ. Case（案例） ··· 60

  1. Establishing Business Relations（出口商寻求建立贸易关系） ········ 60

  2. Enquiry（进口商询盘） ·· 61

  3. Making an Offer（出口商报盘） ··· 62

  4. Reply to Offer（进口商对报盘的回复） ··· 63

  5. Counteroffer（进口商还盘） ·· 64

 Part Ⅳ. Writing Directions（写作指导） ··· 65

 Part Ⅴ. Terms and Sentence Frames（术语与句型） ······························ 66

  1. Terms（术语） ·· 66

  2. Sentence Frames（句型） ··· 68

 Part Ⅵ. Follow Me（跟我写） ·· 70

  1. Offer（出口商报盘） ·· 70

  2. Counter-offer（进口商还盘） ··· 71

 Part Ⅶ. Practical Writing（实训写作） ·· 73

 Part Ⅷ. Linkage（知识链接） ··· 75

 Part Ⅸ. Glossary of Common Sentences（常用语句集） ························ 76

Unit 4　Order（订单） ··· 83

 Part Ⅰ. Objectives（目标） ·· 83

 Part Ⅱ. How to Express（我该怎么说） ·· 83

  1. Placing an Order（进口商下订单） ··· 83

  2. Accepting an Order（出口商接受订单） ··· 84

  3. Refusing an Order（出口商拒绝订单） ··· 84

 Part Ⅲ. Case（案例） ··· 85

  1. Placing a Repeat Order（进口商续订） ·· 85

  2. Refusing an Order（出口商拒绝订单） ··· 86

  3. Placing an Order（进口商下订单） ··· 87

  4. Accepting an Order（出口商接受订单） ··· 88

  5. Concluding a Contract (进口商签合同) ·· 89

 Part Ⅳ. Writing Directions（写作指导） ··· 90

 Part Ⅴ. Terms and Sentence Frames（术语与句型） ······························ 91

  1. Terms（术语） ·· 91

  2. Sentence Frames（句型） ··· 92

Part Ⅵ. Follow Me （跟我写） ········· 94
　　　1. Placing an Order （进口商下订单） ········· 94
　　　2. Accepting an Order （出口商接受订单） ········· 95
　　Part Ⅶ. Practical Writing （实训写作） ········· 96
　　Part Ⅷ. Linkage （知识链接） ········· 99
　　Part Ⅸ. Glossary of Common Sentences （常用语句集） ········· 100

Unit 5　Payment（支付） ········· 104

　　Part Ⅰ. Objectives （目标） ········· 104
　　Part Ⅱ. How to Express （我该怎么说） ········· 104
　　　1. Enquiring about Payment （进口商询问付款方式） ········· 104
　　　2. Asking for Easier Payment Terms （进口商要求宽松的付款方式） ········· 105
　　　3. Urging Payment （出口商催促付款） ········· 105
　　Part Ⅲ. Case （案例） ········· 106
　　　1. Urging Payment （出口商催促付款） ········· 106
　　　2. Informing of Paid （进口商通知已付款） ········· 106
　　　3. Informing of Payment Received （出口商通知收到货款） ········· 107
　　　4. Requesting for Payment Terms （进口商要求付款方式） ········· 108
　　　5. Declining the Request for Payment （出口商拒绝更改付款方式） ········· 109
　　　6. Agreeing to Payment Terms （进口商接受付款方式） ········· 110
　　Part Ⅳ. Writing Directions （写作指导） ········· 111
　　Part Ⅴ. Terms and Sentence Frames （术语与句型） ········· 113
　　　1. Terms （术语） ········· 113
　　　2. Sentence Frames （句型） ········· 114
　　Part Ⅵ. Follow Me （跟我写） ········· 115
　　Part Ⅶ. Practical Writing （实训写作） ········· 116
　　Part Ⅷ. Linkage （知识链接） ········· 119
　　Part Ⅸ. Glossary of Common Sentences （常用语句集） ········· 120

Unit 6　Letter of Credit（信用证） ········· 126

　　Part Ⅰ. Objectives （目标） ········· 126
　　Part Ⅱ. How to Express （我该怎么说） ········· 126
　　　1. Urging Establishment of L/C （出口商催开信用证） ········· 126

  2. Advising Establishment of L/C（进口商通知已开证） ··· 127
  3. Asking for L/C Amendment （出口商要求改证） ··· 127
  4. Asking for L/C Extension （出口商要求展证） ··· 128
 Part Ⅲ. Case（案例） ·· 128
  1. Urging Establishment of L/C（出口商催开信用证） ··· 128
  2. Advising Establishment of L/C（进口商通知已开立信用证） ································ 129
  3. Asking for amendment to L/C（出口商要求改证） ·· 133
  4. Responding to L/C Amendment（进口商回复信用证修改） ··································· 133
  5. Asking for L/C Extension（出口商要求展证） ·· 134
 Part Ⅳ. Writing Directions（写作指导） ·· 135
 Part Ⅴ. Terms and Sentence Frames （术语与句型） ··· 136
  1. Terms（术语） ·· 136
  2. Sentence Frames（句型） ··· 137
 Part Ⅵ. Follow Me （跟我写） ·· 138
  1. Asking for Amendment to L/C （出口商请求进口商修改信用证） ······················· 138
  2. The L/C Extended（进口商延展信用证） ··· 140
 Part Ⅶ. Practical Writing （实训写作） ··· 141
  1. Match the words and phrases with their Chinese meanings. ································ 141
  2. Read the following email and list the sentence patterns applied. ······················· 141
  3. Complete each of the following sentences according to its model given. ············ 142
  4. Complete the following mail with words and phrases given in the box. ············· 143
 Part Ⅷ. Linkage（知识链接） ·· 143
 Part Ⅸ. Glossary of Common Sentences （常用语句集） ·· 145
  1. 出口商 ·· 145
  2. 进口商 ·· 148

Unit 7　Packing（包装） ·· 150

 Part Ⅰ. Objectives（目标） ·· 150
 Part Ⅱ. How to Express（该怎么说） ·· 150
  1. Introducing Packing（出口商说明包装） ·· 150
  2. Raising Packing Requirements（进口商提出包装要求） ······································ 151
  3. Mark Instruction（进口商提出唛头和标志语刷制要求） ····································· 151
 Part Ⅲ. Case（案例） ·· 152

1. Raising Packing Requirements（进口商提出包装要求） ········· 152
2. Introducing Customary Packing （出口商说明包装惯例） ········· 153
3. Accept Packing Method（进口商接受包装方式） ········· 154
4. Mark Instructions（进口商提出刷唛要求） ········· 155
5. Agreeing with Marking Requirements （出口商接受刷唛要求） ········· 156

Part Ⅳ. Writing Directions（写作指导） ········· 157
Part Ⅴ. Terms and Sentence Frames （术语与句型） ········· 158
  1. Terms（术语） ········· 158
  2. Sentence Frames（句型） ········· 160
Part Ⅵ. Follow Me （跟我写） ········· 161
Part Ⅶ. Practical Writing （实训写作） ········· 162
Part Ⅷ. Linkage（知识链接） ········· 164
Part Ⅸ. Glossary of Common Sentences （常用语句集） ········· 165

Unit 8　Shipment　（装运） ········· 171

Part Ⅰ. Objectives（目标） ········· 171
Part Ⅱ. How to Express（该怎么说） ········· 171
  1. Shipping Instruction（进口商发出装运指示） ········· 171
  2. Amending Shipment（出口商更改装运） ········· 172
  3. Urging Shipment（进口商催促装运） ········· 172
  4. Asking for Postponing Shipment （出口商请求延迟装运） ········· 173
  5. Shipping Advice （出口商发出装船通知） ········· 173
Part Ⅲ. Case（案例） ········· 174
  1. Shipping Instruction（进口商发出装运指示） ········· 174
  2. Acknowledging Receipt of Shipping Advice（出口商收到装运指示） ········· 175
  3. Urging shipment（进口商催促装运） ········· 176
  4. Sending Shipping Advice（出口商发送装船通知） ········· 177
Part Ⅳ. Writing Directions（写作指导） ········· 179
Part Ⅴ. Terms and Sentence Frames （术语与句型） ········· 180
  1. Terms（术语） ········· 180
  2. Sentence Frames（句型） ········· 182
Part Ⅵ. Follow Me （跟我写） ········· 183
  1. Replying to Urging Shipment（出口商回复装运催促） ········· 183
  2. Asking for Shipping Amendment （出口商要求更改装运） ········· 185

Part Ⅶ. Practical Writing （实训写作） ··· 186
Part Ⅷ. Linkage（知识链接） ··· 188
Part Ⅸ. Glossary of Common Sentences　（常用语句集） ······················· 189

Unit 9　Insurance （保险） ·· 198

Part Ⅰ. Objectives（目标） ··· 198
Part Ⅱ. How to Express（该怎么说） ··· 198
　1. Introducing Insurance Practice　（出口商介绍保险惯例） ················· 198
　2. Making Demand on Insurance（提出投保要求） ······························ 199
　3. Notifying of Insurance Effected（出口商通知已投保） ····················· 199
Part Ⅲ. Case（案例） ·· 200
　1. Accepting Order（出口商接受订单） ··· 200
　2. Enquiring for the Usual Insurance Practice（进口商咨询投保事宜） ····· 201
　3. Introducing Usual Insurance Practice（出口商说明保险惯例） ············ 202
　4. Making Demand on Insurance（进口商提出投保要求） ····················· 203
　5. Notifying of Insurance Effected（出口商通知已投保） ····················· 204
Part Ⅳ. Writing Directions（写作指导） ··· 205
Part Ⅴ. Terms and Sentence Frames （术语与句型） ······························ 206
　1. Terms（术语） ·· 206
　2. Sentence Frames（句型） ·· 208
Part Ⅵ. Follow Me （跟我写） ··· 209
　1. Entrusting with Insurance （进口商委托代办保险） ························ 209
　2. Accepting to Arrange Insurance （出口商同意代办保险） ················· 210
Part Ⅶ. Practical Writing （实训写作） ·· 211
Part Ⅷ. Linkage（知识链接） ··· 213
Part Ⅸ. Glossary of Common Sentences　（常用语句集） ······················· 215

Unit 10　Complaints and Claims (投诉与索赔) ······························ 219

Part Ⅰ. Objectives（目标） ··· 219
Part Ⅱ. How to Express（该怎么说） ··· 219
　1. Making a Complaint（进口商投诉） ·· 219
　2. Dealing with Complaints　（出口商处理投诉） ······························ 220
　3. Lodging a Claim （进口商索赔） ·· 220
　4. Settling Claim（出口商理赔） ··· 221

  5. Rejecting Claims（出口商拒绝赔付） ·· 221
 Part Ⅲ. Case（案例） ·· 222
  1. Complaining of Wrong Delivery（进口商投诉货物错发） ················ 222
  2. Dealing with Wrong Delivery（出口商处置货物错发） ····················· 223
  3. Making a Claim（进口商索赔） ··· 224
  4. Accepting Claim（出口商同意理赔） ··· 225
 Part Ⅳ. Writing Directions（写作指导） ·· 226
 Part Ⅴ. Terms and Sentence Frames（术语与句型） ································· 227
  1. Terms（术语） ··· 227
  2. Sentence Frames（句型） ··· 228
 Part Ⅵ. Follow Me（跟我写） ·· 229
  Making a Claim(进口商为包装破损索赔) ·· 229
 Part Ⅶ. Practical Writing（实训写作） ·· 230
 Part Ⅷ. Linkage（知识链接） ··· 233
 Part Ⅸ. Glossary of Common Sentences（常用语句集） ························· 234

参考文献 ··· 241

Introduction (简介)

Part Ⅰ. International Business Correspondence（外贸书面通信的方式）

随着通讯技术的高速发展和电子商务的兴起，外贸英语书面通信方式从传统的纸质书信、电报、电传、传真演变过渡到了当今的电子邮件、网络交易平台站内信、短信等。通信手段摆脱了缓慢、费时的传统纸质邮寄，进入了通过互联网即时发送、接受信息的即时通信（Instant Message，简称 IM）时代。

即时通信时代带来了多种多样的网络即时通信工具，这些工具软件安装在电脑和手机上，只要网络畅通，即时交流的渠道就畅通。网络即时通信软件不断更新换代、互相替代，目前在外贸书面通信中最常用的有 Skype、微信（WeChat）、腾讯QQ、TradeManager 等。

1. 电子邮件

目前，英语电子邮件是外贸谈判中使用最频繁、最广泛的书面沟通方式。电子邮件除了速度快、使用简单以外，还便于存档、转发和检索。各类文件，包括文本、图片、音频、视频等，可以通过电子邮件的附件发送给对方，可以帮助买卖双方顺利签署贸易合同。

电子邮件的样例

发件人（From）	Lin Tiantian<Lintiantian@mail.lewawa.com>
收件人（To）	Johnson@yaoo.com
抄送（Cc）	
暗送（Bcc）	salesmanager@mail.lewawa.com
主题（Subject）	Offer for 10,000 small-sized plush monkey toys
附件（Attachment）	An offer sheet

Dear Mr. Johnson,

Thank you for your enquiry yesterday, asking for a 10,000-pieces quotation of our small-sized plush monkey toys made in Jiangsu.

Please find our attached offer sheet. Don't hesitate to let me know if you need any more information.

Best regards
Lin Tiantian
Sales Manager

****

Suzhou Lewawa Toys Co., Ltd.
96　West Street　Wuzhong District　Suzhou　P. R. C. 215000
Email: Lintiantian@mail.lewawa.com
Tel: 0086-512-66866969
Fax: 0086-512-66866868
https://www.lewawa.com
苏州乐娃娃玩具有限公司
地址：中国江苏省苏州市吴中区西大街 96 号
邮编：215000

电子邮件的格式

发件人（From）	（写信人的电子邮箱地址）
收件人（To）	（收信人的电子邮箱地址）
抄送（Cc）	（其他收信人的电子邮箱地址）
暗送（Bcc）	（其他收信人的电子邮箱地址）
主题（Subject）	（电子邮件正文的标题）
附件（Attachment）	（发给收信人的附带文件）

```
（称呼）
（正文）


（结尾敬语）
（署名）
（职位）
*******************************

（发件人的信息，如公司名称、地址、电话、传真以及公司网站、部门负责人等）
```

电子邮件的格式一般都采用齐头式。正文段落之间要有较大的行距，一般是空一行。

电子邮件的格式越来越个性化。越来越多的贸易拥有自己统一的邮箱，统一设置了电子邮件格式。从邮箱抬头、正文、落款到其段落间距、行距、缩进幅度、字号、字体等都做了固定的设计和编排。发件人只要打开邮箱一开始写信，每一部分都会自动进入所预设的格式，邮箱抬头、邮件落款处的署名和公司通讯方式都会自动显示，发件人无需一一输入。

电子邮件的组成部分

1）发件人（From）。写信人的电子邮箱，无需写信人输入，系统会自动生成。

2）收件人（To）。收信人的电子邮箱，需要写信人输入。收件人可以是多个，中间用分号隔开。

3）抄送（Cc）。其他收信人的邮箱。发件人将此邮件发给收件人的同时，如需另发给其他人，就要在此输入被抄送的邮箱。收件人收到邮件后，知道此邮件被抄送给了哪些人。

4）暗送（Bcc）。其他收件人的邮箱。发件人如需将此邮件另发给其他人，又不希望收件人知道，在此输入被暗送的电子邮箱。

5）主题（Subject）。电子邮件正文的标题。收件人打开邮箱，在收件箱列表中首先看到发件人的电子邮箱地址和主题。主题力求简洁有力、清晰具体，要达到一目了然的效果。主题不需要写成完整的句子，不一定非要有主语、谓语或宾语，句尾不加标点符号。

外贸电子邮件的主题十分重要，尤其是促销邮件，如果没有主题，很容易被当成垃圾邮件处理掉。必须注意，主题一定要使用英语，不要使用汉语，汉语在对方的电脑上会变为乱码显示。

6）称呼与结尾敬语。称呼位于正文之前，结尾敬语位于正文之后，二者之间往往是关联的。

十分尊敬、正式的关系

称呼	结尾敬语
Dear Mr. General Manager,（职位：总经理） Dear Mr. President,（职位：会长）	Yours very truly, Very truly yours, Respectfully, Respectfully yours, Yours sincerely, Sincerely yours,

一般关系

称呼	结尾敬语
Dear Mr. Bush,（姓，男性） Dear Mrs. Bush,（已婚女性） Dear Miss Bush,（未婚女性） Dear Ms. Bush,（未知婚否女性）	Sincerely, Yours sincerely, Yours truly, Best regards, Best wishes, Cordially, Cordially yours,

十分亲近的商业伙伴

称呼	结尾敬语
Dear Mary,（名） Hi, Mary,	Best regards, Best wishes, Regards, Kindest regards, Warm regards, All the best,

未知的人士

称呼	结尾敬语
Dear Sir/Madam,（无名、无姓） Dear Sirs,	Yours very truly, Yours faithfully,

电子邮件的称呼和结尾敬语越来越具个性化，不过，专业人士认为商业电子邮件毕竟不同于私人电子邮件，称呼应当采用"Dear"，不要用"Hello""Hi"甚至"Hello all"，结尾敬语要标准通用。

称呼和结尾敬语的后面，习惯上都要加逗号。

7）署名。署名包括发件人的姓名和职位，各占一行。

8）发件人的信息。发件人的信息，如公司名称、地址、电话、传真以及公司网站、部门负责人等，位于署名之后。发件人打开邮箱一开始写邮件，企业统一邮箱都会自动显示这部分，发件人无需输入。

2. 传真

外贸通信当中，虽然传真已经大幅让位于电子邮件，但是，由于传真不存在感染病毒和被黑客拦截的风险，需要保密的一些单据和文件依然通过传真来传输。传真可以传递打印的、手写的或签字的文件，用于传输订单、发票、装箱单、提单、价格表、信用证、报价、工程图纸及数据表格等。

传真没有固定的格式，但传真出去的文件应该附有一份封面，封面一般包括以下内容。

1）发件人的姓名。
2）发件人的地址、传真号码、电话号码。
3）收件人的姓名。
4）收件人的传真号码。
5）收件人的公司与部门。
6）传真的页数（包括封面页）。
7）主题和文号。

传真封面样例

BEIJING SPORTS COMPANY （公司名）	
From (发件人)： Mr. Wang	Receiver (收件人)： Mr. Smith
Department（部门）	To（收件人公司）：ABC Company
TEL（电话）：0086-10-85666666	TEL（电话）：0021-66-6566653
FAX（传真）：0086-10-85666688	Fax (传真)：0021-66-6572849
Subject（主题）：Offer	Pages（页数）：2 （Including this page）
Date (日期)：2015/8/18	
Ref. No.（文号）：F0 1216-01	Ref. No.（文号）：

3. 站内信

随着互联网交易网站的蓬勃兴起，大量贸易通信通过交易网站本身的内部交流渠道进行，这就是站内信。实际上，站内信是另一种形式的电子邮件，它像电子邮件一样可以发信文也可以寄送附件。

阿里巴巴站内信界面

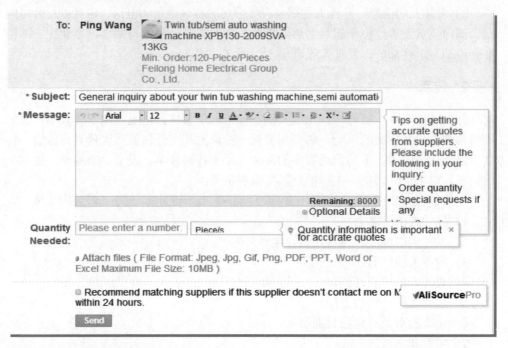

阿里巴巴站内信正文样例

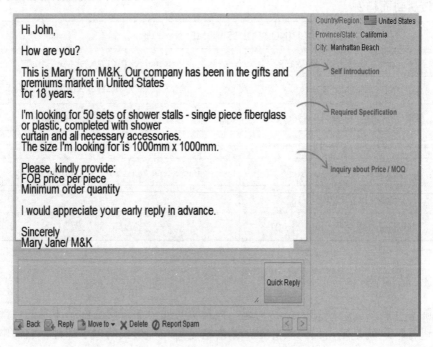

速卖通站内信界面

4. Skype

Skype 是外贸当中常用的交流工具，其文字聊天界面直观简单，使用普遍。

Skype 的文字聊天界面

Introduction (简介)

其实，Skype 真正受欢迎的原因还不在于此，作为一款实时通信软件，它的功能十分强大。Skype 可以视频聊天、语音会议、多人聊天、传送文件等，可以免费高清晰与其他用户语音对话，可以直拨固话、手机，可以呼叫转移、发送短信等。只要网络顺畅，其音质可以超过普通电话。

Skype 于 2003 年 8 月问世至今，被认为是最受欢迎的网络免费电话。2013 年 3 月，微软在全球范围内关闭了 MSN Messenger，由 Skype 取代。Skype 增速惊人，至 2014 年已占据 40% 的国际电话市场。

Part II. Business Correspondence Writing
（信件的撰写）

不论通信方式如何转变，外贸英语信件的撰写总是遵循一定的原则。

1. 传统外贸书信的撰写原则

传统上，外贸英语书信的撰写原则有"3C""6C"和"7C"之说，归纳起来就是：正确（Correctness）、清楚（Clearness）、礼貌（Courtesy）、具体（Concreteness）、简要（Conciseness）、体谅（Consideration）、完整（Completeness）。传统外贸英语书信的撰写原则对于互联网时代的外贸英语信件撰写依然有着巨大的指导意义。

2. 当下外贸信件的特点

口语化

口语化是当下外贸信件英语的显著特点，特别是微信、短信、文字语聊等，双方的交流是一问一答式的，语言轻松随意，可以添加表情符号。口语化式的语言加上表情符号，能迅速拉近双方的距离，是顺利交流的强化剂。

简短化

互联网通信手段速度快，可以随时发送和即时接收，一事一议，这使信文和语言变得非常简短。传统书信由于往来周期长，写信人为了撰写不遗漏，就必须做到面面俱到，因而信文长，语言书面性强。

3. 外贸信件的撰写技巧

为了更好地开展外贸书面交流，写好外贸英语信件，我们应该做到以下几个方面。

1）充分领会传统外贸英语书信的撰写原则，要数据正确、表述清楚、客气礼貌、明确具体、宁短勿长、换位思考、信息完整。

2）交流前要深思熟虑、胸有成竹，要仔细研究对方的兴趣与利益，交流时要有成熟的决策。语言的编辑要仔细谨慎。因为信息的发送只在一点击之中，一经发出对方即可收到，无法修改、无法追回。

3）虽然外贸交流趋向于轻松自然，但毕竟不同于私人交流，它代表着公司的形象，因此，交流的信件，尤其是电子邮件，要正式规范，不要使用表情符号，不要随意使用缩略词，语气要适当，态度诚恳有礼貌。

4）在无把握的情况下，英语措辞切勿采用逐字逐句的英汉翻译，要参照相似或相近的常用英语语句，采用替换、删减、增补、拼接等简单的加工方法。

5）养成良好的撰写习惯，打开拼写检查要防止拼写错误，回复邮件时要注意修改主题，添加附件时要仔细检查防止发错和漏发，点击发送之前要检查。

写好外贸英语信件需要长期不懈的努力。除了读书学习之外，在工作中我们要学习、收集客户的优秀英语信件和优秀语句。对自己已发送的信件，我们要适时回顾，要发现问题，并修改提高。

Part Ⅲ. Practical Writing（实训写作）

把下面各部分分别填写到所给的电子邮件页面框里。

发邮件人

名字：	Fanny Fang
职位：	Sales Manager
公司名称：	Ningbo Bright Lighting Equipment Co. Ltd.
公司地址：	9 Xuefu Rd. Yinzhou District, Ningbo, P. R. China
邮编：	315100
电话：	0086-574-88101234
传真：	0086-574-88101235
电子邮箱：	fangping@nbbrightlighting.com
微信：	123456_PaulFang
Trade Manager：	Paulfang123456 （online time: 12:00am-18:00pm）
SKYPE：	v5.0.0.49777（online time: 12:00am-18:00pm）

收邮件人

名字：	Tony Green
电子邮箱：	TonyGreen@yahoo.com

邮件

称呼：	Dear Mr. Green
结尾敬语：	Yours sincerely
主题：	Thank You for Your Interest in Our Solar Lights
附件：	Company Profile

正文：

We are delighted to learn of your interest in our solar lights. We have specialized in these areas for 14 years and we are vendor of solar lights to Home Depot.

As you know, Home Depot is one of the most famous retailers dealing in solar powered lights. Our solar powered LED lights, solar lights, solar yellow flashing lights, solar cell phone charger, solar flash lights and solar power supply system are all included in the range of products on sale in Home Depot.

Find attached our company profile. Please do not hesitate to contact us for further information.

电子邮件页面框

发件人（From）	
收件人（To）	
主题（Subject）	
附件（Attachment）	

Part IV. Glossary of Common Sentences
（常用语句集）

敦促		It will be highly appreciated（十分感谢）if you give this matter your immediate attention（尽快办理此事）.
敦促		Kindly give this matter your prompt attention. 烦请尽快关注此事。
敦促		We hope you take our suggestion into serious consideration（认真考虑我方建议）。
鼓励	联系	For any information, please don't hesitate （犹豫）to ask me.
鼓励	联系	If you need any further information, please contact （联系）us.
鼓励	联系	Please do not hesitate to contact us if we can be of any assistance（提供帮助）.
鼓励	联系	Please feel free to contact us again if you have any further questions. 如还有疑问，请尽管联系我们。
鼓励	联系	Should you have other questions, please let me know. 如还有疑问，请告知我。
回复		This is in reply to your enquiry of July 6. 兹回复您7月6日的咨询（询价）。
回复		With regard to your enquiry for August 8, we wish to give the following in reply. 关于你方8月8日的咨询，我方回答如下。
回复		It's good to know that everything is going well at your end. 得知你方一切顺利，我很高兴。
回复		Thank you for your email/message. 谢谢您的邮件/短信。
回复		This is in answer to…
回复		This is in response（回答） to your…
期盼	回复	I look forward to hearing from you soon. 期待尽快收到您的回复。
期盼	回复	Please let me know as soon as possible. 请尽快告知我。
期盼	回复	We are anticipating（期盼） your answer.
期盼	回复	We are looking forward to receiving your reply at your earliest convenience. 期待尽早收到回复。
期盼	回复	We are waiting for your feedback（反馈、回复）.
期盼	回复	We await your news with keen interest. 我方热情期待您的消息。
期盼	回复	We expect your early reply. 盼尽早回复。
期盼	回复	We hope to receive your reply at an early date. 盼早日回复。
期盼	回复	We look forward to receiving your favorable reply/response. 期待收到您肯定的回复。
期盼	回复	Will you kindly let us have an early decision? 恳请早日告知我们你方决定。
期盼	回复	Your prompt reply will be greatly appreciated. 如能尽快回复将不胜感激。
收到		We wish to thank you for your fax（传真）of…

收到		We have your message（短信）of...
收到		We have your text（短信）of...
收到		We are in receipt of your letter of 7th July. 我方收到你方7月7日的来信。
收到		Thank you for your enquiry（询价、咨询）for...
收到		We have duly（按时，及时）received your email（邮件）of 5th March.
收到		We have pleasure in acknowledging（确认）the receipt（收到）of your email of 7th July.
收到		We have received your email dated...
遗憾		It is a matter for regret that we cannot ... 十分遗憾我方不能……
遗憾		It is a pity that you cannot ... 很遗憾你方不能……
遗憾		It is most regrettable（遗憾）that...
遗憾		We are regretful（遗憾）that...
遗憾		We are very sorry（遗憾）to know ...
遗憾		We express our regret at ... 我方对……深表遗憾。
遗憾		We regret to inform you ... 很遗憾地告知您……
愿意		It gives us pleasure to do... 我们乐意做……
愿意		It is a pleasure to do... 乐意做……
愿意		It is with pleasure to do...乐意做……
愿意		We are delighted（高兴）to do...
愿意		We are glad（高兴）to do...
愿意		We are happy（高兴）to do...
愿意		We are pleased（高兴）to do...
愿意		We have the pleasure（高兴）in doing...
愿意		We have the pleasure（高兴）of doing...
愿意		We have the pleasure（高兴）to do...
致谢		I appreciate your kindness and hospitality. 谢谢你的友好和热情款待。
致谢		I can't express my gratitude enough. 我怎么表达感激之情也不过分。
致谢		I really can't thank you enough. 我实在对你感谢不尽。
致谢		I truly appreciate it. 我真的很感激。
致谢		It was really kind of you. 你人真好。
致谢		It was so thoughtful of you. 你真体贴人。
致谢		Thank you again for your interest in our company. 再次感谢您对我公司的关注。
致谢		Thank you for the information on your products. 感谢你的产品信息。

续表

致谢		Thank you for your attention to this matter. 感谢您对这一问题予以关注。
致谢		Thank you for your understanding. 感谢您的理解。
致谢		Thank you in advance for your assistance. 提前感谢您的协作。
致谢		Thank you in advance for your cooperation. 提前感谢您的合作。
致谢		Thank you in advance for your kind attention. 提前感谢您的关注。
致谢		Thank you very much for your interest in our company. 非常感谢您对我公司的关注。
致谢		Thank you very much. 非常感谢。
致谢		Thanks for all your efforts. 谢谢你所做出的努力。
致谢		Thanks so much. 多谢。
祝福	假日	I hope that your holiday season is filled with joy and laughter. 祝你假期快乐欢愉。
祝福	假日	I hope you have a wonderful holiday season! 祝你假期过得愉快！
祝福	假日	I wish you health and happiness in the coming year! 祝你明年身体健康、生活愉快！
祝福	假日	I would like to wish you all the best for a wonderful holiday season! 祝你假期快乐，一切顺利。
祝福	假日	We send you our very best wishes for the holidays. 我们寄去最诚挚的祝福，祝您假期愉快！
祝福	假日	We would like to wish you and your family a happy holiday season. 我们祝您和您的家人假期愉快。
祝福	节日	Happy Easter! 复活节快乐！
祝福	节日	Happy Halloween! 万圣节快乐！
祝福	节日	Happy Hanukkah! 光明节快乐！
祝福	节日	Happy Holidays! 节日快乐！
祝福	节日	Happy New Year! 新年快乐！
祝福	节日	Happy Thanksgiving! 感恩节快乐！
祝福	节日	Happy Valentine's Day! 情人节快乐！
祝福	节日	I wish you a Merry Christmas and a Happy New Year! 祝你圣诞快乐、新年快乐！
祝福	节日	May all the joys of Christmas be yours! 祝圣诞节愉快！
祝福	节日	May the coming year bring you happiness, health and prosperity. 祝您在新的一年快乐、健康、兴旺。
祝福	节日	May your new year be filled with health and happiness. 祝您在新的一年里身体健康、生活愉快。
祝福	节日	Merry Christmas! 圣诞快乐！

Unit 1
Establishing Business Relations (建立外贸关系)

Part Ⅰ. Objectives (目标)

After completing this unit, you will be able to

1. know how to establish business relations with new customers by writing English emails;

2. write English emails and messages to express your wishes to establish business relations with new customers, introduce your products to your buyers, promote the sales of your products, ask about the credit status of a new client, or request for goods information from sellers, etc.;

3. know the essential components needed in above emails and messages;

4. become familiar with the typical English terms and sentence patterns commonly used in above emails and messages.

Part Ⅱ. How to Express (我该怎么说)

1. Making Self-Introduction (出口商自我介绍)

A：我是卖方，向新客户发邮件，要做自我介绍。我该怎么说呢？
B：你可以这样说：
1）我是宁波阳光户外家具有限公司的玛丽，通过广交会认识了您。
2）我是宁波永达汽车配件有限公司的汤姆，在阿里巴巴网站上看到您求购汽车刹车片，这正好是我们的经营范围。
3）我是浙江好利服饰有限公司的爱丽丝，您的老朋友王先生把您介绍给我。
A：那么，我用英语该怎么说呢？

B：到"常用语句集"去看看，你先找到同类的句型，然后采用截取、替换、拼接的办法稍做加工，你需要的句子就有了。

A：嘿！瞧瞧，我的英语还不错吧！

----

2. Requesting for Establishing Business Relations（进口商寻求建交）

A：我是买方，我找到了新客户，希望与对方建立外贸关系，开展业务合作。我该怎么说呢？

B：你可以这样说：

1）我从贵公司的网站上看到你们的避震器，特发邮件想了解详细的情况。

2）我从中国驻英大使馆商务参赞处得知贵公司，特发邮件期望与贵方建立贸易关系。

3）我们专营汽车轮胎的进口业务，愿与你们进行交易。

A：那么，我用英语该怎么说呢？

B：到"常用语句集"去看看，你先找到同类的句型，然后采用截取、替换、拼接的办法稍做加工，你需要的句子就有了。

A：嘿！瞧瞧，我的英语还不错吧！

----

3. Asking for Information and Samples（进口商索要资料与样品）

A：我是进口商，想了解对方的产品，希望得到对方的产品资料和样品。我该怎么说呢？

B：你可以这样说：

1）我对贵公司产品很感兴趣，能否发送一份产品目录。

2）对于相机包，能否提供免费样品？

3）为了更好地了解贵公司产品，请贵方能附件发送详细资料。

A：那么，我用英语该怎么说呢？

B：到"常用语句集"去看看，你先找到同类的句型，然后采用截取、替换、拼接的办法稍做加工，你需要的句子就有了。

A：嘿！瞧瞧，我的英语还不错吧！

Part Ⅲ. Case（案例）

1. Requesting for Product Information（进口商索要产品资料）

怀特家具有限公司（White Furniture）位于美国波士顿，为了满足北美家具市场上日益兴起的中式家具热，现正考虑从中国市场寻购中式家具。进口部经理 Johnson White 先生从《今日家具》（Magazine Furniture Today）上找到了一家中国广州的家具出口商——东莞大明家具有限公司。Johnson 访问了该公司网站后，对胡桃木系列（walnut range）家具产生了极大兴趣，于是，决定发电子邮件寻求建立业务关系，并索要全套胡桃木家具的详尽资料。

现在，你是 Johnson，你需要发邮件给东莞大明家具有限公司，对方的电子邮箱为 Exporter@damingfurniture.com，收件人姓氏未知，你的电子邮箱为 Jonhsonwhite@yahoo.com。

Sentence Patterns for Reference（参考语句）

➢ 进口商说明信息来源，表达订购愿望；

➢ 进口商介绍己方公司，索要商品资料；

➢ 进口商期盼回复。

发件人（From）	
收件人（To）	
主题（Subject）	

2. Replying to the Request for Product Information（出口商回复索要产品资料）

东莞大明家具有限公司收到了波士顿怀特家具有限公司索要产品资料的邮件，出口部经理齐芬芬女士马上回复了邮件。邮件首先表示感谢，然后按照对方的要求通过邮件附件向对方寄送全套电子介绍资料——目录（Catalog）、价目表（Price List）和产品介绍（Product Literature）。

作为销售方，齐芬芬觉得这是适度宣传自己公司、促销自己产品的一个大好时机。在满足了对方要求后，她简单介绍了自己公司的发展、生产、市场和主要产品系列，最后期盼对方下试订单。

发件人（From）	Exporter@damingfurniture.com
收件人（To）	Jonhsonwhite@hotmail.com
主题（Subject）	Thank You for Your Enquiry
附件（Attachment）	1. Catalog 2. Price List 3. Product Literature

Unit 1 Establishing Business Relations (建立外贸关系)

Dear Mr. White,

We are so glad that you are interested in our furniture of walnut range. Attached are the latest catalogue, export price list and product literature which will tell you everything about our walnut range as well as other ranges we deal with.

Although established in 2006, we are developing very fast. We pay great attention to design and product quality. We have introduced advanced production equipment from Germany and Italy. Our products are exported to many countries and areas in Americas and the Middle East. The U.S. is our largest market. The two series of "Black Walnut" and "Golden Walnut" are our top sellers.

We look forward to your trial order.

Yours sincerely,

Qi Fenfen

Exporter Manager

Sentence Patterns Applied（语句归纳）
- 出口商感谢咨询，附件寄送产品资料、价目单；
- 出口商介绍己方公司、业务、市场；
- 出口商期盼订购。

3. Requesting for Credit Status（出口商要求提供资信证明）

波士顿怀特家具有限公司通过多番了解和对比，决定先试订胡桃木家具，向东莞大明家具有限公司下10万美元的订单。

（订单邮件略）

东莞大明家具有限公司收到了订单。因为这是与对方的首次合作，且交易量比较大，东莞大明家具有限公司认为有必要调查其资信状况。于是，齐芬芬回复邮件，请求对方提供开户行名称，并承诺一旦查询结果令人满意将立即运作订单。

发件人（From）	Exporter@damingfurniture.com
收件人（To）	Jonhsonwhite@yahoo.com
主题（Subject）	Request for Your Credit Status
附件（Attachment）	

> Dear Mr. White,
>
> We have received your order for walnut range to the value $100,000 with thanks.
>
> Since this is the first order between us, we would highly appreciate it if you could provide us with your bank name. As long as we receiver your credit information from your bank and it is satisfactory, your order will be executed immediately.
>
> We sincerely hope to start long and pleasant business relations with you.
>
> Yours sincerely,
>
> Qi Fenfen
>
> Exporter Manager

Sentence Patterns Applied（语句归纳）
- 出口商收到订单，致谢；
- 出口商请求提供资信证明方（银行名称），承诺运作订单；
- 出口商期盼良好合作关系。

4. Replying to the Request for Credit Status （进口商回复请求提供资信证明）

波士顿怀特家具有限公司收到对方要求提供资信证明的邮件后，Johnson White 马上回复邮件表示理解，欣然提供了公司开户银行的名称与联系方式，并另外提供了两家合作多年的友好贸易公司，以证明自己公司的良好资信状况。开户行与两家公司的名称与联系方式如下：

1）波士顿银行（Boston Bank），地址：波士顿皇家路180号（No. 180, Royal Road, Boston, USA），电话：001-617-566-974，网址：www.Bostbank.com；

2）上海飞虹贸易有限公司（Shanghai Feihong Trading Company），地址：上海西厢路98号（No. 98, Xixiang Road, Shanghai），电话：0086-21-33552266，邮箱：feihong@163.com；

3）凯斯比股份有限公司（Kisby & Co. Ltd.），地址：利物浦13号林森广场28-30楼（28-30/F Latham Square, Liverpool, 13），电话：0044-151-232-356，邮箱：Crisby@yahoo.com。

现在，你是波士顿怀特家具有限公司的Johnson White，你根据以上情况需要向东莞大明家具有限公司回复邮件。

Sentence Patterns for Reference（参考语句）
- 进口商提供资信证明方；
- 进口商列举证明方名称及联系方式（三家）；
- 进口商介绍与证明方的关系；
- 进口商期盼联系证明方。

发件人（From）	
收件人（To）	
主题（Subject）	
附件（Attachment）	

---

5. Asking for Agency（进口商请求充当代理）

波士顿怀特家具有限公司与东莞大明家具有限公司建立了良好的贸易关系，交易量稳步上升。

一年后，波士顿怀特家具有限公司请求在波士顿独家代理销售东莞大明家具有限公司的胡桃木系列家具，而东莞大明家具有限公司以时机尚不成熟为由谢绝了。

一年半后，怀特再次发来邮件，要求为东莞大明家具有限公司充当独家代理（sole agent），帮助其在波士顿批发销售胡桃木家具系列。邮件中说，波士顿怀特家具有限公司已经具备了（be entitled to）独家代理胡桃木家具系列的实力，已经打开了当地市场，形成了可观的销售规模（sizable volume）。邮件还说，如果被授予代理，不但销售规模还有提升，还能帮助出口方消除经不同渠道销售所造成的报价差

（discrepancies）。最后，邮件请求东莞大明有限公司草拟独家代理协议（an exclusive agency agreement）的条款，同意授予他们波士顿独家代理。

发件人（From）	Jonhsonwhite@yahoo.com
收件人（To）	Exporter@damingfurniture.com
主题（Subject）	Request for Sole Agency
附件（Attachment）	

Dear Ms. Qi,

We wish to thank you for your cooperation and assistance over the past 18 months in the sales of your walnut range.

You may recall that last July we brought up the proposal to be your sole agent for your walnut range in Boston. Now we send this email to you again with the same purpose, because we think we are entitled to do so for having built up a sizable volume of business in your products in this market. Such an agreement would not only facilitate our sales promotion, but would also eliminate unnecessary discrepancies between your offers when you are selling through different channels.

If you agree with our proposal, please outline the terms on which you will be prepared to enter into an exclusive agency agreement with us.

We await your favorable reply.

Yours sincerely,

Johnson White

Importer Manager

Sentence Patterns Applied（语句归纳）
- 进口商回顾过去的良好合作，感谢；
- 进口商回顾之前的磋商，请求充当代理商，劝导接受请求（介绍己方的市场、对方产品的销售前景及成本）；
- 进口商敦促草拟代理协议；
- 进口商期盼回复。

6. Offering an Agency（出口商任命代理）

东莞大明家具有限公司经研究，决定授命波士顿 White 家具有限公司为波士顿地区的胡桃木家具系列的独家代理，具体事宜交由出口部经理齐芬芬负责协商，代理条款可参照北美其他地区的代理商协议。于是，齐芬芬起草了一份代理协议，发邮件与对方商谈。

发件人（From）	Exporter@damingfurniture.com
收件人（To）	Jonhsonwhite@yahoo.com
主题（Subject）	Sole Agency for Walnut Range in Boston
附件（Attachment）	A Draft of Agreement

Dear Mr. White,

Thank you for your proposal of acting as a sole agency for our walnut range. Having examined our mutually beneficial collaboration in the past 18 months, we would be very pleased to entrust you with the sole agency for walnut range in Boston.

Attached is the draft of our agreement. Please examine the detailed terms and conditions and let us know whether they meet with your approval.

Yours sincerely,

Qi Fenfen

Exporter Manager

Sentence Patterns Applied（语句归纳）

- 出口商收到愿充当代理的请求，致谢；
- 出口商同意委托代理；
- 出口商寄送协议，请求审议；
- 出口商期盼回复。

Part Ⅳ. Writing Directions（写作指导）

建立外贸关系是开展外贸业务的第一步。不论是出口商还是进口商，都需要主动开拓市场，寻求客户，以便建立更广泛的外贸关系。

出口商寻求建立外贸关系

出口方寻求建立外贸关系的信函包括以下内容：
- ➢ 说明得知对方公司信息的来源；
- ➢ 表达建立外贸关系的愿望；
- ➢ 介绍己方公司、业务等；
- ➢ 介绍产品；
- ➢ 传送电子资料、目录等；
- ➢ 鼓励询价；
- ➢ 期盼回复。

进口商寻求建立外贸关系

进口商寻求建立外贸关系的信函包括：
- ➢ 说明获得对方公司的信息来源；
- ➢ 说明打算进口某产品的意图；
- ➢ 索要产品资料、样品；
- ➢ 介绍己方公司；
- ➢ 提供自己公司的资信状况及证明人；
- ➢ 期盼回复。

出口商回复进口商请求

出口商回复进口商请求建交的信函通常包括：
- ➢ 回应对方的信函；
- ➢ 表示愿意与对方合作；
- ➢ 介绍自己公司；
- ➢ 介绍自己产品；
- ➢ 寄送介绍资料；
- ➢ 期盼回复。

出口商促销

促销信函实际上是一种产品广告。一封好的促销信应具备这四条准则：①吸引客户的注意力；②引起客户的兴趣；③激发客户的购买欲；④促成客户的购买行动。促销信可包括：
- ➢ 说明信息来源；
- ➢ 介绍己方公司；
- ➢ 介绍产品；
- ➢ 介绍价格优势、优惠条件、支付方式、售后服务等；
- ➢ 劝导进一步了解；
- ➢ 提供了解渠道；

- 传送电子资料；
- 承诺；
- 劝导客户采取行动。

促销的信函要开门见山，直奔主题，态度要真挚诚恳，语气要委婉礼貌。介绍自己的公司要客观正面，扬长避短，如有知名客户可以列举一二。在介绍自己的产品时要突出特点和优势。

不要对陌生的欧美客户群发促销信，否则，会被当作垃圾邮件删除，并被拉入黑名单。

进口商请求充当代理

进口商请求充当代理的信函内容有：
- 请求充当代理；
- 回顾良好的合作（对新客户介绍己方公司、提供资信状况）；
- 阐述己方的优势、代理的前景；
- 提议代理期限、区域、权限、佣金等；
- 期盼回复。

出口商委托代理

出口商同意委托代理的信函包括以下内容：
- 感谢来函；
- 同意委任对方为代理；
- 寄送代理协议，期待会签；
- 期盼回复。

委托代理的信函，可将代理性质、期限、地区、付款方式、佣金、销售额等重要条款起草成一份协议，通过邮件附件发送给对方，正文可不细述。

授权代理是供货方对购买商的肯定答复。如果要谢绝对方，需要说明原因，期待以后合作或进行其他方面的合作。

出口商寻求代理

出口商主动寻找代理商时，信函的内容可包括：
- 表达寻求代理的意图；
- 回顾双方的友好合作（对新客户说明得知对方信息的来源）；
- 介绍己方产品；
- 提出代理商应具备的条件；
- 展望前景，劝导对方接受；
- 寄送代理协定；
- 期盼回复。

为了使正文简洁，代理条款通过附件文件传送，正文不细述。

Part V. Terms and Sentence Frames
（术语与句型）

1. Terms（术语）

贸易商
buyer 购买商
seller 销售商
importer 进口商
exporter 出口商
vendor 供应商
retailer 零售商
wholesaler 批发商
agent 代理商
sale agent 销售代理人
trader 经销商
distributor 经销商

代理
agency 代理
general agency 总代理
agency agreement 代理协议
agency commission 代理佣金
duration 代理期
sole agency 独家代理
sole agency agreement 独家代理协议
exclusive agency 独家代理
exclusive right 专卖权
exclusive sales 包销
exclusive distribution 总经销
chain store 连锁店
turnover 营业额，成交量
annual turnover 每年营业额
promotion 促销

商品资料
sales literature 商品宣传资料

leaflet 广告单
brochure 商品小册子，商品说明书
e-brochure 商品电子说明书
pamphlet 商品小册子，商品说明书
booklet 商品小册子，商品说明书
catalog 商品目录，产品目录
e-catalog 电子产品目录
illustrated catalog 有插图的商品目录
sample book 样品册
pattern book （绸缎的）花形本

质量

average quality 平均质量
bad quality 劣质量
best quality 最好的质量
common quality 一般质量
excellent quality 优良质量
fair quality 尚好的质量
fair average quality（F.A.Q）大路货
fine quality 优质量
first-rate quality 头等质量
first-class quality 头等质量
high quality 高质量
inferior quality 次质量
low quality 低质量
selected quality 精选的质量
sound quality 完好的质量
standard quality 标准的质量
top quality 上等质量
usual quality 通常的质量

2. Sentence Frames（句型）

说明信息来源

to learn your name and address from …从……得知你方名称和地址
to have your name and address from …从……得知你方名称和地址
to know your name and address from …从……得知你方名称和地址
to obtain your name and address from …从……得知你方名称和地址

to receive your name and address from…从……得到你方名称和地址

to come to know your name and address through …通过……得知你方名称和地址

through the courtesy of…由于……的好意（介绍）

on the recommendation of…由……推荐

介绍己方公司与业务

to email to introduce… 写邮件介绍……

to introduce…as… 现介绍……为……

to take the opportunity to introduce… 利用此机会介绍……

to deal in… 我方经营……

to handle the import business of … 经营……进口业务

to be specialized in a variety of … 专营各种各样的……

to trade mainly in … 主要做……贸易

… fall within the scope of our business. ……属我们经营的范围

… come within the scope of our business. ……属我们经营的范围

… lie within the scope of our business. ……属我们经营的范围

介绍、评价产品

to be made of… 由……制成

to be moderate in price 价格公道

to be superior in quality 质量上乘

to be excellent in craftsmanship 工艺精湛

to be novel in designs 设计新颖

to be attractive in packing 包装别致

to be elegant in style 款式典雅

to be matching in colors 色泽和谐

to be skillful in workmanship 做工考究

to be of good quality and fair price 物美价廉

to be famous for… 以……著名

to be well-known for…以……著名

to sell well 销路好

to sell fast 销路好

to enjoy fast sales 销路好

to find a ready market 销路好

to find a good market 销路好

to be popular with customers 受到顾客欢迎

to meet with warm reception 很受欢迎

to enjoy great popularity in the global market 信誉全球市场

to win a very high reputation 享有盛誉
to enjoy a very good reputation 享有盛誉

建立关系

to establish business relations with…和……建立贸易关系
to enter into business relations with…和……建立贸易关系
to make business contact with…和……建立贸易关系
to conclude some transactions 达成交易
to be in the market for…求购……

请求、委任代理

to ask to be an agent 要求充当代理
to offer to act as an agent 提出充当代理
to offer one's service as an agent 提出担任代理
to recommend sb. as an agent 推荐某人作为代理
to propose an agency agreement 建议达成代理协议
to appoint … as an agent 任命……为代理
to entrust … with agency 委任……代理

随函附寄

attached please find... 附件请查收……
attached... 附件发送……
accompanying… 一同附寄……
enclosing… 随函附寄……
containing… 随函附寄……
together with… 随函附寄……

快递寄样品

samples to be sent to you by… 通过……将样品寄送给你
to send samples through … 通过……寄送样品

关于

as to … 关于……
with regard to … 关于……
regarding … 关于……
concerning …关于……
relating to …关于……
respecting …关于……
about …关于……

供你参考

for your information 供你参考

for your guidance 供你参考

for your reference 供你参考

for your consideration 供你参考

for your perusal 供你参考

提供资信证明人

as to our financial and credit standing, we refer you to… 关于我方的资信状况，请你方跟……咨询

as to our financial and credit standing, please refer to… 至于我方的资信状况，请咨询……

for information regarding our credit standing, please contact… 至于我方的信誉，请联系……

劝导客户

to recommend you to do something 建议你方做某事

to your advantage to do something 做某事对你方是有利的

to be acceptable to you 你方可以接受

to advise you to work fast 劝你方早做决定

to look forward to doing something 希望做某事

to express one's desire to…愿意……

Part Ⅵ. Follow Me （跟我写）

Request for Establishing Business Relations（出口商请求建立贸易关系）

电子邮件模板

Dear Mr./Ms. （对方的姓），

We have learned from（获知对方公司的信息来源）that you are （说明所了解的情况） in （对方公司所在的国家或地区）. We are glad that you are interested in （对方想要购买的产品）. So, we are willing to establish business relations with you. Attached please find （我方所销售产品的资料）.

We are（我公司的情况）. We export（我公司所出口的产品） to （我产品出口的国家或地区）.

We look forward to receiving your enquiry at an early date.

Yours sincerely,

（署名）

贸易背景

我公司是中国最大的大米经销商（trader），也是中国唯一的（sole）大米出口商。我们向亚洲地区许多国家（many Asian countries）出口大米。

现在，我们从北京的英国驻华使馆（embassy）商务参赞处（Commercial Counselor's Office）获悉，有一家英国（Britain）贸易商对中国的各种大米（China's different kinds of rice）感兴趣，而且对方是英国一家主要的（leading）大米进口商。

于是，我公司销售部经理（Sales Department Manager）张华先生向对方公司的 John Smith 先生发邮件，请求建立贸易关系，并附件寄上最新（latest）产品目录（catalogue）和出口价目表（export price list）。

仿照模板套写

Part Ⅶ. Practical Writing （实训写作）

1. Match the words and phrases with their Chinese meanings.

attachment　　　　　　　电子目录
e-catalog　　　　　　　　附件
vendor　　　　　　　　　厂家
credit status　　　　　　　贸易关系
business relations　　　　　贸易咨询
sales literature　　　　　　商务参赞处
trade reference　　　　　　采购

Commercial Counselor	供应商
procurement	信誉
manufacturer	产品宣传资料

2. Read the following email and list the sentence patterns applied.

How are you doing? Glad to get your business card from China Import and Export Fair（中国进出口商品交易会，即广交会）.

This is Sally from WVC Company. We specialize in parking sensor system（雷达系统）, and all our products are CE（欧盟）/FCC（美国联邦通讯委员会）approved（认证）.

Regarding the FUN MINI DVR you selected in the fair, please find details with best offer in attachment.

Hope to get good news from you. Thanks!

----

3. Complete each of the following sentences according to its model given.

1）We are a specialized corporation, handling the export of animal by-products.

We are a specialized corporation, （经营纺织品出口）_____
_____.

2）We obtained your name and address from the Asian Source, and are glad to know your interest in Chinese bicycles.

We obtained your name and address from （阿里巴巴网站）_____
_____.

3）We are Home Depot's（家得宝） vendor of solar lights.

We are（沃尔玛办公用品的供应商）_____
_____.

4）Our solar power supply system is into the scope of Home Depot's procurement.

Our office equipment is（被列入家乐福的采购名单之中）_____
_____.

5）We are looking for the garden tools and send this mail to ask you for the sales literature.

We are looking for （LED 灯具，特发邮件索要产品资料）_____
_____.

6）It'd be much appreciated if you can add my SKYPE（加我 SKYPE）or call me back for any clarification.

It'd be much appreciated if you（可以加我微信）_____
_____ for any clarification.

7）Attached please find the camping & hiking (露营与徒步) e-catalog.

Attached please find（渔具）_____ e-catalog.

8）Guangbo establishes strategic cooperation（战略合作）partnership with Carrefour.

Haier（与沃尔玛建立了互惠关系）_____
_____.

9）"Bright" is a famous brand in the line of electronic components（电子元件）.

Youngor is（中国服装行业的著名商标）_____
_____.

10）Our products are high quality and samples can be posted if you require them.

Our goods are（美观大方，样品可邮寄）_____
_____.

4. Complete the following with words and phrases given in the box.

| 1）medium price | 2）establish business relations | 3）samples |
| 4）intelligence toys | 5）coincide with | |

We are happy to learn that you, as an exporter of_____, are willing to _____ with us. This happens to _____ our desire.

At present, we are interested in intelligence toys in _____ ranges and shall be pleased if you will kindly send us the _____ and all necessary information.

Meanwhile, please give us your lowest quotation, CIF Auckland, including our 3% commission.

Looking forward to a speedy reply.

Part Ⅷ. Linkage（知识链接）

国内主要银行
Bank of China 中国银行
China Construction Bank 中国建设银行
Agricultural Bank of China 中国农业银行

Industrial and Commercial Bank of China 中国工商银行
China Minsheng Banking Co., Ltd. 中国民生银行
China Merchants Bank Ltd. 中国招商银行
Industrial Bank Co., Ltd. 兴业银行
Bank of Communications 中国交通银行
China Everbright Bank 中国光大银行
Shanghai Pudong Development Bank 上海浦东发展银行
China Development Bank 国家开发银行
China CITIC Bank 中信银行

国际知名银行

Algemene Bank Nederland 荷兰通用银行（荷兰）
BancaNationale del Lavoro 国民劳动银行（意大利）
Banca Commercial Italiana 意大利商业银行（意大利）
Bankers trust New York Corp. 纽约银行家信托公司（美国）
Bancoo Do Brasil 巴西银行（巴西）
Bank America Corp. 美洲银行（美国）
Bank of Tokyo 东京银行（日本）
BanqueNationale de Paris 巴黎国民银行（法国）
Canadian Imperial Bank of Commerce 加拿大帝国商业银行（加拿大）
Chase Manhattan Bank 大通曼哈顿银行（美国）
Chemical New York Corp. 纽约化学银行（美国）
Citibank 花旗银行（美国）
Credit Suisse 瑞士信贷银行（瑞士）
CreditoItaliano 意大利信贷银行（意大利）
Daiwa Bank 大和银行（日本）
First Interstate Bancorp 第一洲际银行（美国）
Fuji Bank 富士银行（日本）
Hongkong and Shanghai Banking Corp. 汇丰银行（中国香港）
Industrial Bank of Japan 日本兴业银行（日本）
InstitutoBancario San Paolo Di Torin 都灵圣保罗银行（意大利）
Lloyds Bank PLC 劳埃德银行（英国）
Mellon National Corp. 梅隆国民银行（美国）
Midland Bank 米兰银行（英国）
Mitsubishi Bank 三菱银行（日本）
Mitsui Bank 三井银行（日本）
Royal Bank of Canada 加拿大皇家银行（加拿大）

Sanwa Bank 三和银行（日本）
Security Pacific Corp. 太平洋安全银行（美国）
Sumitomo Trust & Banking 住友信托银行（日本）
Swiss Bank Corp. 瑞士银行公司（瑞士）
Tokai Bank 东海银行（日本）
Union Bank of Switzerland 瑞士联合银行（瑞士）
Westpac Banking Corp. 西太平洋银行公司（澳大利亚）
Standard Chartered Bank 渣打银行（英国）

Part IX. Glossary of Common Sentences
（常用语句集）

1. 出口商

出口商	促销			We look forward to providing you with high quality products, superior customer service and complete satisfaction. 我方期待为贵方提供高品质的商品和上乘的客服，包您满意。
出口商	促销			We'd like to sell our products in the United States. 我们想在美国销售我们的产品。
出口商	促销			Your reply to this inquiry will enable us to give you priority in supplying your requirement quickly and to provide sufficient quantities for the goods which are going to be best sellers. We hope to provide the best service to you. 你方的回复将使我们优先、迅速地供应你们所需商品，而且对于畅销商品有充足的数量供应。愿我们能为你方提供最佳的服务。
出口商	介绍	公司	规模	This is to introduce the Pacific Corporation as one of the leading exporters of light industrial products having business relations with more than 70 countries in the world. 兹介绍，太平洋公司为最大的轻工业产品出口商之一，和世界上70多个国家有业务关系。
出口商	介绍	公司	声誉	We enjoy an excellent reputation in this field and supply best quality products. 在这个领域里我们享有极好的声誉，可以提供优质的产品。
出口商	介绍	公司	网页	Please visit the websites below for additional information on our products. 请登录下面的网站查询我方产品的更多信息。
出口商	介绍	公司	业务	We wish to inform you that we are specialized in the export of arts and crafts. 现奉告，我方专门经营工艺品出口。
出口商	介绍	公司	资历	Having many years' experience in this particular line of business, we send this email to introduce ourselves as an exporter of fresh water pearls. 发此邮件自我介绍，我方为淡水珍珠出口商，在此行业已有多年经验。

续表

出口商	期盼	合作		We look forward to serving you in the near future. 希望在不远的将来能为您服务。
出口商	期盼	询价		We shall be glad to receive your specific inquiry. 如能得到贵方具体询价，则甚为感谢。
出口商	说明	代理	期限	The Agency Agreement has been drawn up for a duration of one year, automatically renewable on expiration for a similar period unless a written notice is given to the contrary. 代理协议已草拟，期限为一年，除非另有书面通知，否则到期时本协议将自动续延相同的时间。
出口商	说明	代理	佣金	For an old customer like you, we are willing to allow a 15% commission on each machine, plus a special discount of 5% on all orders received before the end of next month. 对于您这样的老客户，我们愿意每一台机器给15%的佣金，此外，对于在下月底之前收到的订单，我们还给予5%的特别折扣。
出口商	说明	信息	来源	Through the courtesy of Mr. White, we are given to understand that you are one of the leading importers of silk in your area. 经由怀特先生，我们得悉贵公司为所在地区中最大的丝绸进口商之一。
出口商	说明	信息	来源	We have heard from China Council for the Promotion of International Trade that you are in the market for Electric Appliances. 从中国国际贸易促进会获悉，你们有意采购电器用具。
出口商	说明	信息	来源	We learn from the Commercial Counselor's Office of our Embassy in your country that you are in the market for Electric Appliances. 我们从我国驻贵国大使馆商务参赞处获悉贵方有意采购家用电器。
出口商	调查	资信		Founder Co. wants to do business with us and has given your details as a referee. 芬德公司欲与我公司开展贸易，并提供贵方为该公司的信用证明人。
出口商	调查	资信		We should be much obliged if you would give us your opinion of their solvency and trustworthiness. 贵方对该公司的付款能力和信用状况持何看法，恳请告知，不胜感谢。
出口商	调查	资信		We would therefore appreciate it if you would let us have information about the financial and business standing of the above firm. 如贵方能将上述公司的财务状况和经营状况告知我方，我方将不胜感激。
出口商	委托	代理		After a careful review of our business relations and your past efforts in pushing the sale of our products, we have decided to entrust you with the exclusive agency for our radio in your country. 鉴于我们之前的合作和你方对我们产品销售所做的努力，我方决定委任你方在你们国家做我们收音机的独家代理商。
出口商	委托	代理		In consideration of your extensive experience in this field, we are glad to appoint you as our sole agent. 考虑贵方在本行业有丰富的经验，我们很高兴任命你方为我公司的独家代理。

续表

出口商	谢绝	代理	请求	As we are now only at the get-acquainted stage, we deem it rather premature to take into consideration the matter of sole agency. In our opinion, it would be better for both of us to try out a period of cooperation to see how things develop. 由于我们还处在初识阶段，我们认为考虑独家代理问题时机尚不成熟。我们认为，尝试合作一段时间看情况如何会对彼此都有好处。
出口商	谢绝	代理	请求	Referring to your request to act as our sole agent for our tractors, we may consider this question seriously when business between us has been further extended. 关于你们要求作为我方拖拉机产品的独家代理一事，我们将在业务有了进一步发展时再慎重考虑。
出口商	谢绝	代理	请求	We don't need a new agent at this stage. 我们现阶段，还不需要新的代理商。
出口商	谢绝	建交	请求	Please accept our regret for having to decline your request for establishment of business relations as the items named in your email have sold out. 很抱歉，我方不得不拒绝你方建立业务关系的要求，因为你方邮件中所要产品已经售完。
出口商	寻求	代理		We'd like you to be our agent if you're interested. 如果您感兴趣的话，我们想让您当我们的代理商。
出口商	寻求	代理		We're looking for an agent to handle our products. 我们正在找代理商，来经销我们的产品。
出口商	寻求	建交		As we deal in tablecloth, we shall be pleased to enter into direct business relations with you. 由于我方经营台布，我们很愿意与你方建立直接贸易关系。
出口商	寻求	建交		In order to extend our export business to your country, we wish to enter into direct business relations with you. 为了向贵国扩大出口业务，我们希望与贵方建立直接的业务联系。
出口商	寻求	建交		We have more than 25 years in selling net ware and obtain a large share of market. We hope we can make co-operate with you. 我们经营网络设备已经超过 25 年了，并占据大部分市场份额，因此，我方很希望与贵方合作。
出口商	询问	代理	条件	In order to enable us to make a careful study of your proposal, we should like to know your plan for promoting the sales of our products, the market consumption and the volume of business which you are able to conclude monthly or quarterly. 为使我方认真研究你方建议，请把你们的我方产品的推销计划、市场销量、你们的月营业额或季营业额通知我方。
出口商	询问	代理	条件	While on the subject of agency, we would ask you to give us an approximate estimate of the volume of business you expect to do annually. 在谈代理问题时，请告知你们预期每年可达成的交易额的约计数。
出口商	询问	代理	销量	Could you give me some idea of your monthly quantity guarantee? 您能告诉我你们每个月能保证完成的销售额吗？
出口商	询问	代理	销量	What are the minimum annual sales you can guarantee? 你们所能保证的最少年销售额是多少？

2. 进口商

进口商	接受	代理	委托	Thank you for offering us the agency in this market for your products. We appreciate the confidence you have placed in us. 谢谢委任我们担任该市场你方产品的代理，并对给予我们的信任深表感谢。
进口商	接受	代理	委托	We appreciate the confidence you place in us by offering a sole agency here in China for your range of beauty products. 感谢你方给予的信任，同意我们在中国为你们的美容产品做代理。
进口商	劝导	代理	委托	We have a wide and varied experience in the trade; we are convinced that we are in a position to promote your product as an agent. 我们有广泛的和各种各样的做贸易的经验，相信作为代理，我方会很好地推广贵公司产品。
进口商	劝导	代理	委托	We have good knowledge of the local customers' needs, and are confident that there is much we can do to extend your business here. 我们对当地顾客的需求很了解，并非常有信心能拓展你方在这里的业务。
进口商	劝导	代理	委托	With many years' marketing experience and good connections in the trade, we offer our service as your agent in Kuwait. 我们在此行业中已有多年的经验和广泛的客户，现提出担任你方在科威特的代理。
进口商	提供	资信	证明	Here's the financial report of our company. 这里是本公司的财务报告。
进口商	提供	资信	证明方	For any information as to our credit standing, please refer to Bank of China, Beijing Branch. 有关我方信誉的任何资料，请向中国银行北京分行查询。
进口商	提供	资信	证明方	We refer you to The Bank of Switzerland if you wish to make any inquiries about our credit standing. 如对本公司信用状况有任何疑问，请向瑞士银行查询。
进口商	寻求	建交		We are very interested in the quality of your products, and we would like open an account with you. 我们对贵公司的产品质量一直深感兴趣，意欲与贵公司开展贸易合作。
进口商	寻求	建交		We have seen your advertisement in "The Overseas Journal" and should be glad to have a price list and details of your terms. 我们看过你方在《海外杂志》的广告，请惠寄你方价目表和条款的详细情况。
进口商	寻求	建交		We shall place regular orders with you if we have established a long and stable relationship and complete the business on the basis of equality and mutual benefits. 如果我们建立了长期稳定的关系，以平等互利的基础做生意，我们会定期向你们订购。
进口商	要求	代理	委托	After making an overall assessment of the business possibilities, we would propose representing you as your sole agent in this territory. 经过全面的估量业务的可能性，我们提出在此地区作你方的独家代理。

续表

进口商	要求	代理	委托	As your agent, we shall spare no effort to promote the sale of your slippers in our market. 作为贵方代理我们将不遗余力地在我们的市场上推销你们的拖鞋。
进口商	要求	代理	委托	Having experienced staff of sales representatives and spacious and well-equipped show rooms, we recommend ourselves to act as your sole agent for your Forever Brand Bicycles in Iran. 我们拥有经验丰富的销售代表和设备良好的宽敞陈列室，现自荐作为你方"永久"牌自行车在伊朗的代理。
进口商	要求	佣金	比例	It will be easier for us to push the sale if you can give us more commission. 如果能多给我们一些佣金，我们推销时会更容易一些。
进口商	要求	佣金	比例	We expect a 5% commission. 我们希望能得到5%的佣金。

3. 资信证明方

证明方	答复	资信	不良	The reports in circulation indicate that they are in an awkward situation for meeting their obligations. 根据通报，该公司履约境况不佳。
证明方	答复	资信	不良	They are known to be heavily committed and have overrun their reserves. Caution is advisable. 据了解他们欠债很多，已超过其储备，建议谨慎处之。
证明方	答复	资信	未知	We are sorry that we cannot furnish you with all the information you desire. 很遗憾我们无法提供你所需要的全部信息。
证明方	答复	资信	未知	We are sorry we are not able to give the precise information you ask. 我们无法向贵公司提供您所需要的确切情报，对此，我们深感遗憾。
证明方	答复	资信	良好	As far as we know their financial standing is sound. 就我们所知，他们的财务状况良好。
证明方	答复	资信	良好	In reply to your inquiry of the June 1, we inform you that our business relationship with the firm has to date been most satisfactory. 兹回复贵方6月1日的查询，本公司与该公司的交易关系迄今为止颇为满意。
证明方	答复	资信	良好	The company was established in 1968, and has supplied our firm with high quality goods for over 20 years. 该公司成立于1968年，所给我方供应品货物品质优良，已逾20年之久。
证明方	要求	资信	保密	This communication is private and confidential for your use only, and without responsibility on our part. 本信息仅供你方参考，我方不承担责任，并请务必保密。
证明方	要求	资信	保密	We accept your assurance that the information we have given will be treated in strict confidence. 我们相信贵公司能恪守承诺，对我方提供的信息严格保密。

Unit 2
Enquiry and Reply
（询价与报价）

Part I. Objectives（目标）

After completing this unit, you will be able to

1. read and write an email or a message relating to enquiry;

2. know the essential components that an enquiry and its reply cover;

3. become familiar with the typical English terms and sentence patterns used in enquiry and its reply.

Part II. How to Express（我该怎么说）

1. Wishing to Buy（进口商寻购）

A：我是买方，要向卖方表达购买的愿望。我该怎么说呢？

B：你可以这样说：

1）我们看到贵公司3月15日在网上发布的纺织品广告。我们现欲购买全棉床单。

2）我们是本市主要的电器进口商，现欲购买你方电扇。

3）我们对你方在广交会上所展出的男士毛衣很感兴趣。

A：那么，我用英语该怎么说呢？

B：到"常用语句集"去看看，你先找到同类的句型，然后采用截取、替换、拼接的办法稍做加工，你需要的句子就有了。

A：嘿！瞧瞧，我的英语还不错吧！

2. Specific Enquiry （进口商具体询价）

A：我是买方，我要向卖方详细了解某种产品及交易条款，该怎么问呢？

B：你可以这样说：

1）我们对你方第 123 号瓷器感兴趣，请寄样品并告知所有必要的信息。

2）我方想询购 100 箱特级红茶。

3）请报 CIF 纽约最低价，并说明最早的船期和付款方式。

A：那么，我用英语该怎么说呢？

B：到"常用语句集"去看看，你先找到同类的句型，然后采用截取、替换、拼接的办法稍做加工，你需要的句子就有了。

A：嘿！瞧瞧，我的英语还不错吧！

3. Responding Enquiries （出口商回复询价）

A：我是卖方，我收到了客户的询价，该怎么回应对方呢？

B：你可以这样说：

1）欢迎贵方 3 月 12 日的询价，并感谢对我们的产品感兴趣。

2）谢谢你方 5 月 14 日的询价，很高兴向你方报该货品的最低价。

3）现回复你方 7 月 6 日的询价，并报 5 公吨核桃仁 CFR 汉堡价。

A：那么，我用英语该怎么说呢？

B：到"常用语句集"去看看，你先找到同类的句型，然后采用截取、替换、拼接的办法稍做加工，你需要的句子就有了。

A：嘿！瞧瞧，我的英语还不错吧！

Part Ⅲ. Case（案例）

1. Establishing Business Relations（出口商寻求建立贸易关系）

宁波汇通股份有限公司（Ningbo Huitong Co., Ltd.）是一家专门从事各类玩具生产和销售的企业。2015年3月1～5日在上海举办的第24届中国华东进出口商品交易会（2015 East China Fair）上，有位加拿大客户Jack Stuart先生对汇通公司展位上的长毛绒玩具（plush toy）很感兴趣。业务员李波和Jack进行了交流，约定展会后再进一步联系。

展会后李波便发邮件与Jack联系，跟进客户。

发件人（From）	Libo@Huitong.com
收件人（To）	Jack@PTtrading.com
主题（Subject）	Plush Toys from East China Fair
附件（Attachment）	Catalogue

Dear Mr. Stuart,

Thank you for your interest in our products during the 2015 East China Fair. As requested, I have sent you some free samples, which we trust will meet your requirements.

We also export other toys covering plastic, wooden, cloth and plush articles, details as per the attached e-catalogue. If you have any specific requirements, please let us know. We can also produce according to your designated styles so long as the quantity is substantial.

We are pleased to add you to our list of clients and look forward to your enquiries.

Yours sincerely,

Li Bo

Sentence Patterns Applied（语句归纳）

➢ 出口商提及之前的联系（华交会会面），寄送样品，评价产品；

➢ 出口商介绍产品范围、服务（按样生产），鼓励联系；

➢ 出口商期盼建交，鼓励询价。

2．Enquiry（进口商询价）

进口方 Jack 收到了李波的邮件，查看了附件中的产品目录，发现其中的一些产品正是己方公司需要购进的。Jack 马上向李波回复了电子邮件，把感兴趣的产品制成了询价单（Enquiry Sheet）放在了附件，要求对方报 CIF 温哥华（CIF Vancouver）最低价，要求说明包装、装运、支付条款，并请求寄来样品。

现在，你是 Jack Stuart，请按照上面的情形给李波先生回复邮件。

Sentence Patterns for Reference（参考语句）
- 进口商收到邮件、产品资料和样品，致谢；
- 进口商表达购买愿望，附寄询价单；
- 进口商请求报价，询问装运、包装、付款，索要样品；
- 进口商劝导报价。

Hints（提示）
所询价的产品名称、价格、等级、数量等信息填写在询价单里，放在邮件的附件中，所以，正文无需细述。

发件人（From）	
收件人（To）	
主题（Subject）	
附件（Attachment）	

An Enquiry Sheet （询价单）

ENQUIRY SHEET（询价单）

TO:	（对方公司名称）		
	Mr.	Enquiry No.	:
	TEL:+ Fax:+	Enquiry Date	:
	E-Mail:	Bid closing date:	

FROM:	（自己公司名称）		
	Address:	Attn	:
（公司标识）	Tel. : Fax :		
	Web : Email :		

Unit：EURO/USD

NO	QTY	UOM	DESCRIPTION	PART NO	UNIT PRICE	TOTAL PRICE
1						0.00
2						0.00
3						0.00
4						0.00
5			TOTAL		0.00	

Please provide the following information:

NO	DESCRIPTION	REMARK
1	Products total weights	
2	Products total volume	
3	Shipping Methods	
4	Freight Cost (CIF/CIP ,including packing, etc)	
5	Delivery Time	

3. Replying to Enquiry（出口商回复询价）

宁波汇通股份有限公司业务员李波收到了 Jack Stuart 的询价，他马上回复邮件进行报价。他告知 Jack，所索要的样品已通过 FedEx 快递寄出，装运期是自收到相关信用证两月之内，支付方式是即期信用证。为了清晰说明，李波把产品的品名、货号、包装数量、价格等信息制成了一张报价单（Quotation Sheet），附件发送给了对方。报价单如下：

Commodity	Article No.	Packing	Cartons per 20'FCI.	CIF Vancouver in USD
New Design Brown Bear	KB0677	8 pcs/ctn	135	13.65 / pc
Bear in Ballet Costume	KB5411	12 pcs/ctn	162	8.12 / pc

发件人（From）	Libo@Huitong.com
收件人（To）	Jack@PTtrading.com
主题（Subject）	Reply to the Enquiry

> 附件（Attachment）　　　Quotation Sheet

Dear Mr. Stuart,

We are pleased to receive your Enquiry of March 13. Attached is our quotation sheet. Quantities less than that are slightly higher in unit price.

Shipment: To be effected within 2 months from receipt of the relevant L/C.

Payment: By sight L/C.

We have also sent the samples you requested by FedEx. In order to assist you in promoting sales at the initial stage, these samples are free of charge.

As we are receiving regular daily orders, our present stocks are nearly exhausted. Therefore, we would advise you to place your order as soon as possible.

We are looking forward to your initial order.

Yours truly,

Li Bo

Sentence Patterns Applied（语句归纳）
- 出口商收到询价单，附寄报价单，说明报价（折扣）；
- 出口商说明装运期；
- 出口商说明支付方式；
- 出口商寄送样品，申明费用（免费）；
- 出口商劝导下订单；
- 出口商期盼订单。

Part Ⅳ. Writing Directions（写作指导）

在询问所需产品信息的同时，询价信函要强调获取信息的重要性和紧迫性，告知对方打算购买，但不承诺购买。询价信函要注重礼貌，语气要谦和，尽量营造愉快的气氛以获取更多的信息。如果对方是陌生的客户，也要尽量把信写成老朋友相见似的叙谈。询价分为一般询价和具体询价。

进口商一般询价

一般询价是对所感兴趣的产品进行一个总体的了解。向陌生客户的首次询价基本上属于一般询价。要点包括：
- 说明获得对方信息的来源；
- 介绍己方公司和业务范围；
- 询问所感兴趣的商品；
- 索要商品目录、价格单、样品；
- 期盼回复。

进口商具体询价

具体询价要求出口方要明确告知产品的详细信息以及交易条件，所询问的目标信息要具体、明确，要有针对性。具体询价的信函一般开门见山，直接切入正题。要点包括：
- 回顾之前的交流（或说明信息来源）；
- 说明打算购买的产品，要求报价；
- 询问品质、折扣、包装、支付方式、交货日期等；
- 要求寄送产品资料、样品等；
- 劝导对方报价；
- 期盼回复。

出口商报价

对于询价信的回复要尽可能迅速及时，因为它意味着一笔生意。其要点有：
- 感谢对方的询价；
- 介绍己方公司、业务；
- 报价；
- 介绍产品；
- 寄送产品资料；
- 承诺；
- 劝导下订单。

Part V. Terms and Sentence Frames
（术语与句型）

1. Terms（术语）

价格
actual price 实际价
bid price 递价

buying price 购入价格
competitive price 竞争价格
cost price 成本价
current price 时价，现行价
exceptional price 特价
export price 出口价
factory price 出厂价格
fair price 平价
firm price 实价
high price 高价
import price 进口价
low price 低价
moderate price 公平价格
new price 新价
market price 市价
offered price 报盘价
original price 原价
present price 现价
quoted price 开价，报价
retail price 零售价
ruling price 行市价格
sale price 出售价格
selling price 出售价格
special price 特价
unit price 单价
wholesale price 批发价

价格术语

EXW（EX Works）工厂交货（……指定地点）
FCA（Free Carrier）货交承运人（……指定地点）
FAS（Free Along Side）船边交货（……指定装运港）
FOB（Free on Board）船上交货（……指定装运港）
CFR（Cost Freight）成本加运费付至（……指定目的港）
CIF（Cost Insurance Freight）成本、保险加运费付至（……指定目的港）
CPT（Carriage Paid to）运费付至（……指定目的港）
CIP（Carriage and Insurance Paid to）运费、保险付至（……指定目的地）
DAT（Delivered at Terminal）终点站交货（……指定目的港或目的地）

DAP（Delivered at Place）目的地交货（……指定目的地）
DDP（Delivered Duty Paid）完税后交货（……指定目的地）

价目单
price list 价格单
price sheet 价格单
enquiry note 询价单
quotation sheet 报价单
offer list 报价单
offer book 报价单

数量
average quantity 平均数量
considerable quantity 大数量
enormous quantity 巨大数量
entire quantity 整个数量
equal quantity 同等数量
estimated quantity 估计数量
extra quantity 额外数量
further quantity 更多的数量
huge quantity 巨大的数量
large quantity 大数量
limited quantity 有限的数量
maximum quantity 最大数量
minimum quantity 最小数量
sizable quantity 可观的数量
small quantity 小数量
substantial quantity 大数量
total quantity 总数量

2. Sentence Frames（句型）

打算购买
to be in the market for... 要购买……
to be desirous of... 想要……
to be interested in... 对……感兴趣
to have an interest in... 对……感兴趣
to feel interested in... 对……感兴趣

to intend to place a large order for… 打算下大订单购买……
to be ready to conclude substantial business 准备达成大笔交易

产品引起兴趣

to be of interest to us 引起我方的兴趣
to interest us 使我方感兴趣

请求（事先感谢）

We thank you in advance for… 我方对……预致谢意
We would be grateful to you for… 我方将十分感激你方……
We would be obliged if… 我方将十分感激如果……
We would appreciate it if… 我方将十分感激如果……
It would be highly appreciated if… 十分感激如果……

询价

to quote us a price for … 向我方报……价
to quote for something at … 报某货价为……
to quote us a firm offer for… 请给我方报……的实盘
to send us your best quotation for… 向我方报……最低价
to make us your lowest quotation for… 向我方报……最低价
to give us your lowest quotation for… 向我方报……最低价
to enquire for… 询购……
to have an enquiry for… 有……的询盘
to send us particulars of… 告知我方……的详细情况
to state terms of… 说明……的条款
to inform us on what terms you can supply… 告知我方在什么条件下你方可供应……

打折优惠

to allow sb. a special allowance 给予某人特别折扣
to allow sb. a special discount 给予某人特别折扣
to give you the first chance 给予你方优先
to give sb. a further reduction of 2% 给予某人再降价 2%
to give you a discount 给你方折扣
to allow you a discount 给你方折扣
to offer you a discount 给你方折扣
to grant you a discount 给你方折扣
to grant a special discount of 3% 给予 3%的特别折扣

Part Ⅵ. Follow Me （跟我写）

Enquiry（进口商询价）

电子邮件模板

Dear Mr./Ms. ___（对方的姓）___,

  We saw your advertisement（广告）posted on ___（对方广告刊登的媒体）___ about ___（对方的产品名称）___. We are interested in ___（我方所感兴趣的产品）___. ___（具体说明产品的材质或规格）___. We would like you to send us some catalogues, price lists and sample books, giving us details on your various ranges, colours, prices, and the materials used.

  We believe in ___（我方的经营理念或宗旨）___. Being in ___（我方所从事的行业）___ for over ___（我方从事该行业的年数）___, our company has an advantage（具有优势）over ___（我方公司超越的方面）___. If you quote us competitive prices, there will be good prospects for your ___（对方的产品名称）___.

  When quoting, please state your terms of payment and time of delivery; and tell us what discount you can allow us.

  We look forward to your prompt reply.

  Yours sincerely,

  ___（署名）___

贸易背景

  我方是经营寝具（bedding business）的一家美国公司，在此行业已经有十多年的历史。与其他经营纺织品的美国公司相比（many other textile businesses across the United States），我公司具有优势。我们的宗旨是：优质的产品和高效的交易（high quality products and efficient transaction）。

  现我公司正在寻购纯棉床单（pure cotton bed-sheet），业务员王晶晶通过互联网（internet）发现了一家卖家，其广告（advertisement）所介绍的纺织产品（your textile products）中的纯棉床单比较符合我方的需求，尺寸是：2.9m×1.6m，2.4m×2.4m，2.4m×1.6m。对方广告提供了联系方式，联系人是 Mr. Nathan Brown。于是，王晶晶需要发邮件询价。

仿照模板套写

_____
_____
_____
_____
_____

Part VII. Practical Writing （实训写作）

1. Match the words and phrases with their Chinese meanings.

special price   最小数量
market price   询价单
minimum quantity   询购……
total quantity   给予某人特别折扣
to be in the market for…   向我方报……最低价
to quote us the lowest price for   特价
to enquire for…   要购买
to send us particulars of…   市价
to allow sb. a special discount   告知我方……的详细情况
enquiry sheet   总数量

2. Read the following enquiry and list its main points.

Dear Sir/Madam,

We have learned from your national trade journal（行业报刊）that you manufacture a range of high-fashion handbags.

We operate a quality retail business and although our sales volume（销量）is not large, we obtain high prices for our high-quality goods.

Would you please send us a catalogue and pricelist, and tell us your terms of business（交易条件）and delivery date?

We look forward to your speedy response.
Yours faithfully,

----

3. Complete each of the following sentences according to its model given.

1）We are interested in your products.
We（对你方质量上乘的瓷器感兴趣）_____
_____.

2）We shall be pleased if you will give us particulars as to your conditions and terms.
We shall be pleased if you will (告知我们付款方式和交货期)_____
_____.

3）When quoting, please state the discount you would allow for a large order.
When quoting, please state (对购买不少于 1000 箱的数量所给予的折扣)_____
_____.

4）Please send us your best quotation for iron nails.
Please (报 100 箱红茶的最低 CIF 价)_____
_____.

5）We may be able to place orders with you if your prices are acceptable.
We may be able (定期下单，如果你方的价格富有竞争力的话。)_____
_____.

6）Thank you for your enquiry of May 12 for frozen rabbit.
Thank you for (2 月 19 日有关 500 公吨化肥的询价)_____
_____.

7）We take pleasure in quoting you our lowest price for black tea.
We take pleasure in (报 5 公吨花生仁 CIF 大阪价)_____
_____.

8）The best we can do is to reduce the price by 2%.
The best we can do is (给你方降价 3%，如你方订单金额超过 10000 美元)_____
_____.

9）You can rest assured of the quality of our products.
You can rest assured (我们会尽最大努力满足你方要求)_____
_____.

10）We are one of the leading exporters of agricultural and animal by-products in this city.
We are (一家专门从事工艺品进出口的大型贸易公司)_____

4. Complete the following email of enquiry with words and phrases given in the box.

1）assure	2）in good demand	3）available
4）detailed	5）receive our careful consideration	

Dear Sirs,

We are in the market for cotton textiles, as they are _____ at this end.

We learn that you are an exporter of the above-mentioned goods. We would therefore, appreciate some _____ information about CIF London prices, discounts and delivery schedule. Please also send us some catalogues if these are_____.

We thank you in advance for your kind attention and _____ you that your offer will certainly_____.

We hope this will be the start for long and mutually beneficial business relations.

Yours faithfully,

（署名）

5. Complete the following email of quotation with words and phrases given in the box.

1）on FOB Ningbo basis	2）illustrated catalogue	3）asked for
4）enquiry	5）competitive	

Thank you for your _____ of March 15 for our pure cotton bed sheets. We attach our _____, price list and a sample book, offering you the detailed information you _____.

Purchases of not less than 200 dozen of any individual item will be allowed a discount of 3%. Payment is made _____, and by confirmed irrevocable L/C at sight.

We are the exporter of varieties of textile items. We provide the highest quality bed sheets at _____ prices. They are soft, durable and very popular on the market both at home and abroad.

We look forward to receiving your first order.

Part Ⅷ. Linkage（知识链接）

装运港船上交货（FOB=Free on Board）
交货地点： 装运港
运输： 买方负责
保险： 买方负责

出口手续： 卖方负责
进口手续： 买方负责
风险转移： 装运港船上
所有权转移： 随交单转移

成本加运费（CFR=Cost+Freight）
交货地点： 装运港
运输： 卖方负责
保险： 买方负责
出口手续： 卖方负责
进口手续： 买方负责
风险转移： 装运港船上
所有权转移： 随交单转移

FOB 与 CFR 的共同点
卖方负责装货并充分通知，买方负责接货；
卖方办理出口手续，提供证件，买方办理进口手续，提供证件；
卖方交单，买方受单、付款；
装运港交货，风险、费用划分一致，以货物装上装运港指定船只为界；
交货方式相同，都是凭单交货、凭单付款；
都适合于海洋运输和内河运输。

FOB 与 CFR 的不同点
FOB：买方负责租船订舱、到付运费，办理保险、支付保险；
CFR：卖方负责租船订舱、预付运费，买方负责办理保险、支付保险。

美国货币
　　美国货币由美元（dollar）和美分（cent）组成，1 美元等于 100 美分。其纸币（bill）有 1、2、5、10、20、50 和 100 美元等面值；硬币（coin）有 1 美分（或 a penny）、5 美分（或 a nickel）、10 美分（或 a dime）和 25 美分（或 a quarter）等。在数字前加$表示美元，如$500 表示 500 美元；在数字后加 C 表示美分，如 50C 表示 50 美分；表示由美元和美分组成的钱数时，常用$表示，如$6.50。

欧元
　　欧元(euro)是欧盟中 19 个国家的货币。欧元的 19 会员国是爱尔兰、奥地利、比利时、德国、法国、芬兰、荷兰、卢森堡、葡萄牙、西班牙、希腊、意大利、斯洛文尼亚、塞浦路斯、马耳他、斯洛伐克、爱沙尼亚、立陶宛、拉脱维亚。1999 年 1 月 1 日在实行欧元的欧盟国家中实行统一货币政策，2002 年 7 月欧元成为欧元区唯一合法货币。欧元由欧洲中央银行和各欧元区国家的中央银行组成的欧洲中央银行系统负责管理。另外欧元也是非欧盟中6个国家的货币，它们是：摩纳哥、圣马力诺、梵蒂冈、黑山、科索沃和安道尔。

自欧元创建以来，其纸币共有七种面额，分别是€5,€10,€20,€50,€100,€200和€500。第一套欧元纸币于2002年1月1日至2013年5月1日期间发行，随后在2013年5月2日起被第二套纸币所取代。与硬币不同的是，纸币的设计在整个欧元区都是一样的。为了使纸币更耐用，并使人们更容易地通过触摸来识别，印制纸币的纸张由纯棉纤维制造。欧元纸币的尺寸最小为120mm×62mm，最大为160mm×82mm；不同的纸币使用不同的主题色调以便区分。

Part Ⅸ. Glossary of Common Sentences
（常用语句集）

1. 出口商

出口商	承诺	报盘	优惠	We will make you a special offer. 我们会给你方一个特价。
出口商	承诺	报盘	优惠	We'll give you our best offer. 我们将给你们最优惠的报盘。
出口商	附寄	产品	资料	Attached you will find our latest catalogue about our products for your information. 附件中附上我方最新产品目录供你参考。
出口商	附寄	产品	资料	For your guidance, our latest illustrated catalogues are attached for you herewith. 最新附图产品目录附件寄给你方以供参考。
出口商	附寄	产品	资料	I have attached our illustrated catalogue and price-list. 附件中附上带图目录册及价格单。
出口商	附寄	产品	资料	To give you a general idea of our company and also the main products we deal in, we attach our latest catalogue and price list for your reference. 为了让你方了解我公司及我公司所经营的主要产品，我们附寄最新的产品目录和价目单供你方参考。
出口商	回复	询价		Thank you for your interest in our food processing machines. 感谢您关注我公司的食品加工机。
出口商	回复	询价		We are very pleased to receive your enquiry of April 10. 非常高兴收到贵方4月10日的询价。
出口商	回复	询价		We welcome your enquiry of May 26th, and thank you for your interest in our products. 欢迎你们5月26日询盘，并感谢你们对我产品的兴趣。
出口商	回复	询价		Your inquiry of June 11 is greatly appreciated. 感谢你们6月11日的询价。

续表

出口商	寄送	产品	目录样品	In order to give you some idea of various qualities of handicrafts we carry, we have pleasure in forwarding you by TNT one catalogue and a few samples for your perusal. 为了让你方了解我方经营的质地各异的手帕，非常高兴通过 TNT 寄给你方我们的产品目录和一些样品供你方参阅。
出口商	寄送	产品	样品	We are sending you some samples by DHL. 本公司通过 DHL 为您寄上一些样品。
出口商	寄送	产品	资料	As per your request, we have sent you a copy of our product brochure by FedEx. 我们已按照您的要求将产品介绍手册通过联邦快递寄出。

2. 进口商

进口商	劝导	报盘	优惠	If your prices are favorable, I can place the order immediately. 如果你方的价格优惠，我方可以马上订货。
进口商	劝导	报盘	优惠	We may be able to place regular orders with you if your prices are competitive. 如果你方价格具有竞争力，我们会定期向你们订购。
进口商	索要	商品	价目表	We shall be pleased if you will send us the lowest quotation for the following. 请寄来下列商品的最低报价单。
进口商	索要	商品	价目表样品	One of our customers is interested in Model 21, and we would like to receive a sample and quotation. 我方一客户想买 21 型号，希望你方寄一份样品和报价单来。
进口商	索要	商品	目录	We are interested in your canned goods and wish to have the catalogues. 我们对你方的罐头食品有兴趣，希望能收到目录。
进口商	索要	商品	目录	We should like you to send us a catalogue and a price list regarding your products. 请给我们寄来你们产品的商品目录和价目表。
进口商	索要	商品	样品	I hope you could also supply samples of these gloves. 希望贵公司顺带惠赐手套样品。
进口商	索要	商品	样品	Please send us some patterns of your newest designs with your best terms. 请选送一些附有最优惠价格的最新花式花样样品。
进口商	索要	商品	样品	We would find it most helpful if you could also supply samples of the various skins from which the handbags are made. 此外，如提供各类皮革手提包样本，不胜感激。
进口商	索要	商品	样品	We would find it most helpful if you could supply samples of your products. 如能提供你们产品的样品将是很有帮助的。
进口商	索要		资料	I would like to request a copy of your company brochure. 我想要一份贵公司的简介。

进口商	索要		资料	Please resend the file in plain text format. 请以纯文本格式再发送一遍文件。
进口商	索要		资料	Please try sending the attachment again. 请再发送一遍附件。
进口商	寻购			We are considering buying Chinese leather shoes. 我们正有意购买中国皮鞋。
进口商	寻购			We are in the market for cotton piece goods. 我们正在寻购棉布。
进口商	寻购			We are interested in the silk made by your company. 我公司对贵方生产的丝绸很感兴趣。
进口商	寻购			We are ready to purchase your Maple Brand Men's Shirts in large quantity. 我公司打算大量购买贵公司的枫叶牌衬衫。
进口商	寻购			We're very interested in the product you exhibited at the international exhibition. 我们对你方在国际展览会上展出的产品,极有兴趣。
进口商	寻购			We intend to book a trial order with you. 我们想向贵方试订一批货。
进口商	询问	价格	大概	Please inform us on what terms you can supply iron nails. 请告知贵方供应铁钉的条件。
进口商	询问	价格	大概	Please let us have information as to the price and quality of the goods. 请告知该商品的价格和质量。
进口商	询问	价格	大概	We would appreciate it if you will please let us know the ruling prices of the goods. 如您能告知该商品的普遍价格,将不胜感激。
进口商	询问	价格	具体	I'd like to have your lowest quotations, C.I.F. Rotterdam. 我想请你们报抵鹿特丹最低到岸价。
进口商	询问	价格	具体	Kindly let us know at what price per ton you are able to deliver quantities of best refined sugar. 请告知我们在大宗订货的情况下每吨优质糖的价格。
进口商	询问	价格	具体	Please quote your lowest price CIF Dalian for each of the following items, inclusive of our 2% commission. 请报下列各种商品的大连到岸价,包括我方2%的佣金。
进口商	询问	价格	具体	The articles we require are listed on the attached sheets. If you have them in stock, please tell us the quantity and also the lowest CIF. Kobe price. 所需品种见附单,如可供现货,请报数量和成本加保险费、运费到神户的最低价。
进口商	询问	价格	具体	We are interested in hand-made gloves in variety of genuine leather. Will you send us a copy of your latest catalogue with details of your prices and terms of payment? 我们想买各种式样的真皮手制手套,请寄你方最新商品目录表一份以及详细的价格和支付条款。
进口商	询问	价格	具体	We shall be pleased if you will give us particulars as to your conditions and terms. 请告知你方交易条款的细节。

续表

进口商	询问	价格	折扣	Could you give us some idea about the discount you can offer on bulk purchase? 能否告知我们批量采购的折扣是多少？
进口商	询问	价格	折扣	When quoting, please state terms of payment and discount you would allow on purchase of quantities of not less than 500 dozen. 报价时，请说明付款条件和对购买不少于 500 打的数量所给予的折扣。
进口商	询问	价格	折扣	Will you please allow us a special allowance on annual total purchase above $500,000? 如果我们每年购买总金额超过 50 万美元，能否给予特别折扣？
进口商	询问	价格	折扣	Your information as to discounts for a large order would be appreciated. 请告知大笔订货的折扣。
进口商	询问	价格		One of our clients takes interest in your products and wishes to have your quotations for the items specified below. 我方一客户对你方产品感兴趣，并希望你方就如下所列商品报价。
进口商	询问	价格		Please inform us of your lowest price for 300 pieces and approximate date of delivery. 请告知 300 件的最低价及大约交货期。
进口商	询问	商品	信息	Could you provide me with information on your T1000-series products? 您是否能提供贵公司生产的 T1000 系列产品的信息？
进口商	询问	商品	信息	I am writing to request information about your latest products. 我想咨询一些有关贵公司新产品的信息。
进口商	询问	商品	信息	Please submit specifications, preferably with illustrations. 请告知规格，最好附有图片说明。
进口商	询问	商品	信息	We should like to have further particulars of your stationary. 我们需要进一步了解你方文具细节。
进口商	询问	商品	信息	We would appreciate receiving details regarding the commodities. 如能告知该商品的详细情况，则不胜感激。
进口商	询问索要	价格样品	大概	Please send me a copy of your glove catalogue, with details of your prices and terms of payment. 请惠寄贵公司的手套目录一份，详述有关价目与付款条件。
进口商	询问索要	价格样品	大概	Please send us samples and quote us your lowest prices for ... 请惠寄样品并报你方……的最低价。

Unit 3

Offer and Counteroffer
（报盘与还盘）

Part Ⅰ. Objectives（目标）

After completing this unit, you will be able to

1. make an offer as a seller, and accept or reject a counteroffer from your buyer by mail;
2. make a counteroffer by mail as a buyer;
3. become familiar with the typical English terms, sentence patterns and essential components in above mails.

Part Ⅱ. How to Express（我该怎么说）

1. Offer（出口商报盘）

A：我是卖方，现收到了客户的询盘，我要报盘。我该怎么说呢？
B：你可以这样说：
1）贵公司昨天的询盘收悉，现就我方洗衣机报盘如下。
2）作为回复，我方报盘如下，以我方最终确认为准。
3）我们向您报以下实盘。
A：那么，我用英语该怎么说呢？
B：到"常用语句集"去看看，你先找到同类的句型，然后采用截取、替换、拼接的办法稍做加工，你需要的句子就有了。
A：嘿！瞧瞧，我的英语还不错吧！

2. Counteroffer （进口商还盘）

A：我是买方，现收到了卖方的报盘。我方无法接受对方的报盘，需要还盘。我该怎么说呢？

B：你可以这样说：

1）非常遗憾，我方不能接受贵方的报盘。

2）我方遗憾地通知你方，交易难以达成，因为……

3）我们不得不做如下还盘，以我方在2015年7月1日或此前收到你方的答复为有效。

A：那么，我用英语该怎么说呢？

B：到"常用语句集"去看看，你先找到同类的句型，然后采用截取、替换、拼接的办法稍做加工，你需要的句子就有了。

A：嘿！瞧瞧，我的英语还不错吧！

3. Asking for a Reduction in Price （进口商要求降价）

A：我是买方，现认为卖方的报价太高，想让对方降价。我该怎么说呢？

B：你可以这样说：

1）除非你方降价10%，否则我们无法接受报盘。

2）如果贵公司降价到50美元每件，我们会考虑下订单。

3）为了拓展贵公司的业务，我们相信你方能给予我方2%的降价。

A：那么，我用英语该怎么说呢？

B：到"常用语句集"去看看，你先找到同类的句型，然后采用截取、替换、拼接的办法稍做加工，你需要的句子就有了。

A：嘿！瞧瞧，我的英语还不错吧！

Part Ⅲ. Case（案例）

1. Establishing Business Relations（出口商寻求建立贸易关系）

林平平是浙江清香茶叶有限公司（Zhejiang Qingxiang Tea Co., Ltd.）的业务员，负责向海内外客户营销各种茶叶和瓷器茶具（teas and porcelain tea sets）。通过互联网搜索，林平平发现名为"Britain Tea Bags (Pvt) Ltd."的一家英国贸易公司正在寻购茶叶，这家公司是英国最大的茶叶进口商之一。林平平随即发出电子邮件表达建立业务关系的愿望，并附寄电子宣传册（E-brochure）向对方介绍己方公司以及所经营的产品。

发件人（From）	Linpingping@qingxiang.com
收件人（To）	import@Britainteabags.com
主题（Subject）	Teas and Porcelain Tea Sets.
附件（Attachment）	E-brochure

Dear Sir or Madam,

We have obtained your name and address from the website: www.alibaba.com. We understand that you are one of the biggest importers of tea in UK and you are now in the market for tea. We are therefore taking this opportunity to approach you in the hope of establishing business relations with you.

To give you a general idea of our products, we attach herewith our E-brochure covering the main items available at present.

If you are interested in any of our products, please email me. We look forward to providing you with high quality products and superior customer service.

Yours faithfully,

Lin Pingping

Salesperson

Sentence Patterns Applied（语句归纳）
- ➢ 出口商说明信息来源，说明所了解的信息，寻求建交；
- ➢ 出口商附寄产品资料；
- ➢ 出口商敦促联系，期盼提供服务。

2. Enquiry（进口商询盘）

Justin Brown 是英国公司 Britain Tea Bags (Pvt) Ltd.的业务员，他收到了林平平的邮件。他仔细查看了附件中的电子宣传册，对一款货号为 M-T16 的名为"梅家坞西湖龙井"的茶叶产生了兴趣，认为这正是己方公司所要购进的，于是，他决定向林平平回复邮件进行询盘。邮件中，Justin 指明所需产品的名称和货号，要求林平平提供产品的详细信息以便于了解其质量，并请求寄送样品。同时，Justin 还询问最早的装运期和最小的起订量（minimum order quantity）。

发件人（From）	import@Britainteabags.com
收件人（To）	Linpingping@qingxiang.com
主题（Subject）	Enquiry for Meijiawu West Lake Longjing Tea
附件（Attachment）	

Dear Mr. Lin,

We thank you for your email and shall be glad to enter into business relations with you.

We have seen your brochure and are interested in Item No. M-T16, Meijiawu West Lake Longjing Tea. We shall be pleased if you would kindly send us samples and email us the necessary information regarding the products so as to acquaint us with the quality. Meanwhile, please quote us lowest price, CIF Liverpool, stating the earliest date of shipment and minimum order quantity.

Should your price be competitive and date of shipment acceptable, we intend to place a large order with you.

Your speedy response will be highly appreciated.

Yours sincerely,

Justin Brown

Salesperson

Sentence Patterns Applied（语句归纳）
- ➢ 进口商收到邮件，同意建立外贸关系；
- ➢ 进口商提及相关产品，索要产品样品，询问产品质量，要求报价，询问装运期与起订量；
- ➢ 进口商劝导报价；
- ➢ 进口商期盼回复。

3. Making an Offer（出口商报盘）

林平平收到了 Justin 的回复，感到很高兴。他认为，对方的询价很具体，很有诚意，是一个潜在的客户，于是，他发邮件报盘。他把产品名称、价格、等级、数量、交货期等信息填写到报盘单（offer sheet），准备放在邮件的附件里，同时，还附件寄送一个电子单页（leaflet）来介绍该产品的详细信息。另外，他同意给对方寄送样品，准备通过联邦快递（FedEx）寄出。

现在，你是浙江清香茶叶有限公司的业务员林平平，请你根据以上情况向 Justin 写一封电子邮件。

Sentence Patterns for Reference（参考语句）
- 出口商收到询价（回复），报价；
- 出口商附寄报盘，附寄产品资料；
- 出口商承诺寄送样品；
- 出口商评价产品质量，评价价格，劝导下订单；
- 出口商期盼回复。

发件人（From）	
收件人（To）	
主题（Subject）	
附件（Attachment）	

An Offer Sheet （报盘单）

报盘单
Offer Sheet

收件人 Attn.	Britain Tea Bags (Pvt) Ltd.	传真号 Fax No.	
发件人 From	Zhejiang Qingxiang Tea Co., Ltd.	日期 Date	2015 Sept. 1
拟制 Drawn By	Lin Pingping	批准 Approved By	

产品名称 Description	物料编码 Part No.	型号规格 Specification	单价 Unit Price
Meijiawu Westlaike Longjing Tea	M-T16	M-T16	$780/Kilo

1、 报价有效期（Period of Validity）：_____。
2、 价格术语（Terms of Price）：__CIF Liverpool__。
3、 付款方式（Terms of Payment）：__Sight L/C__。
4、 平均交货期（Average Lead Time）：__(in stock)__。
5、 最小包装（Minimum of Package）：_____。
6、 每单最小起定量（Min. Quantity Per Order）：__100 kilograms__。

4. Reply to Offer（进口商对报盘的回复）

Justin Brown 收到林平平的报盘后，即刻做出了回复，承诺一收到样品后会马上联系。

发件人（From）	import@Britainteabags.com
收件人（To）	Linpingping@qingxiang.com
主题（Subject）	Meijiawu West Lake Longjing Tea
附件（Attachment）	

Dear Mr. Lin,

Thank you very much for your prompt offer. I will contact you as soon as we receive your samples.

Yours sincerely,

Justin Brown

Salesperson

Sentence Patterns Applied（语句归纳）
- 进口商收到报盘，致谢，承诺联系。

5. Counteroffer（进口商还盘）

Britain Tea Bags (Pvt) Ltd.收到了林平平寄来的样品，经查看发现，样品质量比本地市场上销售的日本茶叶稍好，但价格比日本茶叶高出 20%。公司决定还盘：如对方降价 15%，可以考虑订购。

现在，你是 Justin，你需要写邮件向林平平还盘。

Sentence Patterns for Reference（参考语句）
- 进口商收到样品，致谢；
- 进口商评价价格，对比产品价格，评价产品质量；
- 进口商要求价格打折，要求降价；
- 进口商劝导接受还盘；
- 进口商期盼回复。

发件人（From）	
收件人（To）	

主题（Subject）	
附件（Attachment）	

....
....
....
....
....
....
....
....
....
....
....
....
....

Part Ⅳ. Writing Directions（写作指导）

出口商报盘

报盘是卖方对询价或询盘的回复。报盘是在全面权衡各个交易条件的基础上产生的，所以比报价更加具体、准确。为了抓住交易机会，报盘一定要及时。报盘的内容可包括：

➢ 感谢对方的询盘；
➢ 介绍己方公司与业务（初次）；
➢ 介绍产品；
➢ 报盘，说明产品数量、单价、目的港等；
➢ 明确报盘的条件（实盘或虚盘）；
➢ 说明产品包装、支付方式、交货期；
➢ 劝导对方接受；
➢ 期盼回复。

报盘信函一般采用附件传送的报盘单报盘，所以，实际正文比较简洁。

进口商还盘

当进口商不接受出口商的报盘时,可以进行还盘。还盘函的内容一般包括:
- 感谢报盘;
- 表示不能接受报盘,表示歉意;
- 说明不接受报盘的理由;
- 提出己方的条件或要求;
- 劝导接受;
- 期盼回复。

进口商还盘大多是因为对方所报的价格太高,但也有其他情况下的还盘,比如交货期、付款条件、包装等。在指明不能接受的条款时,要说明不能接受的原因,并适时提出己方的建议。

进出口双方都可以还盘,往复多次,没有限制。如果实在达不成一致,也要展示出友好的态度。

还盘函要直奔主题,注意礼貌,要清晰地表明自己的态度。

出口商谢绝报盘

出口方在收到进口商的询盘后,发现由于缺货或其他原因无法满足对方要求而不能报盘时,就不得不谢绝报盘。谢绝报盘要解释不能报盘的原因,要展示出真诚良好的合作态度,给对方留下友好的印象。
- 感谢对方的询价;
- 对不能报盘表示歉意;
- 说明不能报盘的原因;
- 介绍替代产品(如缺货);
- 期盼回复。

报盘和还盘措辞要谨慎,防止含混或引起误解。

Part V. Terms and Sentence Frames
(术语与句型)

1. Terms(术语)

报盘
offeror 发盘人,报盘人
offeree 受盘人
offer 报盘

counteroffer 还盘，还价
official offer 正式报盘
preferential offer 优先报盘
special offer 特殊报价
offer price 售价

虚盘

non-firm offer 虚盘
an offer subject to our final confirmation 以我方最后确认为准的报盘
an offer subject to the goods being unsold 以货物尚未出售为有效的报盘
an offer subject to prior sale 以先售为条件的报盘
an offer subject to change without notice 不经通知可以改变的报盘
an offer without engagement 无约束性的报盘
an offer without obligation 无约束性的报盘
an offer subject to market fluctuation 以市场浮动为准的报盘

实盘

firm offer 实盘
an offer subject to your reply reaching here by… 以你方在……之前回复为有效
an offer subject to your reply reaching here within…days 以你方在……天内回复为有效
an offer subject to your reply received by us before… 以我方在……之前收到你方的回复为有效

交易条件

price terms 价格条件
payment terms 付款条件
discount 折扣
packing 包装
delivery date 交货日期
shipment 装运
time of shipment 装运时间

市场

market condition 市场状况
market fluctuation 市场波动
market information 市场信息
market price 市场价格

market research 市场研究
market survey 市场调查
domestic market 国内市场
foreign market 国外市场
overseas market 国外市场
product market 产品市场
market quotation 市场价格
market shortfall 市场供应不足
market transaction 市场交易

2. Sentence Frames（句型）

报盘

to offer 报盘
to offer CIF 报盘到岸价
to offer as follows 报盘如下
to make sb. an offer 向某人报盘
to make an offer for something 就某商品报盘
to give sb. an offer 向某人报盘
to entertain an offer 考虑报盘
to accept an offer 接受报盘

报实盘

to offer firm 报实盘
to remain effective for…days 有效期为……天
to remain good for…days 有效期为……天
to remain available for…days 有效期为……天
to remain firm for…days 有效期为……天
to remain valid for…days 有效期为……天
to remain open for…days 有效期为……天

说明折扣、支付方式、包装、装运等

to allow a discount of… 打折……
(payment is) to be made by… 货款支付方式为……
(shipment is) to be made during… 装运在……进行
(goods are) to be packed in … 货物用……包装

提供优惠条件；

to give you the first chance 给予你方优先

to give you a discount 给你方折扣
to allow you a discount 给你方折扣
to offer you a discount 给你方折扣
to grant you a discount 给你方折扣

说明市场行情
to be active （市场）活跃的
to be advancing （市场）旺盛的
to be weak （市场）疲软的
to be declining （市场）衰退的
to be depressed （市场）不景气的
to be inactive （市场）不活跃的
to be overstocked （市场）存货过多的
to be steady （市场）稳定的
to be flat （市场）平稳的
to be firm （市场）稳定的
to be quiet （市场）平静的
to be sluggish （市场）滞缓的
to be dull （市场）迟缓的，呆滞的
to be feverish （市场）波动的
to be panicky （市场）恐慌的

比较产品
to compare favorably with... 比……要好
to make a comparison 做比较
to be ... than... 比……要……
a comparison will convince you of.... 通过比较使你相信……

评价报盘
to be unworkable （报盘）不可行的
to be unrealistic （报盘）不现实的
to be unacceptable （报盘）不可接受的
to be infeasible （报盘）不可行的
to be on the high side （报盘）偏高
to be out of line with the market （报盘）与市场不一致
to be too high to be acceptable （报盘）太高不能接受

还盘
to counteroffer 还盘

to make a counteroffer 还盘

to make reduction in your price 降价

to make concession in your price 降价

to reduce your price by… 你方把价格降低……

to reduce your price to… 你方把价格降低到……

Part Ⅵ. Follow Me （跟我写）

1. Offer（出口商报盘）

电子邮件模板

Dear Mr. /Ms. <u>对方的姓</u>,

Thank you for your enquiry of <u>（对方询价的日期）</u>, asking for quotation on <u>（对方打算购买的数量）</u> of our <u>（我方产品的名称）</u> made in <u>（产品生产地）</u>. We are pleased to offer the following:

  Commodity: <u>（产品名称）</u>
  Specifications: <u>（产品规格）</u>
  Material: <u>（产品材质）</u>
  Stuffing: <u>（产品内部填充物）</u>
  Colors: <u>（产品颜色）</u>
  Place of Origin: <u>（产品原产地）</u>
  Quantity: <u>（数量）</u>
  Price: <u>（价格）</u>
  Payment: <u>（付款方式）</u>
  Packaging: <u>（包装方式）</u>
  Shipment: <u>（交货期）</u>

The above offer is firm until <u>（报盘有效终止日）</u>. If you think our offer is satisfactory, please let us know on or before <u>（期限）</u>. You can be assured of our best service.

Yours sincerely,

  <u>（署名）</u>

贸易背景

我公司生产并出口毛绒玩具猴（plush monkey toys）。毛绒玩具猴的规格分为大号、中号、小号（big size, medium size, small size）三种，分别为80cm、50cm 和 30cm。毛绒玩具猴采用全棉法兰绒（100% cotton flannel fabric）面料制作，颜色有橘色和棕色（orange and brown），内部用 PP 棉（polyester fiber）填充，生产地在江苏。按照包装惯例，小号玩具猴是一个纸盒（carton）装一打，一个木箱（wooden case）装十个纸盒，出口纽约的到岸价（CIF New York）是每打 298 美元，付款方式一律采用不可撤销的即期信用证（irrevocable L/C at sight），装运期是收到对方信用证后的 30 日之内。

2015 年 7 月 2 日，美国纽约一家公司的 William Taylor 先生发邮件向我公司询价 8 000 打小号毛绒玩具猴。我公司业务员王碧琳需要回复邮件报盘，报盘有效期至 7 月 10 日。

仿照模板套写

2. Counter-offer（进口商还盘）

电子邮件模板

Dear Mr. /Ms. （对方的姓），

We thank you for your offer of（对方的报盘日期）, offering us（产品的数量）（产品的名称） made in （产品生产地）at （对方所报的价格）.

We regret to inform you that we cannot accept your offer as （不接受报盘的理由）. We would like you to consider our counter offer and send your response reaching us on or before （要求对方回复的最后期限）.

　　Counteroffer: （产品的数量） （产品的名称） made in （产品生产地） at （我方还盘价）. We are satisfied with the other terms in your offer.

　　We look forward to your favorable response.

　　Yours sincerely,

　　（署名）

贸易背景

　　我公司位于美国纽约，现收到中国江苏出口商王碧琳女士2015年7月3日关于8 000打小号毛绒玩具猴的报盘。王碧琳的报价是每打298美元纽约到岸价。我方无法接受这个价格，因为我们从其他卖家已收到几个报价，都比对方报的价格低10美元每打（lower by $10 per dozen）。

　　于是，William Taylor先生需要回复邮件进行还盘，提出8 000打江苏产小号毛绒猴每打288美元纽约港到岸价，要求对方于7月12日或之前答复。至于其他内容，我们无异议。

仿照模板套写

Part VII. Practical Writing （实训写作）

1. Match the words and phrases with their Chinese meanings.

offer	实盘
counteroffer	虚盘
firm offer	正式报盘
non-firm offer	报盘
official offer	接受报盘
offer price	报虚盘
accept an offer	报盘如下
make a firm offer	报实盘
offer as follows	报盘价
offer without engagement	还盘

2. Read the following email and list the sentence patterns applied.

We thank you for your enquiry of 10th September for Groundnuts（花生）CFR Antwerp（安特卫普）.

In reply, we make a firm offer, subject to your reply reaching us on or before September 20th for 250 metric tons of Groundnuts, Handpicked（手捡的）, Shelled（去壳的）and Ungraded（不分等级的）at US$ 200 net per metric ton CFR Antwerp and any other European Main Ports. Goods will be shipped within 30 days after receipt of your sight L/C.

Please note that we have quoted our best price and are unable to entertain any counteroffer.

----

3. Complete each of the following sentences according to its model given.

1）This offer is subject to the goods being unsold.
This offer (以你方7日内回复为有效)_____.

2）The offer is valid for 7 days.
The offer is (在5月15日前有效)_____.

3）We regret to inform you that your price is so high that we cannot accept it.
We regret to inform you that (你方的价格太高，我方很难将其推销出去)_____

_____
_____.

4) Information indicates that some parcels of similar quality are being sold at prices about 10% lower than yours.

Information indicates（美国进口的相同质量的商品卖价比你方低 8%）_____
_____
_____.

5) We do not deny that the quality of your product is slightly better. However, in no case should the difference in price be as much as 10%.

We do not deny that (你方产品款式新颖)_____
_____. However,（价格上的差异无论如何也不可能高达 20%）_____
_____
_____.

6) Market is weak and in a state of decline.

Market is (坚挺并有上扬趋势)_____
_____.

7) Your offer is out of line with the market price. Therefore, we make a counteroffer as follows.

Your offer (脱离行情，所以我方不能接受)_____
_____.

8) Let's meet each other half way（各退让一步）and reduce the price by 2%

Let's meet each other half way（将价格降到 10 美元每件）_____
_____.

9) Since you are a valued（受重视的） customer, we are giving you this opportunity of accepting your counteroffer.

（为了双方建立长期友好的贸易关系）_____
_____, we are giving you this opportunity of accepting your counteroffer.

10) In view of the fact that we have given you the most favorable price and the quality of our products is excellent, we trust you will place an order with us.

In view of the fact that we have given you the most favorable price and the quality of our products is excellent,（我们相信你方会接受我方报盘）_____
_____.

4. Complete the following email of offer with words and phrases given in the box.

| 1) subject to | 2) for | 3) confirmation |
| 4) email | 5) making | |

Thank you for your _____ of enquiry _____ our leather bags. In reply, we take pleasure in_____ you an offer attached with our catalogues.

Please note that this offer is _____ our final _____.

We trust you will find our offer competitive and assure you of our best services at all times.

5. Complete the following email of counteroffer with words and phrases given in the box.

1）for	2）making	3）on the high side
4）to accept	5）at	6）out of line
7）per	8）reduce	9）counter-offer
10）by		

We thank you for your offer _____ 1000 sets of Butterfly Brand sewing machines _____ $ 60 _____ set CIF London.

However, we regret to state that our end-users here find your price _____ and _____ with the prevailing market level. As you know, the prices of sewing machines have declined since last year. You may be aware that some dealers are lowering their prices. Under these circumstances, it is impossible for us _____ your price. If you can _____ your price _____ 5%, there is a possibility of getting business done.

We are _____ this counteroffer based on the long-standing business relationship between us. As the market is declining, we hope you will consider our _____.

We would appreciate a speedy response.

Part Ⅷ. Linkage（知识链接）

报价与报盘（Qotation and Offer）

报价和报盘都是卖方向买方提供商品的交易信息，但二者所报的内容有差别。

报价一般只包括商品的品名、规格和单价3项，有的报价中也包括数量和交货期2项。报价通常是卖方对一个新客户第一次询价的答复。

报盘又称发盘，它包括商品的品名、规格、数量、单价、包装、交货期、付款方式7项。报盘是双方经过磋商后，卖方向买方正式的、完整的报价。

虚盘与实盘（Non-firm Offer and Firm Offer）

虚盘是无约束力的报盘。一般情况下，多数报盘均为虚盘，虚盘不规定报盘的有效日期，并且附有保留条件，如：The offer is subject to our final confirmation.（该报盘以我方最后确认为准。）

实盘规定有效日期，而且一旦被买方接受，报盘人就不能撤回。

如果说，虚盘包括7项交易信息，那么，实盘包括8项，多一个有效期。

Part IX. Glossary of Common Sentences
（常用语句集）

1. 出口商

出口商	报盘	实盘		We are in a position to make you a firm offer for T-shirt. 我们现向你方报 T 恤的实盘。
出口商	报盘	实盘		We offer you firm, as follows. 我们向你方报以下实盘。
出口商	报盘	实盘		We're willing to make you a firm offer at this price. 我们愿意以此价格为你方报实盘。
出口商	报盘	虚盘		As requested, we are offering you the following subject to our final confirmation. 根据要求，现我方就如下货物向贵方报盘，以我方最后确认为准。
出口商	报盘	虚盘		We make you the following offer, subject to the goods being unsold. 我方做如下报盘，以货物未经出售为有效。
出口商	报盘	虚盘		We offer you without engagement the following. 我方向你方报虚盘如下。
出口商	报盘			In reply to your enquiry dated Dec. 10, we quote you the price CFR Hamburg for 5m/t Walnut meat. 现回复你方 12 月 10 日询盘，报 5 公吨核桃仁 CFR 汉堡价。
出口商	报盘			Thank you for your enquiry of May 21. We are pleased to send you our best quotation for Men's Shirts. 谢谢你方 5 月 21 日询盘，现高兴地向你方报男衬衫最低价。
出口商	报盘			We take pleasure in quoting you our lowest price for black tea. 现报红茶最低价。
出口商	承诺	报盘		We have received your enquiry and will give you a quotation for 30 long tons of Tin Foil Sheets as soon as possible. 我们已收到你方询盘，将尽快给你方 30 长吨锡箔的报价。
出口商	承诺	报盘		We'll let you have our firm offer next Sunday. 下星期天我们就向你们发实盘。
出口商	承诺	产品	质量	We offer a 100% satisfaction guarantee on all of our merchandise. 我们保证我们的所有商品都能让您百分之百满意。
出口商	承诺	产品	质量	You can rest assured of the quality of our products. 你可以对我们产品的质量放心。
出口商	承诺	产品	质量	You may rest assured that you will be satisfied with our goods. 贵方可放心，您会对我方货物感到满意。
出口商	发盘	实盘		We offer, subject to your reply reaching us on or before February 28th, 500 Phoenix Brand bicycles at 50 USD per set CIF London for shipment in April. 我方提供 500 辆凤凰牌自行车，每辆 50 美元 CIF 伦敦价，4 月份装运。本报价为你方 2 月 28 日或之前答复有效。

续表

出口商	发盘	虚盘		In response to your enquiry of May 1st, we quote, subject to our final confirmation, Butterfly Brand Sewing Machine, model JB1 at 240 USD per set Rangoon. Time of shipment depends on the quantity ordered. 兹答复你方5月1日的询盘：蝴蝶牌洗衣机，型号JB1，每台240美元CIF仰光。装运时间视订单数量而定。本报价以我方最后确认为准。
出口商	回绝	还盘	价格	It is regrettable that it is impossible for us to accept your counter-offer, even to meet you halfway. 很遗憾，我们没法接受贵方还盘，甚至折中价。
出口商	回绝	还盘	价格	The price quoted to you is very reasonable, and we regret that your counteroffer is not acceptable to us. 我方发盘十分合理，因此很遗憾不能接受贵方还盘。
出口商	回绝	还盘	价格	We are not in a position to entertain business at your price, since it is far below our cost. 我们不能以此价格和你方达成交易，因为这一价格远远低于我们的成本。
出口商	接受	还盘		Although your price is below our level, we accept, as an exception, your order with a view to initiating business with you. 尽管你们的价格低于我们的标准，但因首次与您开展业务，我们破例接受此订单。
出口商	接受	还盘		As a token of friendship, we accept your counter-offer. 考虑到双方的友谊，我们接受贵方还盘。
出口商	接受	还盘		Your counterbid is well founded. We will consider accepting it. 你方还价很合理，我们准备接受你方还盘。
出口商	拒绝	报盘	缺货	As recently the goods are in extremely short supply, we regret being unable to make an offer. 因近期货源紧张，很抱歉不能报盘。
出口商	拒绝	报盘	缺货	Owing to heavy commitments, we cannot accept fresh business at present. 由于订单太多，请恕我方不能接受新业务。
出口商	拒绝	报盘	缺货	Thank you for your inquiry, but the goods are now out of stock. 谢谢你的询问，可是现在库存无货。
出口商	拒绝	价格	下调	After careful thought, we must state that our price is moderately fixed and we are not in a position to grant the reduction you asked for. 经过深思熟虑，坦白说，我们的价格已确定，无法给予贵方要求的降价。
出口商	拒绝	价格	下调	Although we are anxious to begin business with you, we regret that we cannot allow the reduction asked. Our prices have been cut to the lowest possible point. 尽管我渴望与贵方开展贸易，但很抱歉不能接受贵方的降价要求，我方价格已削减到了最低。
出口商	拒绝	价格	下调	The price you counter offered is not in line with the prevailing market. We find it too low to be acceptable. 你方还盘与现行市场价不符。我方觉得太低，无法接受。
出口商	开列	报盘	项目	Referring to your email dated July 10 in which you inquire for shirts, we have pleasure in giving you following offer. 关于贵方7月10日对衬衫的询盘，现报盘如下。

续表

出口商	开列	报盘	项目	Replying to your enquiry of the 8th May, we have pleasure quoting our sateen as follows. 贵公司5月8日询盘收悉,现对我公司的贡缎报价如下。
出口商	开列	报盘	项目	We acknowledge with thanks receipt of your email of March 11 enquiring for peanuts. Our offer is as follows. 收到你方3月11日对花生的询盘,我方不胜感激,现报价如下。
出口商	评价	报盘	价格	Given the high quality of our merchandise, we believe that this is a reasonable price. 鉴于我们的商品品质优秀,我们认为目前的价格是合理的。
出口商	评价	报盘	价格	This is a special offer and is not subject to our usual discount. 本报价很优惠,而且给予特殊折扣。
出口商	评价	报盘		This offer is based on an expanding market and is competitive. 此报盘着眼于扩大销路而且很有竞争性。
出口商	评价	报盘		We feel sure that a fair comparison in quality between our electric fans and those of other suppliers will convince you of the fairness of our quotation. 我们确信公正地比较我们的电扇和其他供应商的电风扇的质量会使你相信我们的报价是适当的。
出口商	评价	产品	工艺	Chinese Cloisonne is famous in the world for its unique craftsmanship. 中国景泰蓝以它独特的工艺闻名于世界。
出口商	评价	产品	价格	Our goods are moderate in price, about 10% lower than our competitors'. 我们的货物价格公道,大约比我们竞争者的货价要低10%。
出口商	评价	产品	价格	The price of our product is 15% lower than that of similar product of Indian origin. 我们产品的价格要比印度产的同类产品价格低15%。
出口商	评价	产品	价格	The prices of our products are in line with the prevailing market level. 我们产品的价格与现行的行市水平相一致。
出口商	评价	产品	款式	The gloves are made of superior genuine leather and can be supplied in various designs and colors. 手套是用上乘真皮制成,有多种式样和颜色可供应。
出口商	评价	产品	款式	The product is guaranteed long wear, attractiveness and real comfort. 产品保证耐用、美观、舒适。
出口商	评价	产品	款式	They are really beautifully designed. 它们确实设计得很漂亮。
出口商	评价	产品	声誉	Chinese silk pieces enjoy great popularity in South Asia. 中国丝绸享誉南亚。
出口商	评价	产品	声誉	Our products enjoy great popularity in this line. 我方产品在这方面享有盛誉。
出口商	评价	产品	声誉	The goods are unanimously acclaimed by our customers. 该产品得到我方客户一致好评。
出口商	评价	产品	销路	Our T-shirts can find a ready market in the eastern part of your country. 我公司的T恤在贵国东部市场很畅销。
出口商	评价	产品	销路	The goods are most popular with our customers. 该产品受到我方客户的极大欢迎。

出口商	评价	产品	销路	This item, being quite popular, will also command / find a ready sale in your market. 这种畅销品在你方市场上也会有好销路。
出口商	评价	产品	质量	Our products have competitive price and of high quality. 我们的产品价格很有竞争力,质量始终如一,品质上乘。
出口商	评价	产品	质量	The quality and prices of our products compare favorably with those of Japanese makes. 我们产品的质量比日本货的质量要好,价格也便宜。
出口商	评价	产品	质量	The quality of Art. No. 401 is better than that of Art. No. 301. 第401号商品的质量要比第301号商品好。
出口商	评价	产品		Being moderate in price and attractive in packing, our toys are very popular with customers in the U.S. 我们的玩具由于价格公道,包装别致,在美国很受顾客欢迎。
出口商	评价	产品		Excellent in craftsmanship and novel in designs, our silk garments command a ready sale in your market. 我们的丝绸服装工艺精湛,设计新颖,在你们的市场上很畅销。
出口商	评价	产品		Our blanket is a perfect combination of durability, warmth, softness and easy care. 我们的毛毯经久耐用,柔软温和,使用方便。
出口商	评价	产品		Our competitive prices, superior quality and efficiency have won confidence and goodwill among our business clients. 我们具有竞争性的价格,上乘的质量和卓越的效率已经在我们的客户中赢得信誉。
出口商	评价	产品		Our silk garments are made of pure silk of the best quality. They are moderate in price, excellent in craftsmanship and unique in design. 我们的丝绸服饰采用上乘纯真丝制成,价格公道,工艺精湛,设计独特。
出口商	评价	价格	合理	Our offer was reasonable instead of wild speculations. 我们的报价合理,而不是漫天要价。
出口商	评价	价格	合理	Our price is reasonable, compared with that in the international market. 我方价格与国际市场相比还是合理的。
出口商	评价	价格	合理	The price comes in line with the ruling price in the world market. 这价格与世界市场上的通行价格是一致的。
出口商	评价	价格	优惠	I'm afraid you won't find another company who will give you cheaper prices than ours. 恐怕不会再有其他公司可以提供比我们更低的价格。
出口商	评价	价格	优惠	If it had not been for our good relationship, we couldn't have made you a firm offer at this price. 要不是为了我们的友好关系,我们是不以这个价格报实盘的。
出口商	评价	价格	优惠	Our price is lower than that in the international market. 我们的价格比国际市场价格要低得多。
出口商	评价	价格	优惠	We've kept the price close to the costs of production. 我们已经把价格压到生产费用的边缘了。
出口商	评价	价格	优惠	You'll see that our offer compares favorably with the quotations you can get elsewhere. 你会发现我们的报价比别处要便宜。

续表

出口商	劝导	订购		A trial order will convince you that the products will meet your needs to your satisfaction. 一次试订货便会使你相信，这种产品会满足你方要求。
出口商	劝导	订购		As for the above offer, it is extremely probable that the price will rise still more and it would therefore be to your interest to place your orders without delay. 对于以上报盘，产品价格极有可能上升，因此，从你方利益考虑，应及早订货。
出口商	劝导	订购		Because of the heavy demands for the limited supply of this velvet in stock, we would advise you to place your order without delay. 由于丝绒需求量大且库存有限，我们建议你方及早订货。
出口商	劝导	订购		The quality of our products is good and the prices are favorable, so we recommend that you accept our offer. 我们的产品质量好，价格优惠，因此我们推荐贵方接受我方的报价。
出口商	劝导	订购		We deem it to your advantage to avail yourselves of our offer. 我们认为你方接受我方报盘是有利的。
出口商	劝导	订购		We trust you will find our quotation satisfactory and look forward to receiving your order. 我们相信你方会十分满意我方报价，盼望收到你方订单。
出口商	申明	实盘	有效期	Our offer remains effective for 10 days. 本报盘有效期为10天。
出口商	申明	实盘	有效期	The above offer is valid for one month. In case of order, you must arrange it to reach us before October 31. 上述报盘的有效期为一个月。若要订购，订单必须在10月31日之前抵达我方。
出口商	申明	实盘	有效期	The offer will remain firm until May 31, beyond which date the terms and prices must be renegotiated. 报价有效期到5月31日，过了这个日期，条件和价格必须重新商议。
出口商	申明	虚盘		Please note that our quotation may change without notice. 请注意，我方报价如有变更，不另通知。
出口商	申明	虚盘		The offer is subject to the seller's final confirmation. 本盘以卖方最终确认为准。
出口商	申明	虚盘		The offer is without obligation. 本报盘无约束力。
出口商	同意	价格	打折	Based on your purchase volume, we are prepared to offer you a 2% discount. 根据您购买的数量，我们打算给您2%的优惠。
出口商	同意	价格	打折	Considering our longstanding cordial business relationship, we can allow you a reduction of 4% in our price. 考虑到我们双方的长期友好贸易关系，我们同意在原价基础上让利4%。
出口商	同意	价格	打折	In order to conclude the business, we are prepared to lower our price by 30 percent. 为了达成这笔买卖，我们准备降价30%。
出口商	同意	价格	打折	The best we can do is to make a reduction of 3% in our quotation. 我方能做出的最大让步就是在我们的报价中降低3%。

续表

出口商	同意	价格	打折	The highest discount we can allow you on this article is 8%. 这种商品我们所能给的最高折扣是8%。
出口商	同意	价格	打折	We are prepared to offer you 8% reduction. 但是我们可以考虑给你们便宜8%。
出口商	同意	价格	打折	We have decided to meet you half way by allowing you 5% discount on this transaction. 我们决定各让一步，对这笔交易给予你5%的折扣。
出口商	同意	价格	下调	If your order is large enough, we can consider making a further concession in our price. 如果你们订货数量较大，我们可以考虑在价格上再做一些让步。
出口商	同意	价格	下调	Taking into consideration our cordial business relations, we will exceptionally comply with your request by reducing our price to 5 USD per piece CIF San Francisco. However, this should not be taken as a precedent for the future. 考虑到我们良好的业务关系，我们愿意破例满足你方要求，把价格降到每件5美元CIF旧金山价，但是下不为例。
出口商	同意	价格	下调	We could bring it down to $340 per unit. 我们可以把价格压到每台340美元。

2. 进口商

进口商	还盘	价格	打折	A discount on prices will make it easier for us to promote sales. 价格上打点折扣便于我们推销。
进口商	还盘	价格	打折	If you can grant us a special discount of 20%, we will place an order for 20,000 yards. 如能给20%的特别折扣，我们将订购20000码。
进口商	还盘	价格	打折	Should you be ready to reduce your price by, say 5%, we might conclude terms. 如果贵方愿意减价，比如5%，我们就可以成交。
进口商	还盘	价格	打折	To conclude this business, you need to lower your price at least by 10%. 要达成这笔交易，贵方至少要降价10%。
进口商	还盘	价格	打折	To expand your business, we believe you should offer us a reduction of 10%. 为拓展公司业务，我们相信贵方能给予10%的降价。
进口商	还盘	价格	打折	Would you please reduce the price by 5%, otherwise we cannot accept your offer. 贵方能否给予我方5%的降价，否则我们无法接受报盘。
进口商	还盘	价格	打折	You could benefit from higher sale with a little concession, say a 2% reduction. 你方只要稍做让步，比方说降价2%，就可得到一大笔交易。
进口商	还盘	价格	下调	If you can lower the unit price by USD 2.00, we will increase our purchase volume to 500 units. 如果您能把单价降低2美元，我们就会把订购数量增加到500个。

续表

进口商	还盘	价格	下调	Would you consider reducing the unit price from 750 RMB to 700 RMB? 可不可以把单价由 750 元降到 700 元？
进口商	拒绝	报盘	价格	It will be rather difficult for us to push any sales if we buy it at this price. 如果按这个价格买进，我方实在难以推销。
进口商	拒绝	报盘	价格	We have received your offer but regret that your price is too high to be acceptable. Unless you reduce your price in line with the market conditions here, we do not think any business can be done. 我们已收到你方的报价，很遗憾你方的价格太高，不能接受。除非你们降价，与这儿的市场行情一致，否则，我们认为没有生意可做。
进口商	拒绝	报盘	价格	We regret to inform that that we cannot make use of your kind offer at present as similar but well-established products of the same quality are available at much lower prices. 很遗憾我们目前无法接受贵方报价，因为同样质量的广为接受的产品价格更低一些。
进口商	拒绝	报盘	价格	We regret to say that we cannot accept your offer because your price is rather on the high side. 很遗憾，由于贵方价格过高，我方无法接受贵方报盘。
进口商	拒绝	报盘	价格	While appreciating the good quality of your shirts, we find your price is rather too high. 尽管贵方衬衫质量很好，但是我方认为价格过高。
进口商	接受	报盘	附条件	Subject to your shipment in June, we will order 300 tons. 如果你方 6 月装运，我方将订购 300 吨。
进口商	接受	报盘	附条件	We accept your price if you take the quantity we offer. 如果你方接受我们提出的数量，我们便接受你们的价格。
进口商	接受	报盘		We have decided to accept your offer for 200 tons of edible oil at $56 CIF US per ton. 我们决定接受你方关于 200 吨食用油的报盘，单价每吨 56 美元 CIF。
进口商	评价	价格	太高	I think it would be difficult for us to make any sales at such a price. 我认为按这种价格买进，我方实在难以推销。
进口商	评价	价格	太高	To be frank with you, some countries are actually lowering their prices. 坦率地说，一些国家正在降价出售。
进口商	评价	价格	太高	Your unit price is two hundred dollars higher than we can accept. 你们提出的单价比我们可以接受的价格高 200 美元。
进口商	劝导	接受	还盘	We hope that this counter offer will meet with your approval and we shall place regular orders with you on receipt of your confirmation. 希望此还盘能够得到贵公司的同意，一旦收到贵方的确认，我们将定期订货。
进口商	劝导	接受	还盘	We hope you will accept our terms and make preparation for an early delivery. 我们希望你方能接受我方条件，早日做好装船准备。

Unit 4

Order（订单）

Part Ⅰ. Objectives（目标）

After completing this unit, you will be able to

1. read and write English emails and messages relating to an order either as an importer or an exporter;

2. know the essential components of the mails of this kind;

3. become familiar with typical English terms and sentence patterns which are commonly used in the emails and messages above.

Part Ⅱ. How to Express（我该怎么说）

1. Placing an Order（进口商下订单）

A：我是进口方，现在要下订单。我该怎么说呢？
B：你可以这样说：
1）请按照我方第 AS505 号订单供货。
2）我们认为你方价格令人满意，因此很高兴向你们订购 2 000 台长虹电视机。
3）谢谢你方近期的报盘，现向你方订购下列商品。
A：那么，我用英语该怎么说呢？
B：到"常用语句集"去看看，你先找到同类的句型，然后采用截取、替换、拼接的办法稍做加工，你需要的句子就有了。
A：嘿！瞧瞧，我的英语还不错吧！

2. Accepting an Order （出口商接受订单）

A：我是出口方，现收到了进口方的订单，想告诉对方接受订单。我该怎么说呢？

B：你可以这样说：

1）谢谢你方123号订单。我们接受此订单，并尽早交货。

2）很高兴地告知贵方，我们已经接受了贵方订购50吨绿茶的第333号订单。

3）现确认接受你方上周的订单。

A：那么，我用英语该怎么说呢？

B：到"常用语句集"去看看，你先找到同类的句型，然后采用截取、替换、拼接的办法稍做加工，你需要的句子就有了。

A：嘿！瞧瞧，我的英语还不错吧！

3. Refusing an Order（出口商拒绝订单）

A：我是卖方，现收到了订单，但是由于某种原因而不得不谢绝订单。我该怎么说呢？

B：你可以这样说：

1）由于订单太多，请恕我方不能接收新订单。

2）感谢贵方有意购买我方货号为123的自行车，但是我们已经停止生产此产品了。

3）因为原材料供应的问题，非常抱歉我们不能接受你方的续订货。等到供应情况一有好转，我们会马上与你方联系。

A：那么，我用英语该怎么说呢？

B：到"常用语句集"去看看，你先找到同类的句型，然后采用截取、替换、拼接的办法稍做加工，你需要的句子就有了。

A：嘿！瞧瞧，我的英语还不错吧！

Part III. Case（案例）

1. Placing a Repeat Order（进口商续订）

Robert Smith 先生是澳大利亚 Jemala Texture 公司进口部的经理助理。半年多来，Robert Smith 从中国广东祈顺丝绸进出口有限公司几次订购桑蚕丝（mulberry silk），双方交易顺利，丝绸在澳大利亚市场畅销。现在，为了迎接圣诞节购物旺季，Jemala Texture 公司准备再次订购。下面是 Robert Smith 发出的订购邮件。

发件人（From）	robertsmith@hotmail.com
收件人（To）	liuming@mail.qishunsilk.com
主题（Subject）	A Repeat Order for Mulberry Silk
附件（Attachment）	Order No. AB2323

Dear Mr. Liu,

Thanks for your cooperation in the supply of mulberry silk under order No. 1616 for last season. Our customers are all satisfied with the dependable quality and the colours of your products. There is a great demand for your products here.

Please find the attached order No. AB2323. We expect you will allow us the same terms of payment for this repeat order. Meanwhile, we have to lay emphasis upon the point that shipment must be made before Christmas.

We are looking forward to your immediate confirmation.

Sincerely,

Robert Smith

Assistant Manager

Sentence Patterns Applied（语句归纳）
➢ 进口商回顾之前的交易并致谢，评价产品，表达订购愿望；

- 进口商附寄订单，对付款方式提出要求，对装运期提出要求；
- 进口商期盼确认订单。

An Order Form（订单）

Order Form

Order number:	
Date:	
Salesperson:	

Buyer's name:		Phone Number:	
Shipping/Delivery Address:			

Quantity	Item	Price Each	Subtotal
		Total:	
		Sales Tax:	
		Shipping/Delivery Charge:	
		Grand Total:	

2. Refusing an Order（出口商拒绝订单）

刘明先生是广东祈顺丝绸进出口有限公司的销售部经理，他收到了老客户 Robert Smith 的续订单。然而，因为由于公司接受的订单太多，桑蚕丝货源紧缺，实在无货可供。于是，刘明发邮件给 Robert Smith，推荐替代产品——柞蚕丝（tussah silk）。

发件人（From）	liuming@mail.qishunsilk.com
收件人（To）	robertsmith@hotmail.com
主题（Subject）	Tussah Silk as Good as Natural Silk

Dear Mr. Smith,

Thank you for your order No. AB2323.

While we appreciate your efforts in pushing the sales of our products, we regret that we are not in a position to offer you the desired goods, owing to excessive demand. However, we should like to take this opportunity to offer the following material as a close substitute for your consideration.

500 yards Tussah Silk, Item No. 6103, at USD 4.80 per yard CIF Melbourne, including your commission of 3 %.

The sample cutting and color are shown in the sample book which we sent to you a short time ago. If you are able to accept this offer, please reply to us as soon as possible for our confirmation.

Yours sincerely,

Liu Ming

Sales Manager

Sentence Patterns Applied（语句归纳）
- 出口商收到订单，致谢；
- 出口商谢绝订单，致歉（表达遗憾）；
- 出口商推荐产品替代，报价，说明佣金；
- 出口商介绍产品，期盼回复。

3. Placing an Order（进口商下订单）

Robert 收到刘明的邮件后，马上向公司做了汇报。Jemala Texture 公司反复查看了剪样（sample cutting）和花色，认为可以接受刘明推荐的替代品，决定订购货号为 6103 的柞蚕丝绸 500 码，要求其他交易条款（terms and conditions）要和此前十月份成交的编号为 AB1616 的订单相同，尽快装运。

现在，你是 Robert，你需要向刘明发邮件下订单。订单编号：AB2325，订单放在邮件附件中发送给对方。

Sentence Patterns for Reference（参考语句）
- 进口商收到报盘，致谢；
- 进口商接受报盘；
- 进口商附寄订单，对交易条款提出要求；
- 进口商催促尽早装运。

发件人（From）	
收件人（To）	
主题（Subject）	
附件（Attachment）	

4. Accepting an Order（出口商接受订单）

刘明收到了订单，确认接受，通过电子邮件附件向对方发送电子合同，要求对方会签。

发件人（From）	liuming@mail.qishunsilk.com
收件人（To）	robertsmith@hotmail.com
主题（Subject）	500 Yards of Tussah Silk Item No. 6103
附件（Attachment）	Sales Contract No. 223

Dear Mr. Smith

Thank you for your order No. AB2325. We are pleased to confirm with you a transaction of 500 yards of Pongee Silk 6103.

Attached you will find our Sales Contract No. 223 in PDF. Please countersign it and return one copy to us for our file.

We trust you will open the relative L/C as soon as possible.

Yours sincerely,

Liu Ming

Sales Manager

Sentence Patterns Applied（语句归纳）
- 进口商收到订单，致谢，确认接受订单；
- 进口商寄送合同，要求合同会签；
- 进口商要求（催促）开立信用证。

5. Concluding a Contract (进口商签合同)

Robert 收到了刘明寄来的编号为 223 的销售合同，经下载、打印、签署之后，又扫描、发送给了对方。同时，Robert 还告知刘明相关信用证正在开立，承诺信用证开好后会马上打电话通知，要求刘明尽快安排装运。

现在，你是 Robert，你需要向刘明回复邮件。

Sentence Patterns for Reference（参考语句）
- 进口商收到合同，会签合同，附寄合同；
- 进口商通知信用证正在开立，承诺将电话通知信用证开立；
- 进口商提醒、催促安排装运；
- 进口商劝导、期盼订单运作。

发件人（From）	
收件人（To）	
主题（Subject）	
附件（Attachment）	

Part Ⅳ. Writing Directions（写作指导）

进口商下订单

一般来说，下订单之前双方已经经历了反复的磋商，交易条款已经谈妥，或者，订单邮件附带的订单表本身附有各项交易条款，在这种情况下，信文内容往往十分简略。然而，如果进口方以下订单的方式利用信文展开谈判，那么，就必须提及商品名称、规格、数量、金额以及支付方式、包装、装运等交易条款。必要时，对商品的质量、交货期等要做出补充。下订单的信函表述必须要清楚、准确。

➢ 提及之前的信件；
➢ 确认订购某商品；
➢ 说明商品规格、数量、价格等；
➢ 提出要求；

- 劝导执行订单；
- 期盼回复。

偶尔也有向陌生客户下订单的，如果是这样，首先要做自我介绍并说明如何得知对方公司信息。

订单邮件越来越多地利用附件寄送订单表，换言之，信文越来越简略了。

出口商接受订单

接受订单的信件内容有：

- 感谢订购；
- 接受订单；
- 寄送销售确认书或销售合同，要求会签；
- 提出要求，如开立信用证；
- 承诺执行订单；
- 期盼回复。

接受订单的信件一般要重复对方来函中的重要内容如商品名称、规格、数量、价格、包装、交货期、装运、付款等。重复对方信函中的重要内容是外贸信函写作的一个惯例，这显得郑重其事，等于告诉对方：我方将照单执行，不会出错，请放心。

出口商谢绝订单

出于礼貌谢绝订单的信函一定要说明原因，如果是缺货，要不失时机地推荐其他商品，或提议今后合作；如果不能接受对方的某个条款，要加以解释，并提出己方的变通办法。

- 感谢订购；
- 拒绝订单，致歉；
- 拒绝订单的原因；
- 推荐替代商品，或提出其他变通建议；
- 劝导接受；
- 期盼回复。

Part V. Terms and Sentence Frames
（术语与句型）

1. Terms（术语）

订单

order sheet, order form, order blank, order note 订单

sales order 销货订单
trial order 试订单
verbal order 口头订单
split order 分批订单
order on hand 已收到订单
original order 原始订单
received order 收到订单
formal order 正式订单
export order 出口订单
import order 进口订单
first order 首批订单
initial order 首批订货
new order 新订货单
pending order 未完成的订单
repeat order 再次订货，续订单
block order 整批预订

发票
commercial invoice 商业发票
customs invoice 海关发票
provisional invoice 临时发票
consular invoice 领事发票
official invoice 正式发票
proforma invoice 形式发票

2. Sentence Frames（句型）

下订单
to place an order with sb. for something 向某人订购某物
to send sb. an order 向某人下订单
to give sb. an order 向某人下订单
to order something at a price… 按……价格订购
to order from… 向……订购
to place an order elsewhere 向别处订购
to place a trial order 下试订单
to order something as a trial 下试订单
to attach an order 附寄订单
to increase an order 增加订货

to duplicate an order 将订货增加一倍

to be on order 已订购（尚未发货）

接受订单

to take an order 接受订货

to accept an order 接受订单

to entertain an order 接受订单

to confirm acceptance of an order 确认接受订单

执行订单

to execute an order 执行订单

to fulfill an order 执行订单

to fill an order 执行订单

to work on an order 执行订单

to carry out an order 执行订单

to ensure the fulfillment of an order 保证订单的执行

完成订单

to close an order 决定成交

to complete an order 完成订货

to dispatch an order 发货

暂停执行订单

to suspend an order 暂停执行订单

to hold up an order 暂停执行订单

谢绝订单

to decline an order because… 因为……谢绝订单

to refuse an order because… 因为……谢绝订单

to be unable to accept an order 无法接受订单

to be not in a position to accept an order 无法接受订单

to turn down an order 谢绝订单

取消订单

to withdraw an order 取消订单

to rescind an order 取消订单

to revoke an order 取消订单

to cancel an order 取消订货

to cut an order 取消订单

缺货
to be not available 无货可供
to be out of stock 无存货

一式多份
in duplicate 一式两份
in triplicate 一式三份
in quadruplicate 一式四份
in quintuplicate 一式五份
in sextuplicate 一式六份
in septuplicate 一式七份
in octuplicate 一式八份
in nonuplicate 一式九份
in decuplicate 一式十份

Part Ⅵ. Follow Me （跟我写）

1. Placing an Order（进口商下订单）

电子邮件模板

Dear Mr. /Ms. （对方的姓），

Thank you for your timely reply of （对方回复询价的日期，即报盘的日期） to our enquiry about （我方询价的产品）. We are very satisfied with the trade terms you offer. And the prices are acceptable. Therefore, we now email you our purchase order （我方订单的编号） in the attached file.

We will open （我方将开立的信用证类型） in your favor as soon as possible through （将开立信用证的银行）, for the total value of （信用证总金额） as stated in this order. Please inform us of the shipping date （提前告知装船的天数） in advance after you receive our L/C.

We look forward to your confirmation of the acceptance of our order.

Yours sincerely,

（署名）

贸易背景

我公司位于美国纽约，正在寻购印刷用纸（printing paper）。公司业务员 William Monahan 收到一家出口商关于五种印刷用纸的报盘，报盘人是张田先生，报盘日期是 3 月 8 日。我方认为该报盘价格合理，其他交易条件也可以接受。

现在，William Monahan 要回复邮件下订单，订单编号为 PP238。邮件需要告知对方，我方将尽快通过中国银行纽约分行（Bank of China, New York Branch）开立以对方为受益人的不可撤销的即期跟单信用证（an irrevocable documentary L/C at sight），总额为 180 万美元，要求对方至少提前两天将装船日期通知我方。

仿照模板套写

....

....

....

....

....

....

....

....

....

....

....

....

....

....

2. Accepting an Order（出口商接受订单）

电子邮件模板

Dear Mr. /Ms. （对方的姓），

We confirm our acceptance to your order （对方订单的编号） you email us （对方邮件的发送时间） for （对方订购的产品）. And we welcome you as one of our customers.

We are pleased to send you in the attached file the Sales Confirmation （销售合同的编号） for your e-signature. Please sign it and return it to us for our file. And please open your L/C （开立信用证的期限）. Shipment will be made （我方发货的时间）.

Your cooperation is highly appreciated. We assure you of our best service and look forward to receiving more orders from you.

Yours sincerely,

（署名）

贸易背景

今天上午，我公司业务员张田收到了 William Monahan 发来的订购五种印刷用纸（five kinds of printing paper）的编号为 PP238 的订单，公司同意接受此单。

现在，张田要给对方回复邮件，并附件传送编号为 PP080315 的销售合同，要求对方会签后发还供我方存档。邮件还需要叮嘱对方在本月底以前开立相关信用证，并承诺一收到信用证后马上发货。

仿照模板套写

....
....
....
....
....
....
....
....
....
....
....
....
....
....

Part Ⅶ. Practical Writing （实训写作）

1. Match the words and phrases with their Chinese meanings.

trial order	履行订单
accept an order	达成交易
out of stock	试订单
fulfill an order	拒绝订单
repeat order	正式订单
confirm an order	替代品
conclude an order	续订单

replacement	无现货
formal order	接受订单
decline an order	确认订单

2. Read the following email and list the sentence patterns applied.

We have received the captioned（标题项下的）shipping ex s.s. "Dongfeng"（经"东风"号）and are very pleased to inform you that we find the goods quite satisfactory.

As we believe we can sell additional quantities in this market, we wish to place with you a repeat order for 1 000 doz. of the same style and sizes.

If possible, please arrange early shipment of this repeat order, as we are badly in need of the goods.

----

3. Complete each of the following sentences according to its model given.

1）We have pleasure in sending you an order for cosmetics.

We have pleasure in sending you（给贵方寄去洗衣机订单）_____

_____.

2）We have the pleasure of ordering the following goods.

We have the pleasure of ordering（兹订购 900 架钢琴）_____

_____.

3）Thank you for your quotation of September 17 as we are pleased to place a trial order for your electrical products.

Thank you （感谢贵方报盘）_____ as we are pleased to place a trial order for your electrical products.

4）We appreciate your enquiry for our schoolbags and welcome you as one of our customers.

We appreciate （感谢你方订购我们的咖啡）_____ and welcome you as one of our customers.

5）Much to our regret, we cannot at present accept any fresh orders for Tiantan Brand Men's Shirts, owing to heavy commitments.

Much to our regret, we cannot at present accept any fresh orders for Tiantan Brand Men's Shirts, owing to heavy commitments. （一旦补足货源，我们会很高兴满足你方要求）_____

_____

_____.

6) We regret we cannot entertain your order No. 789 due to heavy commitments.

We regret we cannot entertain （非常抱歉我们不能考虑你方的续订单）_____
_____ due to heavy commitments.

7) Now we can supply bed-sheets from stock, and they are of the same quality and also fashionable.

Now we can supply bed-sheets from stock, and they are （它们和贵方订购的货品质量相似而且工艺精湛，设计新颖）_____
_____.

8) Unfortunately, your order goods Model No. 84 are now out of stock, but we recommend No. 85 as a substitute which is very close to your choice in quality though slightly higher in price.

（我们很遗憾地告知你方）_____ that your order goods Model No. 84 are now out of stock, but we recommend No. 85 as a substitute which is very close to your choice in quality though slightly higher in price.

9) We strongly advise you to accept catalogue MX1O1 as the type you selected is no longer obtainable.

We strongly advise you to accept catalogue MX1O1 （这是一个非常好的替代品）
_____.

10) We accept your order and are sending you herewith our sales contract in PDF for your signature.

We accept your order and are sending you herewith （兹寄上我方编号为 123 的售货合同，供贵方签署）_____
_____
_____.

4. Complete the following email of offer with words and phrases given in the box.

1) arrange	2) for	3) further
4) accept	5) receive	

We are very pleased to _____ your Order No. 543 _____ bed sheets and pillow cases. We accordingly _____ the order and shall _____ delivery as soon as possible.

We hope they will reach you in good time and that we may have _____ orders from you.

5. Complete the following email with words and phrases given in the box.

1) recommend	2) Attached	3) contact
4) inconvenience	5) unable	

We are very sorry that we are _____ to fulfill（履行） your order for ten Topline LCD Screens（Topline 液晶屏幕）. Topline has recently ceased production（停止生产） of all smaller-sized LCD screens and our previous stock（目前的库存） has been depleted（耗尽，售完）. We are very sorry for the_____.

Topline is not expected to produce home or business-sized（家用或商用） screens again in the near future.

We_____ Starbyte and Ace screens（Starbyte 和 Ace 的液晶屏幕） as similar in function and price to the Topline products.

Please find_____ another copy of our current catalog. Again, we are sorry that we are unable to provide you with the Topline screens. Please feel free to____ me with any questions you may have. I will be happy to recommend other products for your specific needs.

Part Ⅷ. Linkage（知识链接）

计量单位

在国际贸易中，由于商品的种类和性质不同，计量的方法也不同，又由于各国采用的度量衡制度不一样，计量单位的名称和其表示的实际数量也不一样。

1）重量（weight）。公吨（metric ton, m/t），长吨（long ton, l/t）（英），短吨（short ton, s/t）（美），千克（kilogram, kg），克（gram, g），盎司（ounce, oz），磅（pound, lb）（英、美）。

2）长度（length）。米（meter, m），英尺（foot, ft），码（yard, yd）。

3）面积（area）。平方米（square meter），平方英尺（square foot），平方码（square yard）。

4）体积（volume）。立方米（cubic meter），立方英尺（cubic foot），立方码（cubic yard）。

5）容积（capacity）。公升（liter, l），加仑（gallon, gal），蒲式耳（bushel）。

6）数量（number）。件（piece, pc）、双（pair）、套（set）、打（dozen）、袋（bag）、包（bale）。

毛重（gross weight）和净重（net weight）

毛重指加包装物（没去皮重）的重量。

净重指除去包装物（去皮）的商品重量，但有时商品的包装不便与商品分别计算（如捆麻袋片的盘条等），特别是某些农副产品，习惯上将包装视同商品本身，忽略不计皮重，这种规定称之为"以毛作净"（gross for net）。

Part IX. Glossary of Common Sentences
（常用语句集）

1. 出口商

出口商	承诺	订单	运作	We assure you that our best attention will be given to the execution of this order. 我们保证将尽全力关注并执行本订单。
出口商	承诺	订单	运作	We assure you that this order and further orders shall have our immediate attention. 我们向你方保证将立即运作本次订单及后续订单。
出口商	承诺	订单	运作	We have received your Order No. 751 and it will be executed to your satisfaction. 我们收到你方751号订单，请放心订单运作会让你方满意。
出口商	承诺	订单	运作	Your order is receiving our immediate attention. You can depend on us to make shipment well within your time limit. 我们将立即办理你们的订货。你们尽管放心我们完全可以在你们规定的时间内交货。
出口商	接受	订单		Thank you for your Order No. 123. We accept it and will dispatch the goods early June. 谢谢你方123号订单。我们接受此订单，并将于6月初交货。
出口商	接受	订单		This email is to confirm your order for 2,000 pounds of California pistachios. 发本邮件确认您订购2 000磅加州开心果。
出口商	接受	订单		We are glad to inform you that we have accepted your Order No. 22 for 1,000 tons of black tea. 很高兴地告知你们，我们已经接受了贵方第22号订单，订购1 000吨红茶。
出口商	接受	订单		We have pleasure in informing you that we have accepted your order No. 234. 我们高兴地告知已接受你方第234号订单。
出口商	接受	订单		With reference to the goods you ordered, we have decided to accept your order at the same price as that of last year. 关于你方订购货物，我们决定按去年价格接受你方订单。
出口商	收到	订单		Further to our telephone conversation this morning, I should like to confirm details of the order. 继今天上午我们的电话交谈，我想确认订货的具体内容。
出口商	收到	订单		Thank you for placing an order for our dark chocolate. 感谢您订购我们的黑巧克力。
出口商	收到	订单		We acknowledge with thanks your order of June 1. 我们确认收到你方6月1日订单。
出口商	收到	订单		We are very pleased with your order, because it represents our first deal with you. 我们很荣幸能收到你方的订单，这标志着我们的首次合作。

续表

出口商	收到	订单		We confirm your order dated May 9 for "Apple" brand MP3. 我们确认你方 5 月 9 日"苹果"牌 MP3 的订单。
出口商	通知	订单	运作	Your order is booked and we are working on it. 已接受你方订单，现正在执行中。
出口商	通知	订单	运作	Your order is receiving our immediate attention and we will keep you informed of the progress. 我们正在迅速处理你方订单，并将随时告知你方进展情况。
出口商	推荐	产品	替代	In order to meet your demand, we would recommend an excellent substitute; it is as good as the inquired article in quality. 为满足你方需求，我们推荐一种优秀的替代品，在质量上，他与询价的商品一样好。
出口商	推荐	产品	替代	Unfortunately, your order goods Model No. 84 are now out of stock, but we recommend No. 85 as a substitute which is very close to your choice in quality though slightly higher in price. 很抱歉，你方所订购的 84 型产品目前已无存货，故推荐 85 型产品，此产品与贵方指定的产品在质量上极相近，只是价格稍贵些。
出口商	推荐	产品	替代	We now have a new product, which is an excellent replacement. 我们现在有一个非常好的替代品。
出口商	谢绝	订单	过多	Due to heavy orders recently received from India, we cannot make delivery before June. 由于最近接到印度来的大量订单，我们无法在 6 月前交货。
出口商	谢绝	订单	过多	In view of our heavy bookings, we are not in a position to commit ourselves to new orders. We hope you will understand the position we are facing. 鉴于我方已收到大量订单，我们不能承担新订单，希望贵方能理解我方目前的处境。
出口商	谢绝	订单	过多	Owing to heavy commitments, we cannot accept fresh business at present. 由于订单太多，请恕我方不能接收新业务。
出口商	谢绝	订单	过多	We regret being unable to accept your order because orders currently on hand are too many. 由于目前我们手头的订单太多，很遗憾我们无法接受贵方订单。
出口商	谢绝	订单	价格	As wages and prices of materials have risen considerably, we regret we are not in a position to book the order at the prices we quoted half a year ago. 由于工资和原料价格大幅度上涨，很抱歉无法按我方半年前报价格接受订单。
出口商	谢绝	订单	价格	To our regret, we are unable to accept your order at the price requested, since our profit margin does not allow us any concession by way of discount of price. 很抱歉，我们不能按你方所要求的价格接受订单，因为我方利润已不允许我们再做出让步，给予你方折扣。
出口商	谢绝	订单	缺货	Due to heavy demand, we can accept orders only for August delivery and not in a position to entertain new booking for the moment. 由于需求量大，我们只接受 8 月份交货的订单，目前无法处理新订单。

续表

出口商	谢绝	订单	缺货	In view of the heavy backlog of orders that we have to execute, we hope you will wait for some time to cover your requirements elsewhere in this particular case. 鉴于我们未履行的订单积压太多，希望你们等一些时候，或者在这种特殊情况下从别处进货。
出口商	谢绝	订单	缺货	We regret that, owing to a shortage of stocks, we are unable to fill your order. We will, however, contact you by email once supply improves. 因为存货短缺，未能供应贵公司所需货品，特此致歉。一旦供应情况改善，我们将发邮件通知贵公司。
出口商	谢绝	订单	缺货	We regret to inform you that we are not in a position to cover your need for the said goods. Once our supplies are replenished, we shall be only too pleased to return to this matter. 很遗憾地通知你方我们无法满足你方的要求不能提供你方所说的产品。一旦补足货源，我们会很高兴再谈此事。
出口商	谢绝	订单	缺货	We thank you for your order of March 8 for electric motors, but regret to inform you that because of our stringent supply position we are unable to make supply immediately. 感谢你方3月8日关于电动机的订单，但很遗憾地通知你们，由于我们供货紧张，无法立即供货。
出口商	谢绝	订单	停产	We appreciate your interest in our product, but we no longer supply it as the production has been discontinued. 感谢贵方有意购买我们的产品，但是我们已经停止生产此产品，所以无法提供。
出口商	谢绝	订单	停产	We regret to tell you that the article you order is not available because the demand for this article has fallen to such an extent that we have ceased to produce it. 很遗憾地告知贵方，您所订购的货物目前无货可供，因为对这种产品的需求下降，我方已经停止生产了。
出口商	谢绝	订单	停产	We regret we cannot entertain your repeat order owing to the uncertain availability of raw materials. We shall contact you again once supply position improves. 非常抱歉我们不能考虑你们的续订货，因为不清楚是否有原材料。一旦供应情况有了好转，我们会再与你们联系。

2. 进口商

进口商	催促	订单	运作	Since the traditional season is approaching, we have to ask you to reply by the end of this month. 因为传统的销售季节即将来临，我方要求你们本月底前答复。
进口商	催促	订单	运作	We trust that you will give this order your prompt and careful attention. 我们相信贵方能对此单给予认真及时的安排。
进口商	催促	订单	运作	Your prompt attention to this order will be highly appreciated. 请从速办理本订单，不胜感谢。
进口商	签订	合同		We have counter-signed the contract and now return one copy for your file. 我们已会签了合同并寄回一份供你方存档。

续表

进口商	劝导	订单	运作	If the first order is satisfactorily executed, we shall place further orders with you. 如果第一份订单执行令人满意，我们将向你下更多的订单。
进口商	劝导	订单	运作	If this order is executed to our satisfaction, substantial orders will follow. 如果订单的执行是令人满意的，将会有大量的订单。
进口商	劝导	订单	运作	If this order proves satisfactory, we shall be happy to place further orders with you. 如果这次订货令我方满意，我方会再次订购。
进口商	劝导	订单	运作	We will submit further orders if this one is completed to our satisfaction. 如果这次的订单完成情况令我们满意，我方将继续订购。
进口商		订单		Please supply the corresponding goods in accordance with the details in our order No. 202. 请照我方第202号订单供货。
进口商		订单		We are pleased to place an order with you for 1,000 cases of canned peaches. 我们想订购1 000箱贵公司的蜜桃罐头。
进口商		订单		We find the quality and prices of your product satisfactory and are pleased to place an order with you. 我们认为你们产品的质量和价格是令人满意的，因此很高兴向你们订购。
进口商		订单		We request that you acknowledge acceptance of our order, and confirm the condition stated above. 请接受我方订单，并请确认上述交易条件。
进口商		订单		We thank you for your quotation of May 20 and now place an order with you for the following items. 谢谢你方5月20日报价，现向你方订购下列商品。
进口商	协商	订单	起订量	We are very interested in your watches but because your minimum limit for an order is too big for this market, we have difficulty in inducing buyers to place trial orders for your products. 我们对贵方的手表很感兴趣，可是由于贵方的最小起订量对这个市场来说太大了，我们难以劝导买主试购贵方产品。
进口商	询问	订单	起订量	We would also like to know the minimum export quantities per color and per design. 我们还想了解各类商品的每种颜色和式样的最低出口起售量。
进口商	询问	订单	起订量	What is the minimum quantity of an order for your goods? 你们这种产品的起订量是多少？
进口商	要求	货物	质量	Please see to it that the goods are exactly the same as our sample. 请确保货物与样品完全一致。
进口商	要求	货物	质量	The goods must be equal to our samples in all aspects. Inferior goods will be rejected. 货物必须完全符合样品。劣质产品将被拒收。
进口商	要求	货物	质量	The quality of the order must be exactly the same as that of your sample. Any goods inferior to the sample shall be rejected. 所订货物品质须与贵方样品完全相同。我们拒收一切质量低于样品的货物。

Unit 5

Payment（支付）

Part Ⅰ. Objectives（目标）

After completing this unit, you will be able to

1. read and write English messages and emails to discuss various methods of business payment terms with your business clients either as an importer or an exporter;

2. become familiar with the typical English terms and sentence patterns and important components used in above messages and emails.

Part Ⅱ. How to Express（我该怎么说）

1. Enquiring about Payment（进口商询问付款方式）

A：我是进口方，想了解出口方的付款方式。我该怎么说呢？

B：你可以这样说：

1）你们希望用什么方式付款？

2）你们通常采用什么样的付款方式？

3）请告知你方付款方式。

A：那么，我用英语该怎么说呢？

B：到"常用语句集"去看看，你先找到同类的句型，然后采用截取、替换、拼接的办法稍做加工，你需要的句子就有了。

A：嘿！瞧瞧，我的英语还不错吧！

_____

_____

_____

_____

2. Asking for Easier Payment Terms （进口商要求宽松的付款方式）

A：我是进口方，希望出口方在付款方面能给予更加宽松的方式。我该怎么说呢？

B：你可以这样说：

1）如果你们可以提供较为宽松的支付方式，我方有可能下大订单。

2）由于该合同金额少于 2 000 美元，因此希望贵公司接受我们用付款交单方式来支付货款。

3）信用证付款方式不符合我们通常的做法，我们建议采用承兑交单。

A：那么，我用英语该怎么说呢？

B：到"常用语句集"去看看，你先找到同类的句型，然后采用截取、替换、拼接的办法稍做加工，你需要的句子就有了。

A：嘿！瞧瞧，我的英语还不错吧！

3. Urging Payment（出口商催促付款）

A：我是卖方，现买方没有按时付款，我要催促付款。该怎么说呢？

B：你可以这样说：

1）由于我们一直能按时收款，这次你们延迟付款必定有特殊原因。

2）贵方欠款 5 000 美元，现在已过期 20 天，我们不明白你们为什么还不能结账。

3）我们现在必须坚持要求你们在 7 天内付款。

A：那么，我用英语该怎么说呢？

B：到"常用语句集"去看看，你先找到同类的句型，然后采用截取、替换、拼接的办法稍做加工，你需要的句子就有了。

A：嘿！瞧瞧，我的英语还不错吧！

Part III. Case（案例）

1. Urging Payment（出口商催促付款）

吴丹丹女士是杭州机械进出口有限公司的销售部经理，一直负责与尼日利亚拉各斯机械进出口公司的业务往来。此前，拉各斯机械进出口公司的购买量一直不是很大，一般都在几千美元至5万美元之间，但每次都能按时付款，从不拖延。然而，最近一次，一笔1万美元的货款已经到期5天，对方还未支付。于是，吴丹丹发邮件催促对方付款。考虑到之前的友好合作，邮件中吴丹丹措辞十分委婉，充分顾及到了对方的感受。

发件人（From）	wudandan@hotmail.com
收件人（To）	alfredjackson@mail.yahoo.com
主题（Subject）	USD 10 000 under Invoice No. 1879

Dear Mr. Jackson,

We are writing to inform you that the USD10 000 under invoice No. 1879 is now 5 days overdue. As we have always received your payment punctually, we are puzzled to understand your delay in payment this time. We are assuming this is merely an oversight on your part.

Please remit the above payment within the next 5 days.

We appreciate your cooperation in this regard.

Kind regards,

Wu Dandan

Sales Manager

Sentence Patterns Applied（语句归纳）
- 出口商提出货款到期，询问延迟付款原因；
- 出口商指定付款期限；
- 出口商敦促、劝导付款。

2. Informing of Paid（进口商通知已付款）

Alfred Jackson先生是拉各斯机械进出口公司的业务部经理助理，负责与杭州机械进出口有限公司的业务联系。Alfred 收到吴丹丹的催款邮件后马上进行了追查，发现是公司会计部门（accounting department）忽视（made an oversight）了这笔汇款。Alfred 当即安排汇款，并向吴丹丹回复邮件致歉，态度十分诚恳。

现在，你就是 Alfred，你需要回复邮件。

Sentence Patterns for Reference（参考语句）
- ➢ 进口商收到催款，致谢；
- ➢ 解释付款延误，致歉；
- ➢ 进口商通知付款，提醒核查；
- ➢ 进口商良好祝愿。

发件人（From）	
收件人（To）	
主题（Subject）	

3. Informing of Payment Received （出口商通知收到货款）

吴丹丹收到了对方通知已付款的邮件，经查账，拉各斯机械进出口公司汇出的 1 万美元已经到账。吴丹丹发邮件告知 Alfred 货款收到，并期盼收到对方更多订单。

发件人（From）	wudandan@hotmail.com
收件人（To）	alfredjackson@mail.yahoo.com
主题（Subject）	USD10,000 Received

Dear Mr. Jackson,

We have just received USD10,000 under invoice No. 1879. Thank you for your speedy response.

We are looking forward to further orders from your company.

Wu Dandan

Sales Manager

Sentence Patterns Applied（语句归纳）
- 出口商通知收到货款，致谢；
- 出口商期盼（更多）订单。

4. Requesting for Payment Terms（进口商要求付款方式）

从杭州机械进出口有限公司进口的货物在尼日利亚市场越来越畅销，市场前景相当良好，拉各斯机械进出口公司决定大量续订。Alfred 向吴丹丹发出了 30 万美元的订单，订单放在邮件附件中，订单编号为 262。

之前，由于订单金额都在 5 万美元之下，加上双方长期友好的贸易关系，付款方式均采用前 50%T/T+后 50%T/T，即 50%电汇预付款，剩余见提单复印件支付。因此，对于此次的大笔订购，拉各斯机械进出口公司特别强调，付款沿用之前的方式。

发件人（From）	alfredjackson@mail.yahoo.com
收件人（To）	wudandan@hotmail.com
主题（Subject）	Repeat Order for 500 Tool Machines
附件（Attachment）	Order No. 262

Dear Ms. Wu,

The demand for your products in this market is great, and we are pleased to place with you a repeat order No. 262 for 500 tool machines with the total amount of USD 300,000. Please see attachment for details.

We expect you will allow us the same terms of payment for this repeat order, that is, 50% T/T in advance and the balance against the copy of B/L.

Kind Regards,

Alfred Jackson

Manager Assistant

Sentence Patterns Applied（语句归纳）
- 进口商表达订购愿望（求购），下订单，寄送订单；
- 进口商要求付款方式，说明付款方式。

5. Declining the Request for Payment（出口商拒绝更改付款方式）

收到30万美元的大订单，令吴丹丹十分高兴，可是，付款方式又令她犯难。按照公司惯例，5万美元以上的订单必须要采用即期信用证支付。面对不可更改的公司规定和30万美元的订单，吴丹丹必须做到左右兼顾，既要坚守公司惯例，又要留住订单。

于是，吴丹丹向 Alfred 发邮件，耐心说明付款方式是公司的惯例，不能更改，即只能采用即期信用证付款。对于公司的惯例，吴丹丹在邮件中显得十分无奈，请求对方能够理解，同时，回顾双方之前的友好合作，试图打友情牌说服对方。邮件如下：

发件人（From）	wudandan@hotmail.com
收件人（To）	alfredjackson@mail.yahoo.com
主题（Subject）	Payment Terms of Order No. 262

Dear Mr. Jackson,

We would like to confirm and accept your order No. 262 for 500 tool machines, CIF Lagos, with the total amount of USD 300,000, for shipment before this December.

However, as to payment, we have considered your proposal, but regret to say that we have to adhere to our usual practice, that is, payment by L/C at sight. As you know, we always agree with you on payment terms when the amount is less than USD50, 000.

We much appreciate the support you have given us in the past and would be grateful if you would accept our terms of payment this time.

Kind regards,

Wu Dandan

Sales Manager

Sentence Patterns Applied（语句归纳）
- 出口商收到订单，确认接受；
- 出口商拒绝付款方式要求，表达遗憾，说明（解释）付款惯例；
- 出口商回顾合作，劝导接受付款方式。

6. Agreeing to Payment Terms（进口商接受付款方式）

对于拉各斯机械进出口公司来说，通常不使用信用证支付。但是，面对此笔交易，拉各斯公司通过综合考虑，决定退让一步，同意接受即期信用证支付，并要求寄来形式发票（proforma invoice）以便办理手续（follow usual procedure）。

现在，你是 Alfred，你需要向吴丹丹回复邮件，你在表示同意用即期信用证付款的同时，也要表明这次让步是为了双方利益，要让对方感受到你公司所做的努力。

Sentence Patterns for Reference（参考语句）
- 进口商收到订单确认，致谢；
- 进口商说明己方的付款惯例；
- 进口商破例接受即期信用证付款方式；
- 进口商索要形式发票。

发件人（From）	
收件人（To）	
主题（Subject）	

....
....
....
....
....
....
....

Proforma Invoice （形式发票）

形式发票是一份标有货物名称、规格、单价等信息的非正式的参考性发票，简称 PI。它是应进口商的要求，由出口商开出的。进口商常常需要形式发票来申请进口和外汇。

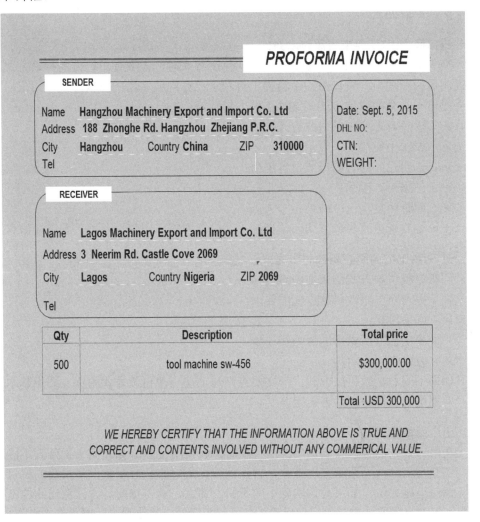

Part Ⅳ. Writing Directions（写作指导）

出口商说明付款方式

应进口商的询问，或者需要特加说明时，出口商要把己方的付款方式明确地告知进口方，并提出具体的要求，详细说明付款方式、时间、总额等。有时还要对采用这一付款方式做出必要的解释，其目的是希望对方接受。要点包括：

- 感谢、确认对方的订购；
- 说明己方所要求的付款方式；
- 说明采用这一付款方式的理由；

> 劝导接受；
> 期盼回复。

进口商/出口商要求更改付款方式

交易中的一方如果不能接受另一方的付款方式时，需要提出己方的付款方式，并说明原因和理由。进口方往往会提出有利于己方的较宽松的付款方式，而出口方则会提出更安全的付款方式。这种信件内容包括：

> 提及对方要求的付款方式；
> 表明不能接受，表示歉意；
> 说明己方的付款方式及其理由；
> 说服对方接受；
> 期盼回复。

不论是要求更改付款方式还是拒绝更改付款方式，语气要友善，态度要诚恳。

进口商/出口商同意更改付款方式

同意更改付款方式的信文内容包括：

> 提及对方更改付款方式的要求；
> 同意接受；
> 表明己方所做出的努力和让步；
> 敦促下一步运作。

如果不同意更改付款方式，信文要点则与上述更改付款方式的信文要点基本一样，差别是前者肯定而后者否定。

出口商催款付款

当出口方未能按时收到进口方的付款时，就得要催款。如果第一次催款不能奏效，还要写第二次乃至第三次催款。首次催款提醒对方按时付款，尽早履约就可以了，切勿小题大做。如果对方的确不闻不问，那么，就得提醒对方注意违约的责任后果，告诫将采取法律措施。但无论如何，绝不恐吓、攻击对方，更不能人身侮辱，做到有礼有节。催款信大致包括以下一些内容：

> 提及货款，或上次发出的催款信，或前几次催款的种种努力；
> 希望解释迟付的原因；
> 给对方限定一个合理的最后期限；
> 提出警告；
> 期盼回复。

进口商请求延期付款

进口方到期无法付款时，需要向出口方解释原因并请求延期付款。要点包括：

> 陈述对某笔货款一时无法支付；
> 致歉，并说明原因；

- 提出偿付的期限;
- 说服对方接受。

Part V. Terms and Sentence Frames
(术语与句型)

1. Terms (术语)

付款

payment in advance 预付货款
deferred payment 延期付款
cash payment 现金付款
down payment 付款定金
extension of payment 延长付款
full payment 全额付款
non-payment 不付款
partial payment 部分付款
account payable 应付款
account receivable 应收款

汇票

bill of exchange (简称 bill, draft) 汇票
banker's draft 银行汇票
commercial draft 商业汇票
clean draft 光票
documentary draft 跟单汇票
sight draft 即期汇票
time draft 远期汇票
endorsement 背书
holder 持票人
drawer 出票人
payer 付款人
payee 受款人

汇付

remittance 汇款

mail transfer（简称 M/T）信汇
telegraphic transfer（简称 T/T）电汇
demand draft（简称 D/D）票汇
check 支票
cash 现金

托收

clean collection 光票托收
documentary collection 跟单托收
documents against payment（简称 D/P）付款交单
documents against payment at sight（简称 D/P at sight）即期付款交单
documents against payment after sight（简称 D/P after sight）远期付款交单
documents against acceptance（简称 D/A）承兑交单

2. Sentence Frames（句型）

支付方式

to make payment by L/C 用信用方式支付
to pay under (on)…terms 按……方式支付
to pay on …basis 按……方式支付
to accept D/P terms as a special accommodation 接受付款交单支付方式作为特殊照顾
to remit… 汇款……
to pay in advance 预付
to pay by installments 分期付款
to pay on delivery 货到付款
to pay by D/P at sight 即期付款交单方式支付
to pay by D/A 承兑交单方式支付
to pay by cash against documents on arrival of goods 货到凭单付现

汇票

to draw a draft on sb. 向某人开出汇票
to accept a draft 承兑汇票
to honor a draft 承兑汇票
to dishonor a draft 拒付汇票

计额

in the amount of 金额计
to the amount of 金额计
for the amount of 金额计

Part VI. Follow Me （跟我写）

Requesting for Easier Payment Terms（进口商请求宽松的付款方式）

电子邮件模板

Dear Mr./Ms. （对方的姓），

Thank you for your quotation of （对方报价的日期）.

We would be happy to place another order with your company, provided that you kindly agree to a change in payment method from （变更前的付款方式） to （变更后的付款方式）, which will help us （变更后的付款方式所带来的好处）.

Since we believe we have already established a good working relationship with your company and have proved that we are reliable buyers, please give our request your most serious consideration.

We await your positive reply.

Yours sincerely,

（署名）

贸易背景一

Jean Helen 收到卖方陈凯文先生 2015 年 11 月 3 日的报价后，同意下订单，但要求变更付款方式，从现在的即期信用证（L/C at sight）变更为付款交单（Documents against Payment），理由是可以减少成本（reduce costs）。

现在，需要写出 Jean Helen 要求变更付款方式的邮件。

仿照模板套写

贸易背景二

王梦梓收到卖方 Jessie Alba 女士 2015 年 9 月 8 日的报价后，同意下订单，但要求变更付款方式，从现在的即期付款交单（D/P at sight）变更为承兑交单（D/A），理由是缓解公司资金周转的困难（alleviate the liquidity problem of the business）。

写出王梦梓要求变更付款方式的邮件。

仿照模板套写

Part VII. Practical Writing （实训写作）

1. Match the words and phrases with their Chinese meanings.

payment in advance	预付
commercial draft	商业汇票
D/P after sight	预付货款

pay in advance	即期付款交单方式支付
time draft	远期付款交单
pay by installments	货到付款
pay on delivery	跟单汇票
pay by D/P at sight	承兑交单方式支付
documentary draft	远期汇票
pay by D/A	分期付款

2.Read the following email and list the sentence patterns applied.

With regard to your Sales Confirmation No. 113 for selling the Fleece Zip Jacket（羊毛带拉链夹克） in the amount of US $310,000, we wish to propose an easier payment arrangement.

Our past purchases from you have been paid, as a rule, by confirmed irrevocable letter of credit. It has cost us a great deal on this basis. From the time we open the credit to the time our buyers pay us, the tie-up（冻结）of our funds lasts for about four months. This situation is particularly taxing（难以负担的）owing to the tight money（资金紧张）conditions and the prevailing high bank interest rate（银行高利率）.

In view of our long business relationship and the small amount involved in this transaction, we hope you can consider easier payment terms. We propose either cash against documents on arrival of goods（货到凭单付现）, or drawing on us（开具汇票向我方索款） at three months' sight（见票三个月付款）.

---

3. Complete each of the following sentences according to its model given.

1）We regret it is against our policy to quote on FOB basis, as it is our general practice to do business with all our clients on CIF terms.
  It is （我方惯例是按照到岸价交易）_____
_____.

2）We regret that we can't agree to draw at 30 days D/A.
  We regret（很抱歉，我们不能接受以"货到交单付现"方式付款）_____
_____.

3）We must now ask you to settle this account within the next few days.
  We must now ask you （请您务必在2015年12月20日前结清这笔账款）____
_____.

4）We regret to inform you that it is our usual practice not to accept payment by D/A.
  We regret to inform you （我们的惯例是用即期信用证支付）_____

5）Payment is to be effected before the end of this month.
Payment is（在这几日内应该付款）_____
_____.

6）As a special accommodation, we agree to your proposal and accept payment by D/P at sight, but this should not be regarded as a precedent.
As a special accommodation,（我们同意你方建议，接受远期付款交单）_____
_____.

7）In view of our long business relation, we will make an exception to our rules and accept L/C at 30 days（after）sight.
In view of our long business relation,（我们这次破例）_____
_____.

8）For future transactions, D/P will be accepted if the amount is under USD 2,000.
For future transactions,（如果金额不超过 200 美元，我们同意接受承兑交单的付款方式）_____
_____
_____.

9）For payment, we require 100% value, confirmed, and irrevocable Letter of Credit with partial shipment and transshipment allowed clause, available by draft at sight, against surrender of full set of shipping documents to the negotiating bank here.
For payment,（我们需求按发票金额的 100%、凭保兑的、不可撤销的、凭即期汇票付款的信用证）_____
_____
_____.

10）Reluctantly compelled to say that, failing receipt of your cheque by next Monday, we must have resource to legal proceedings for its recovery（下星期一以前，如应收款不能收回，我们只好诉诸法律，特此奉告）.
Reluctantly compelled to say that, [5 天之内，如应收款不能收回，我们将通过律师（attorney）督促付款] _____
_____
_____.

4. Complete the following email with the words and phrases given in the box.

1）dozen	2）sight L/C	3）to accept
4）at	5）accept	

We are in receipt of your bid（递盘） yesterday for 100,000 piece of our latest toy products FX41000 _____ $246 per _____, CIF New York. However, you didn't mention specific payment terms.

We'd like to tell you that we only accept payment by_____. Generally speaking, Letter of Credit is considered to be a reliable and safe method of payment in international trade. It protects the rights and interests of both of us. It is our usual case_____ sight L/C when we do business internationally. We wonder whether you _____ this kind of payment.

Thank you in advance for your prompt reply.

Part VIII. Linkage（知识链接）

支付方式

国际贸易的支付方式，可以概括为顺汇和逆汇两类。

1）顺汇是付款人主动将款项付给收款人，也就是汇款。汇款分为电汇（Telegraphic Transfer，T/T）、信汇（Mail Transfer，M/T）、票汇（Demand Draft，D/D）。

2）逆汇是指托收和信用证。托收是指卖方凭汇票或单据委托当地银行转托进口地银行向买方收款的一种结算方式。

根据托收单据的不同，托收可分为光票托收和跟单托收。光票托收是卖方仅凭汇票而不附带任何货运单据委托银行办理托收。跟单托收是卖方将汇票连同货运单据一起交银行委托托收。货运单据主要包括发票、提单、保险单等。在这种方式下，根据向进口商交付货运单据的条件不同，托收可分为三种。

1）即期付款交单（Documents against Payment at sight）。即期付款交单（简称D/P at sight），是指出口人装运之后，开具即期汇票，连同装运单据交给当地银行，通过银行向进口人提示，进口人见票后须立即付款，付清货款后，领取装运单据，即通常所说的"一手交钱，一手交货"。

2）远期付款交单（Documents against Payment after Sight）。远期付款交单（简称D/P after sight），是指出口人装运后，开具远期汇票连装运单据交给当地银行，通过银行向进口人提示，由进口人承兑远期汇票，于汇票到期日付清货款后领取装运单据。

3）承兑交单（Documents against Acceptance）。承兑交单（简称D/A），是指出口人装运之后，开具远期汇票连同装运单据交给银行，通过银行向进口人提示，由进口人承兑远期汇票之后，即可取得装运单据，提取货物，待汇票到期再付清货款。

Part IX. Glossary of Common Sentences
（常用语句集）

1. 出口商

出口商	催促	付款	委婉	As we have always received your payment punctually, we are puzzled to understand your delay in payment this time. 由于我们一直能按时收款，所以这次我们不明白你们为何迟付。
出口商	催促	付款	委婉	No doubt there is some special reason for the delay in payment and we should welcome an explanation and also your remittance. 你们延迟付款无疑有特殊的原因，请说明，并寄汇款。
出口商	催促	付款	委婉	Please kindly send us the cheque for the settlement of your account to the end of last year at your earliest convenience. 请尽快寄给我方支票以结清去年年底之前的账款。
出口商	催促	付款	严厉	As you seem to take advantage of our leniency on this matter, we now give you the final notice that, unless we shall receive a substantial amount on account by reply, we shall adopt other measures for its recovery. 对于此事，贵方似乎在趁机利用我方的宽容态度。本次系最后通告，贵方回复时请汇足够金额以结此账，否则，我方只好采取其他措施结账。
出口商	催促	付款	严厉	If you fail to make your payment, we shall be compelled to enforce payment through the hands of attorney. 如你方不付款，我们不得不通过律师强制执行付款。
出口商	催促	付款	严厉	In spite of your repeated promises to let us have a cheque, we are still without a settlement of your outstanding account, and therefore, unless same is settled by the end of this month, we shall be compelled to hand over the matter to our solicitor. 贵方虽多次答应付款结账，但迄今尚未结清。如在本月底以前，贵方尚未拨款结清，我们只好委任法律顾问处理。
出口商	催促	付款	限期	Payment is to be made before the end of this month. 这个月末以前应该付款。
出口商	催促	付款	限期	Reluctantly compelled to say that, failing receipt of your cheque by next Monday, we must resort to legal proceedings for its recovery. 下星期一以前，如应收款不能如期收回，我们只好诉诸法律，特此奉告。
出口商	催促	付款	限期	Unless your cheque is in my hands on or before the 20th May, I shall immediately take steps to enforce payment. 5月20日以前，如尚未收到贵方支票，本人将立刻采取措施强制付款。
出口商	催促	付款	限期	We must now ask you to settle this account within the next few days. 请您务必在这几日内结清这笔账款。

续表

出口商	催促	付款	限期	We must now insist that you send your payment within the next five days. 我们现在必须要求你们在 5 天内付款。
出口商	催促	付款	限期	We wish to state that if the account is not paid by next Monday, we shall be forced to place the matter in the hands of our solicitors. 下星期一以前未能结清本件款项，不得已，我们将委任我公司法律顾问处理。
出口商	催促	付款	强制	Having made repeated applications for payment of this amount without avail, we now give you notice that we shall take out a summons for recovery of the same. 为结清本账目，我方多次催促，但未有任何效果。现通知你方，我方准备向法院起诉。
出口商	催促	付款	强制	Respecting our overdue account, we have today placed the matter in the hands of our solicitors. 由于逾期未获付款，本日已移交我们公司法律顾问处理。
出口商	催促	付款		It is now several weeks since we sent you out first invoice and we have not yet received your payment. 我们的第一份发票已经寄出有好几周了，但我们尚未收到您的任何款项。
出口商	催促	付款		Please honor our draft on presentation. 请见票即付。
出口商	催促	付款		Please pay the outstanding balance of USD 325.75 as soon as possible. 请尽快支付 325.75 美元的未付货款。
出口商	催促	付款		The following items totaling $400 are still open on your account. 以下产品的欠款总计为 400 美元，你方尚未偿付。
出口商	催促	付款		This is a reminder that payment for your last order has not yet been received. 现提醒您尚未支付上次订单的货款。
出口商	催促	付款		We cannot understand why you have not settled your account of USD 5,000, which is now 30 days overdue. 贵方欠款 5 000 美元，现在已过期 30 天，我们不明白你们为什么还不能结账。
出口商	催促	付款		We have to remind you that the freight is still due on Invoice No. 1223. 我们得提醒你们 1233 号发票中的运费仍未支付。
出口商	接受	付款	方式	As a sign of trust, we'll consider accepting payment by D/P at this sales-purchasing stage. 在此推销阶段我们信任贵方，将考虑接受付款交单。
出口商	接受	付款	方式	As a special accommodation, we agree to your proposal and accept payment by D/P at sight, but this should not be regarded as a precedent. 作为特殊照顾，我们同意你方建议，接受即期付款交单，但是这不应视为先例。
出口商	接受	付款	方式	For future transactions, D/P will be accepted if the amount is under USD 2,000. 对于今后的交易，如果金额不超过 2000 美元，我们同意接受付款交单的付款方式。
出口商	接受	付款	方式	In compliance with your request, on this occasion we accept delivery against D/P at sight, but this should not be taken as a precedent. 按照你方要求，我们破例地接受即期付款交单交货，但这种情况下不为例。

				续表
出口商	接受	付款	方式	In order to pave the way for you to push the sale for our products in your market, we agree to payment for this transaction under D/A terms. 为了给贵公司销售我们的产品铺平道路，我们同意本笔交易以承兑交单付款。
出口商	接受	付款	方式	In view of our long business relationship, we will make an exception to our rules and accept L/C at 30 days after sight. 鉴于我们长期的业务关系，我们破例接受信用证30天付款。
出口商	接受	付款	方式	We agree to draw at 30 days D/P. 我们同意开立30天期的付款交单汇票。
出口商	接受	付款	方式	We'll agree to change the terms of payment from L/C at sight to D/P at sight. 我们同意将即期信用证付款方式改为即期付款交单。
出口商	介绍	付款	惯例	In general practice, we require the payment by L/C. 日常操作中，我们要求以信用证付款。
出口商	介绍	付款	惯例	L/C at sight is normal for our exports to France. 我们向法国出口一般使用即期信用证付款。
出口商	介绍	付款	惯例	Our terms of payment is by confirmed, irrevocable letter of credit by draft at sight. 我方支付条款是凭保兑的、不可撤销的即期信用证付款。
出口商	介绍	付款	惯例	Our terms of payment is by confirmed, irrevocable Letter of Credit in our favor, available by draft at sight, reaching us one month ahead of shipment, remaining valid for negotiation in China for another 21 days after the prescribed time of shipment, and allowing transshipment and partial shipments. 我们的付款条件是用保兑的、不可撤销的、以我方为受益人的信用证，凭即期汇票付款，在装运前一个月抵达我处，在中国议付有效到规定的装运期后第21天，并且允许转船和分批装运。
出口商	介绍	付款	惯例	Payment by L/C is our method of financing trade in such commodities. 对这种商品，以信用证付款是我们做贸易的方法。
出口商	介绍	付款	惯例	The term of payment we usually adopt is confirmed and irrevocable L/C. 我们通常采用的付款方式是保兑的不可撤销的信用证。
出口商	拒绝	付款	方式	Owing to the fluctuation of US dollar, we cannot accept payment using this currency. 由于美元的波动性，我们不同意使用美元结账。
出口商	拒绝	付款	方式	We can't agree to draw at 30 days D/A. 我们不同意开具30天期的承兑交单汇票。
出口商	拒绝	付款	方式	We never accept "Cash against Documents" on arrival of goods at destination. 我们从不接受"货抵目的地付款交单"方式付款。

续表

出口商	拒绝	付款	方式	We regret our inability to make any arrangement contrary to our usual practice, which is payment by confirmed, irrevocable Letter of Credit payable against presentation of shipping documents and valid for at least 15 days beyond the promised date of shipment. 非常抱歉，我们无法进行任何有违我们惯例的调整，我们通常的支付方式是保兑的、不可撤销信用证见单付款，在规定的装运期至少15天有效。
出口商	拒绝	付款	方式	We regret that we are unable to consider your request for payment under D/A terms. 对你方要求以承兑交单方式付款一事，我们抱歉难以考虑。
出口商	拒绝	付款	方式	We regret to inform you that it is our usual practice not to accept payment by D/A. 我们遗憾地通知你方，我们的惯例是不接受承兑交单的支付条件。
出口商	拒绝	付款	方式	We regret we cannot accept "Cash against Documents on arrival of goods at destination". 抱歉，我方不能接受"货到目的地后凭单付款"的条件。
出口商	拒绝	付款	延期	Any further delay in paying your balance due cannot be accepted. 我们不能接受你们继续延迟付款了。
出口商	拒绝	付款	延期	We can't accept payment on deferred terms. 我们不能接受延期付款。
出口商	同意	付款	方式	In view of the small quantity you have ordered, we are in a position to accept payment by D/P at sight for the value of the goods shipped. 鉴于您所订购的数量比较小，我们准备接受即期付款交单作为付款方式。
出口商	同意	付款	方式	We are prepared to accept payment for your trial order on D/P basis. 对你方这批试订购的货物，我们准备接受付款交单方式付款。
出口商	坚持	付款	方式	Regarding payment, we require 100% value, confirmed, and irrevocable Letter of Credit with partial shipment and transshipment allowed clause, available by draft at sight, against surrender of full set of shipping documents to the negotiating bank here. 关于支付，我们需求按发票金额的100%、凭保兑的、不可撤销的信用证，允许分批装运和转船，凭即期汇票付款，并凭出示全套装运单据给我处的议付银行行为有效。
出口商	坚持	付款	方式	The terms of payment is confirmed as irrevocable L/C. 付款条件确定为不可撤销信用证。
出口商	坚持	付款	方式	We insist on payment by L/C. 我们坚持用信用证支付。

2. 进口商

进口商	拒绝	付款	方式	We find your price and quality satisfactory; however we would suggest that your terms of payment should be altered. 我方认为贵方所报的价格以及产品的质量都很令人满意，但是我方建议对付款方式进行修改。
进口商	拒绝	付款	方式	Your offer is acceptable but we are not in a position to make payment by L/C at sight as it will cost us more. 你方报价可以接受，但是我们无法接受即期信用证的付款方式，因为成本太高。
进口商	请求	付款	分期	Please understand why we have not found it possible to settle our account in full. 我公司不能一次付清货款，敬请谅解。
进口商	请求	付款	宽松	Could you please consider an exception and accept D/A? 您能否考虑一次例外，接受承兑交单的付款方式？
进口商	请求	付款	宽松	If you could offer us easier payment terms, it would probably lead to an increase in business between our companies. 如果你们可以提供较为宽松的支付方式，就可能增加我们两公司之间的业务。
进口商	请求	付款	宽松	In order to save a lot of expenses on opening the letter of credit, we will remit you the full amount by T/T when the goods purchased by us are ready for shipment and the freight space is booked. 为了节省开立信用证的大量费用，我们将在我方购买的货物已备齐待运，舱位已订下时，电汇全部金额。
进口商	请求	付款	宽松	It would help me greatly if you would accept D/P or D/A. 如果您能接受付款交单或承兑交单方式付款，那可帮了我们的大忙。
进口商	请求	付款	宽松	Since the contract is less than USD 3,000 in value, we would like you to ship the goods to us on D/P basis. 由于该合同金额少于 3 000 美元，因此希望贵公司允许我们用付款交单来支付货款。
进口商	请求	付款	延期	I should appreciate an extension of one month for the payment of my bill of $6,500 due April 5. 我方应于 4 月 5 日付款 6 500 美元，如能延期 1 个月，将不胜感激。
进口商	请求	付款	延期	We should like to request an extended payment plan with your company. 我们想向贵公司请求延迟付款。
进口商	请求	付款	延期	We would greatly appreciate it if you could grant us a 10-day payment extension. 如果您能将付款期限推迟 10 天我们将不胜感激。
进口商	请求	付款	延期	Would it be acceptable to remit payment by September 5th? 能否将支付期限延至 9 月 5 日？
进口商	请求	付款	延期	Would it be possible to extend the payment deadline until the end of the month? 可不可以将支付期限延长到月底？
进口商	提议	付款	方式	I suppose D/P or D/A should be adopted as the mode of payment this time. 我建议这次用付款交单或承兑交单方式来付款。

续表

进口商	提议	付款	方式	It is against our usual practices to accept D/A payment, so we propose paying by T/T. 承兑交单付款方式不符合我们通常的做法，我们建议电汇付款。
进口商	提议	付款	方式	It's better for us to adopt D/P or D/A. 最好是采用付款交单方式或承兑交单方式。
进口商	提议	付款	方式	We'd like to pay by T/T. 我们乐意使用电汇方式付款。
进口商	提议	付款	方式	You would be kind enough to send us a trial delivery for sale on D/A terms. 如能以承兑交单方式适销发货，我们将十分感激。
进口商	通知	货款	已付	The amount has already been remitted by cheque. 款项已经以支票形式汇出。
进口商	通知	货款	已付	This amount has been passed to your credit in settlement of your account. 该货款已汇入贵方账户，已结清账款。
进口商	通知	货款	已付	We have made the payment of USD 10,000 to you today through Bank of China; please check your bank account accordingly. 我方已于今日通过中国银行将 10 000 美金的货款支付给你方，请查收。
进口商	通知	货款	已付	We have remitted the captioned amount to you by T/T through Agricultural Bank of China 我方已将上述货款通过中国农业银行电汇你方。
进口商	通知	货款	已付	We have to inform you that, in accordance with your instructions, we have this day drawn upon Tanaka & Co. at 60 d/s for $200,000, inclusive of charges. 遵照贵方指示，我们已于本日向田中公司开出见票后 60 日付款的面额 200 000 美元汇票一张，费用包括在内。
进口商	协商	付款	方式	From the moment we open the credit until our customer pays us normally ties up funds for about 3 to 4 months. This is a particularly serious problem for us in view of the difficult economic climate and the prevailing high interest rates. 从我们开立信用证到我们的客户支付我们，通常要占用 3~4 个月的资金。鉴于经济气候不佳和现行的高额利率，占用资金问题就尤为严重。
进口商	协商	付款	方式	Is it possible to find alternative terms for our future business? 今后的交易有没有可能谋求其他付款方式？
进口商	询问	付款	方式	Please let us know the terms of payment. 请告知付款条件。
进口商	询问	付款	方式	What is the mode of payment you wish to employ? 您希望用什么方式付款？
进口商	询问	付款	方式	What's your regular practice concerning terms of payment? 你们通常采用什么样的付款条件？
进口商	询问	付款	方式	Will you let us know what your terms of payment are? 请告知你方付款条件。
进口商	要求	付款	分期	We would adopt the terms of payment by installment for present purchase. 这次交易我们将采用分期付款方式。

Unit 6

Letter of Credit（信用证）

Part Ⅰ. Objectives（目标）

After completing this unit, you will be able to

1. read and write English emails and messages relating to L/C, such as, as an exporter, urging establishment of L/C, asking for amendment to L/C or extension of L/C, and as an importer, advising the establishment of L/C, agreeing or refusing to extend L/C etc.;

2. know the essential components that the above emails cover;

3. become familiar with typical English terms and sentence patterns commonly used in the emails and messages above.

Part Ⅱ. How to Express（我该怎么说）

1. Urging Establishment of L/C（出口商催开信用证）

A：我是出口方，进口商所订购的货物已备妥待用，交货期临近，而进口方的信用证尚未开立，我要催促对方。我该怎么说呢？

B：你可以这样说：

1）请尽量加快有关信用证的开立，以便我们能顺利执行订单。

2）装船日期日益临近，但我们至今未收到相关信用证，请立即给我们答复。

3）由于所订货物已备妥待运，请立即开立信用证。

A：那么我用英语该怎么说呢？

B：到"常用语句集"去看看，你先找到同类的句型，然后采用截取、替换、拼接的办法稍做加工，你需要的句子就有了。

A：嘿！瞧瞧，我的英语还不错吧！

2. Advising Establishment of L/C（进口商通知已开证）

A：我是进口方，现已开立信用证，需要告知对方。我该怎么说呢？

B：你可以这样说：

1）现通知你方，我们已通过东京银行开立了以你方为受益人的第 C019 号信用证。

2）以你方为受益人、金额为 5 000 美元的有关这笔订货的不可撤销信用证已开出，有效期至 2015 年 5 月 15 日止。

3）我们已通过国家银行开出了以史密斯公司为受益人，金额为 50 000 美元的 500 件男士羊绒衫的信用证。

A：那么我用英语该怎么说呢？

B：到"常用语句集"去看看，你先找到同类的句型，然后采用截取、替换、拼接的办法稍做加工，你需要的句子就有了。

A：嘿！瞧瞧，我的英语还不错吧！

3. Asking for L/C Amendment（出口商要求改证）

A：我是卖方，现收到买方的信用证。但是经过审核，发现信用证有不符之处，我必须要求对方修改信用证。我怎么说呢？

B：你可以这样说：

1）很遗憾，我方发现信用证有些不符之处。

2）你方信用证的规定与合同不一致，请按合同进行修改。

3）请将信用证 H5541 作如下修改：

① 信用证到期地应是"中国"而不是"在我国"；

② 信用证应凭"即期"汇票付款，而不是"30 天远期汇票"；

③ 删掉"不准分批和转运"条款。

A：那么我用英语该怎么说呢？

B：到"常用语句集"去看看，你先找到同类的句型，然后采用截取、替换、拼接的办法稍做加工，你需要的句子就有了。

A：嘿！瞧瞧，我的英语还不错吧！

4. Asking for L/C Extension （出口商要求展证）

A：我是出口方，发现信用证所规定的期限内无法完成装运，现在不得不请求进口商延展信用证的装运期和有效期。我该怎么说呢？

B：你可以这样说：

1）请将345号信用证有效期延期至11月15日。

2）由于舱位不足，请求延长信用证的有效期至4月10日。

3）请将你方第BX182号信用证的装船期和有效期分别延展至8月30日和9月10日，并请将修改通知于7月15日之前送达我方。

A：那么我用英语该怎么说呢？

B：到"常用语句集"去看看，你先找到同类的句型，然后采用截取、替换、拼接的办法稍做加工，你需要的句子就有了。

A：嘿！瞧瞧，我的英语还不错吧！

Part Ⅲ. Case（案例）

1. Urging Establishment of L/C（出口商催开信用证）

赵明是江苏国盛进出口贸易股份有限公司（Jiangsu Guosheng Import & Export Trading Co., Ltd.）的业务员，代表公司在2015年8月2日与日本东京国际贸易株式会社（Tokyo International Trading Co., Ltd.）签订了一份销售合同，向对方出口5 480

个毛绒熊。双方商定用即期信用证付款，在 2015 年 9 月 26 日前装运。可是，直至 8 月 26 日，赵明还没有收到对方开来的信用证，因此赵明给对方的业务员 Takada Chisato 发邮件催促，说明交货期临近，希望对方尽快开来相关信用证。

发件人（From）	Zhaoming@guosheng.com
收件人（To）	Takada@tokyointernational.com
主题（Subject）	Urging Establishment of L/C
附件（Attachment）	

Dear Takada Chisato,

Referring to the goods under our Sales Confirmation No. E034579, we wish to draw your attention to the fact that the date of delivery is approaching, but we have not received the covering L/C.

To secure punctual fulfillment of the contract, please do your best to speed up the establishment of the relative L/C. We hope that the L/C will reach us within 10 days.

In order to avoid subsequent amendment, please ensure that the L/C stipulations are in conformity with those in the Sales Confirmation.

We hope to receive your favorable reply soon.

Best regards,

Zhao Ming

Sentence Patterns Applied（语句归纳）
- 出口商提醒交货期，未收到信用证；
- 出口商催促开立信用证，限定信用证开立期限；
- 出口商对信用证条款提出要求；
- 出口商期盼回复。

2. Advising Establishment of L/C（进口商通知已开立信用证）

Tokyo International Trading Co., Ltd.的业务员 Takada Chisato 收到赵明的催促开立信用证的邮件后，迅速联系三菱东京银行（The Bank of Tokyo-Mitsubishi UFJ）于 8 月 28 日开出了以对方为受益人（in your favor）的第 CBY-142880 号信用证，金额为 43 840 美元，有效期截止为 10 月 26 日。之前没有尽早开证的原因是由于员工的疏忽（due to an oversight of our staff）。

现在，你是 Takada Chisato，请你向赵明回复邮件。

Sentence Patterns for Reference（参考语句）
- 进口商收到催开信用证的邮件；
- 进口商解释信用证延误，致歉；
- 进口商通知已开证，说明开证行、证号、金额、有效期等；
- 进口商提醒、催促尽快装运；
- 进口商期盼装运通知。

发件人（From）	
收件人（To）	
主题（Subject）	
附件（Attachment）	

An L/C （信用证）

ISSUE OF A DOCUMENTARY CREDIT
15/08/28-09:30:34　　　　LocalSwiftAcks-8414-136437

Message Header

Swift Input:	FIN 700 Issue of a Documentary Credit	
Sender:	BANK OF TOKYO-MITSUBISHI UFJ	
	CHIYODA, TOKYO	
Receiver:	BANK OF CHINA	
	JIANGSU CN	
MUR:	2010030502001540	

Message Text

SEQUENCE OF TOTAL	*27:	1 / 1
FORM OF DOC, CREDIT	*40A:	IRREVOCABLE
SENDER'SREF.	*20:	HX0190123
DOC. CREDIT NUMBER	*21:	CBY-142880
DATE OF ISSUE	31:	150828
APPLICABLE RULES	*40 E:	UCP LATEST VERSION
EXPIRY	*31 D:	DATE 151026 IN CHINA
APPLICANT	*50:	TOKYO INTERNATIONAL TRADING Co., LTD.,
		14/F EMPIRE BLD, TOKYO, JAPAN
		TEL:81(0)5221-7636-333
BENEFICIARY	*59:	JIANGSU GUOSHEN IMPORT & EXPORT
		TRADING CO., LTD.
		NO.110. JIANYE ROAD,
		NANJING, 210004 CHINA
		TEL:86-25-84469999
AMOUNT	*32 B:	USD43480, 00
AVAILABLE WITH / BY	*41 D:	ANY BANK IN CHINA BY NEGOTIATION
DRAFTS AT	42 C:	DRAFTS AT SIGHT FOR
		FULL INVOICE COST
DRAWEE	52 A:	THE BANK OF TOKYO-MITSUBISHI UFJ
		CHIYODA, TOKYO
PARTIAL SHIPMENTS	43 P:	PROHIBITED
TRANSSHIPMENT	43 T:	PROHIBITED
LOADING ON BOARD	44 A:	ANY PORT IN CHINA
FOR TRANSPORT TO	44 B:	TOKYO
LATEST DATE OF SHIPMENT	44 C:	150926
DESCRIPTION OF GOODS	45 A:	5480　PCS　FLUFFY　BEAR　ART.　NO.
		BFTOO8

OTHER DETAILS AS PER S/C NO E034579
INCOTERM: CFR TOKYO

DOCUMENTS REQUIRED 46 A:

1. SIGNED COMMERCIAL INVOICE IN TRIPLICATE
2. FULL SET OF CLEAN ON BOARD OCEAN BILLS OF LADING, MADE OUT TO ORDER OF SHIPPER AND BLANK ENDORSED AND MARKED "FREIGHT PREPAID"AND NOTIFY APPLICANT.
3. PACKING LIST IN DUPLICATE
4. CERTIFICATE OF QUALITY IN 2 ORIGINALS ISSUED BY MANUFACTURER
5. CERTIFICATE OF ORIGIN ISSUED BY THE CHINA'S CHAMBER OF COMMERCE ORIGINALS. IN ADDITON, THECERTIFICATE OF ORIGIN MUST STATE THAT THE COUNTRY OF ORIGIN OF GOODS SHIPPED HAS BEEN MENTIONED ON EACH CARTON OF THE CONSINGMENT
6. BENEFICIARY'S CERTIFIED COPY OF FAX DISPATCHED TO THE APPLICANT WITHIN 7 DAYS AFTER SHIPMENT ADVISING THE CONTRACT NUMBER, NAME OF COMMODITY, QUANTITY, INVOICE VALUE, BILL OF LADING NO., BILL OF LOADING DATE, THE ETA DATE AND SHIPPING CO.

ADDITIONAL CONDITIONS 47A:

1. SHIPMENT MUST NOT BE MADE EARLIER THAN THE CREDIT ISSUING DATE.
2. ONE SET OF NON-NEGOTIABLE SHIPPING DOCUMENTS TO BE SENT TO THE APPLICANT THROUGH COURIER SERVICE WITHIN 03 WORKING DAY AFTER SHIPMENT AND A COURIER RECEIPT OF WHICH MUST ACCOMPANY THE ORIGINAL DOCUMENTS SATATED ABOVE
3. DISCREPANCY FEE OF USD35.00 WILL BE DEDUCTED FROM THE PROCEEDS OF EACH PRESENTATION OF DISCREPANT DOCUMENTS.
4. ALL DOCUMENTS MUST BE FORWARDED IN ONE LOT BY EXPRESS
5. ALL DOCUMENTS MUST INDICATE LC NO. CONTRACT NO AND NAME OF ISSUING BANK

CHARGES 71B:

All BANKING CHARGES OUTSIDE THE OPENING BANK ARE FOR BENEFICIARY'S ACCOUNT.

PERIOD FOR PRESENTATION 48: 21 DAYS FROM THE DATE OF SHIPMENT, BUT NOT LATER THAN THE CREDIT VALIDITY.

CONFIRMATION INSTRUCTION 49: WITHOUT

3. Asking for amendment to L/C（出口商要求改证）

赵明收到了经三菱东京银行开立、由中国银行江苏分行转交的第 CBY-142880 号信用证。经过单证员的仔细审核，发现信用证有一些条款与双方之前达成的销售合同条款不符（discrepancy）。为此，赵明发邮件给 Takada Chisato 要求修改信用证。

发件人（From）	Zhaoming@guosheng.com
收件人（To）	Takada @tokyointernational.com
主题（Subject）	Asking for L/C amendment
附件（Attachment）	

Dear Mr. Chisato,

Thank you for your L/C CBY-142880 issued by The Bank of Tokyo-Mitsubishi UFJ, however, after careful examination we have found some discrepancies. We, therefore, request the following amendments:

1. The amount in figures should read "USD 43840.00";

2. The name of the beneficiary should read "Jiangsu Guosheng Import & Export Trading Co., Ltd. ";

3. The place of expiry should be "in China" instead of "in Japan";

4. the Bill of Lading should be marked "Freight Prepaid" instead of "Freight Collect";

5. Delete the clause "Partial shipments and transshipment prohibited".

As our goods have been ready for shipment for quite some time, please make the necessary amendments as soon as possible.

Best regards,

Zhao Ming

Sentence Patterns Applied（语句归纳）
- 出口商收到信用证，致谢，发现信用证差错，要求修改；
- 出口商指出信用证差错，要求修改信用证；
- 出口商说明装运进展，催促修改信用证。

4. Responding to L/C Amendment（进口商回复信用证修改）

收到赵明要求修改信用证的邮件后，Takada Chisato 迅速联系三菱东京银行对第

CBY-142880 号信用证进行修改。同时，回复邮件给赵明，请求在收到修改后的信用证以后，全速安排装运。

发件人（From）	Takada @tokyointernational.com
收件人（To）	Zhaoming@guosheng.com
主题（Subject）	Amendment to L/C No. CBY-142880

Dear Mr. Zhao,

In reply to your requirement of L/C amendment, we would like to express our apology to the errors in opening L/C No. CBY-142880.

We have already contacted our banker to make all amendments in line with your requirements.

On receipt of the notification of L/C amendment, you are requested to effect the shipment with all speed.

Best regards,

Takada Chisato

Sentence Patterns Applied（语句归纳）
- 进口商收到要求修改信用证的邮件，致歉；
- 进口商修改信用证；
- 进口商提醒、催促尽快装运。

5. Asking for L/C Extension（出口商要求展证）

昨天，赵明收到了进口商所修改的信用证。但是，由于进口方 Tokyo International Trading Co., Ltd. 之前未及时开立信用证，加上随后修改信用证所耽搁的时间，出口方江苏国盛进出口贸易股份有限公司已经来不及按照合同所规定的"9月26日前"进行装运。于是，赵明不得不请求进口方延展信用证，要求对方把信用证的装运期和有效期分别延展至10月15日和10月30日，并要求延展后的信用证要在9月底抵达出口方。

现在，你是赵明，请根据以上交易情形发邮件给 Takada Chisato。

Sentence Patterns for Reference（参考语句）
- 出口商收到修改后的信用证，致谢；
- 出口商解释装运延期，致歉；
- 出口商要求延展信用证；
- 出口商期盼延展后的信用证。

发件人（From）

收件人（To）

主题（Subject）

Part Ⅳ. Writing Directions（写作指导）

关于信用证的内容比较多。从出口商的角度有：要求开证、催证、确认收到信用证、要求改证、请求延展信用证等。从进口商的角度有：通知已开证、已修改信用证、同意或拒绝延展信用证等。

出口商催开信用证
出口商催促开立信用证，其内容包括：
➢ 提及相关的订单或合同；
➢ 说明货物备好，或装运期临近等；
➢ 说明延误导致的后果，如不能如期装运；
➢ 催促开立信用证；
➢ 期盼回复。

进口商通知已开证
进口商开立信用证后要及时通知对方，内容包括：
➢ 提及相关的订单或合同；

- 告知相关信用证已开立；
- 说明信用证编号、金额、开证行等；
- 叮嘱装运等；
- 期盼回复。

出口商要求修改信用证

收到信用证后，出口方如发现其条款与合同、销售确认书不相符时，必须要求进口方修改信用证。其要点包括：
- 确认收到相关信用证；
- 说明信用证有不符之处；
- 指出具体的错误；
- 要求修改；
- 期盼回复。

出口商要求延展信用证

当出口商在信用证规定的期限内不能装运时，就得请求进口商延展信用证的装运期和有效期，其内容一般包括：
- 指出相关信用证及期限；
- 请求延展信用证；
- 说明延展的理由；
- 说明延展的期限；
- 期盼回复。

有关信用证的信函语言要简洁，语气要诚恳。如果是己方不慎给对方带来了麻烦，一定要道歉，同时，对于对方的要求在不影响己方利益的前提下要尽量满足。

Part V. Terms and Sentence Frames
（术语与句型）

1. Terms（术语）

信用证种类

Letter of Credit (L/C) 信用证
form of credit 信用证形式
sight L/C 即期信用证
usance L/C 远期信用证
irrevocable L/C 不可撤销的信用证

confirmed L/C 保兑的信用证
unconfirmed L/C 不保兑的信用证

信用证内容
opening bank 开证行
issuing bank 开证行
beneficiary 受益人
validity of L/C 信用证效期
expiry date 效期
date of issue 开证日期
issuing date 开证日期
L/C amount 信用证金额
L/C number 信用证号码
bill of lading (B/L) 提单
bill of exchange 汇票
draft 汇票
date of shipment 装船日期
partial shipment 分批装运
part shipment 分批装运
transshipment 转船
allowed 允许
prohibited 不允许
freight prepaid 运费预付
freight paid 运费已付
freight collect 运费到付

信用证操作
establishment of an L/C 开立信用证
advice of establishment of L/C 通知开立信用证
amendment to L/C 修改信用证
extension of L/C 延展信用证
discrepancy 不符之处

2. Sentence Frames（句型）

催开信用证
to speed up the L/C 催开信用证
to expedite the L/C 催开信用证

to hasten the establishment of the L/C 催开信用证

to have not received your relative L/C 还未收到你方相关信用证

开立信用证

to open a credit 开立信用证

to issue a credit in one's favor 以某人为受益人开出信用证

to establish a credit through bank 通过银行开立信用证

to arrange a credit with bank 通过银行开立信用证

to cancel a credit 取消信用证

修改信用证

to make the following amendment 做如下修改

please amend L/C No.... as follows 请按下列意见修改第……号信用证

the name of the beneficiary should read... 受益人应为……

please insert the word "about" before... 请在……（信用证的数量或金额）前插入"大约"。

the amount both in figures and in words should respectively read "..." 大小写金额应分别为"……"

the bill of lading should be "..." instead of "..." 提单应为"……"，而不是"……"

to delete the clause "..." 删除……条款

to amend your L/C No.... to allow partial shipment 修改你方第……号信用证以允许分批装运

延展信用证

to extend the date of shipment to ... 将装运期延期至……

to extend the validity of the L/C to ... 将信用证的有效期延期至……

to extend the date of shipment and validity of the L/C to ... and ... respectively 将信用证的装运期和有效期分别延期至……和……

Part VI. Follow Me （跟我写）

1. Asking for Amendment to L/C （出口商请求进口商修改信用证）

电子邮件模板

Dear Mr. /Ms. （对方的姓）,

We are glad to receive your L/C No. （对方信用证的编号） under the S/C No. （我

方销售合同的编号）.

We have carefully observed the terms and conditions stipulated in your L/C, but we regret to inform you that we found some discrepancies in the L/C which you have to instruct your opening bank to make the following amendments.

1. （信用证中不符的项目） of the L/C should be "（应当正确的写法）", instead of "（对方错误的写法）".

2. （信用证中不符的项目） of the L/C is "（应当正确的写法）", not "（对方错误的写法）".

We hope the amendment to the L/C can reach here before （修改后信用证应当抵达的期限）, or the shipment will not be effected as requested. Your immediate response is being expected.

Yours sincerely,
（署名）

贸易背景

马凯任职的公司和进口商 Allen Bledel 女士的公司签订了编号为 AD-MASSC02 号的不锈钢茶具（Stainless Steel Tea Set）买卖合同，马凯收到了编号为 MAS-ADLC02 信用证。经单证员审核，该信用证存在三处不符之处：

1) 总金额的大小写应为：USD118 422.00，即十一万八千四百二十二美元，而不是 USD119420.00，即十一万九千四百二十美元；

2) 不锈钢茶具的货号（Article No.）应为 S5130，而不是 S5310；

3) 信用证付款期限为"即期"，不是"30 天远期"。

马凯需要发邮件要求 Allen Bledel 女士修改信用证，修改后的信用证于 2015 年 4 月 30 日前抵达。

仿照模板套写

----

2. The L/C Extended（进口商延展信用证）

电子邮件模板

Dear （对方的名），

We have received your email of （对方邮件的日期）, contents of which have been noted by us.

In compliance with your request, we have already instructed our bank to extend the dates of shipment and validity of our L/C to （延展后的装运期） and （延展后的有效期） respectively. You can be assured that the extension advice of the L/C should reach you in due time.

Please make necessary arrangements to have the goods shipped before or on （装运期截止日） and present the documents required by our L/C to the negotiating bank with the least possible delay.

We look forward to your shipping advice.

Yours truly,

Yours sincerely,

（署名）

贸易背景

Lucy 小姐所在的公司向 AndrewTunik 所在的公司出售一批产品，双方签订了合同，Lucy 收到了相关的信用证。可是，由于供货的原因，Lucy 发现无法按照原先的最迟装运期（2015 年 11 月 10 日）将所有货物备好。因此，Lucy 于 2015 年 11 月 3 日发邮件给 Andrew，请求将信用证的装运期和有效期分别延展至 2015 年 11 月 30 日和 2015 年 12 月 15 日。

Andrew 收到了 Lucy 的请求后，马上联系开证行修改延展信用证。现在 Andrew 需要回复邮件，告知 Lucy 信用证已按请求延展，要求抓紧时间在 11 月 30 日前装运，并向议付行提交装运单据。

仿照模板套写

Part Ⅶ. Practical Writing （实训写作）

1. Match the words and phrases with their Chinese meanings.

beneficiary	有效期
letter of credit	提单
sight L/C	即期信用证
B/L	信用证
validity	受益人
to open an L/C	开立信用证
to extend the date of shipment	催开信用证
to amend the L/C	延展装运期
to be ready for shipment	备妥待运
to speed up the establishment of the L/C	修改信用证

2. Read the following email and list the sentence patterns applied.

Further to our email of February 2nd urging you to establish the L/C, we are very disappointed that we have not received any news from you on this matter.

We would like to remind you that it is stipulated in our Sales Confirmation that shipment should be effected during March. The goods concerned have been ready for shipment for quite some time. If we do not receive your L/C by the end of February, we will not make the shipment in the stipulated time.

We hope this matter will receive your prompt attention.

Unit 6　Letter of Credit（信用证）

3. Complete each of the following sentences according to its model given.

1) It is advisable for you to open the covering L/C immediately so as to enable us to effect shipment within the stipulated time limit.
Please do your best to (立即开立有关信用证，以便我们能及时执行订单) _____.

2) The goods against your Order No. 110 have been ready for shipment for a long time.
The goods ordered are (已备妥待运) _____.

3) We have established a letter of credit in your favor through Tokyo Bank.
We have opened L/C No.123 (通过中国银行开立，以你方为受益人) _____.

4) We have opened a credit with the National Bank for the amount of USD50, 000 covering 1000 pieces of men's cashmere sweaters.
We have opened a credit（金额为 12 000 欧元的 100 打女士棉衬衣）_____.

5) The credit is valid until December 20, 2015.
The credit is (有效期至 2016 年 10 月 18 日) _____.

6) Please amend your L/C No.3429 as follows.
Please (将第 3379 号信用证修改为允许转船) _____.

7) The bill of lading should be "freight prepaid" instead of "freight collect".
(信用证的到期地) _____ should be "in China", (而不是"在我国") _____.

8) Thank you very much for your L/C covering your order No.CB256.
Thank you very much for your L/C No. AG795 (第 CNF4467 号销售确认书项下的) _____.

9) Please extend the validity of the L/C No.345 to November 15.
Please extend（第 789 号信用证的有效期延展至 7 月 10 日）_____.

10) Please extend the date of shipment and the validity of your L/C No. BX182 to August 30 and September 30 respectively.
Please extend（装船期和有效期）_____ of your L/C No. BX276(分别延展至 9 月 15 日和 10 月 15 日) _____.

4. Complete the following mail with words and phrases given in the box.

| 1）shipping advice | 2）with | 3）issued |
| 4）cover | 5）effected | |

Immediately on receipt of your email dated July 10 advising that the covering export license had been_____, we opened L/C No. 3005 in your favor _____Bank of Copenhagen for €16,000 to _____ our order for 4,000 Cotton T-shirts.

Please see to it that the shipment of this order is _____ during this month, since punctual shipment is one of the important considerations in dealing with our market.

We should be glad if you could manage to arrange shipment by "Rose" sailing on or about the 25th, and send us your _____ immediately after the departure of the vessel.

Part Ⅷ. Linkage（知识链接）

信用证

信用证（Letter of Credit，，L/C）是银行根据开证申请人的请求和指示，向受益人开具的有一定金额、并在一定期限内凭规定的单据承诺付款的书面文件。

信用证的当事人

1）开证人（Applicant，Opener）
2）开证行（Opening Bank， Issuing Bank）
3）通知行（Advising Bank， Notifying Bank）
4）受益人（Beneficiary）
5）议付行（Negotiating Bank）
6）付款行（Paying Bank， Drawee Bank）

信用证的结算程序

1）进口商申请开证
2）开证行开证
3）通知行通知、转递受益人
4）受益人审查信用证与开证人修改信用证
5）议付行向受益人议付，向开证行索偿
6）开证行验单付款
7）开证人付款赎单与提货

信用证的种类

1）跟单信用证和光票信用证

2）可撤销信用证和不可撤销信用证
3）保兑信用证
4）公开议付信用证和限制议付信用证
5）付款信用证
6）承兑信用证
7）即期信用证（单到付款信用证和电报索偿信用证）
8）远期信用证
9）假远期信用证
10）迟期付款信用证
11）预支信用证
12）循环信用证
13）对开信用证
14）背对背信用证
15）可转让信用证

信用证的内容

1）开证行名称、地址、信用证的类型、名称、证号、开证日期、金额、受益人、开证申请人、付款人、汇票期限、金额等。

2）汇票条款、单据、货物条款、装运条款、其他条款、开证行担保条款、开证文句。

信用证的审核

1）信用证的性质：是否为不可撤销。

2）适用惯例：是否申明所适用的国际惯例规则。

3）信用证的有效性：检查是否存在限制生效及其他保留条款，注意电开信用证是否为简电信用证。

4）信用证当事人：对开证申请人和受益人的名称和地址要仔细加以核对。

5）信用证到期日和到期地点：到期日应符合买卖合同的规定，一般为装运日后15 天或20 天，到期地点一定要规定在出口商所在地，以便做到及时交单。

6）信用证金额、币种、付款期限规定是否与合同一致。

7）商品品名、货号、规格、数量规定是否与合同一致。

8）信用证中的装运条款包括装运期限、装运港、卸货港、分批装运之规定是否与合同一致。

9）对信用证项下要求受益人提交议付的单据通常包括：商业发票、保险单、海运提单、装箱单、原产地证明、检验证书以及其他证明文件，要注意单据由谁出具、能否出具，信用证对单据是否有特殊要求，单据的规定是否与合同条款一致，前后是否有矛盾。

Part IX. Glossary of Common Sentences
（常用语句集）

1. 出口商

出口商	催促	信用证	开立	As the goods against your Order No. 118 have been ready for a long time, it is advisable for you to open the covering L/C immediately so as to enable us to effect shipment within the stipulated time limit. 你方第118号订单项下的货物备妥待运已有相当时日，我们提请你方立即开出相关信用证，以便我方能在规定的时间内交货。
出口商	催促	信用证	开立	As the goods ordered are ready for shipment, please expedite your L/C. We will effect shipment as soon as it reaches us. 由于所订货物已备妥待运，请即开立信用证。我方一收到信用证，立即装船。
出口商	催促	信用证	开立	If your L/C fails to reach us by the end of March, we will be forced to cancel your order. 如信用证不能在3月底前开到我处，我方将被迫取消你方订单。
出口商	催促	信用证	开立	In spite of our repeated requests, we still have not received your letter of credit. Please open the credit immediately; otherwise, we cannot effect shipment in January. 尽管再三催请开立信用证，但信用证仍未收到。请立即开立，否则不能1月份交货。
出口商	催促	信用证	开立	Please do your best to set up the covering L/C allowing us to ship the goods on receipt of your L/C. 请尽量加快有关信用证的开立，以便我们能顺利执行订单。
出口商	催促	信用证	开立	Please establish the covering L/C as soon as possible so we can ship goods. 请务必尽早开立相关信用证，以便我们安排装运。
出口商	催促	信用证	开立	Please speed up the L/C covering S/C No. 2345 so that we may execute the order smoothly. 请速开2345号合同项下信用证，以便订单顺利执行。
出口商	催促	信用证	开立	The date of shipment is approaching, but we have not received your relevant L/C up to date, please let us have your reply promptly. 装船日期日益临近，但我们至今仍未收到相关信用证，请立即给我们回复。
出口商	催促	信用证	开立	We are sorry that we could not ship the goods by a May vessel due the delay in setting-up your L/C. Please open the said L/C at once. 我们感到遗憾，由于贵方信用证耽误，我们的货不能装5月份的船。请速速开立上述信用证。
出口商	催促	信用证	开立	We should request you to expedite the establishment of the L/C so that we may effect shipment by the direct steamer scheduled to arrive here about 28th. 我方要求你方尽快开出信用证，以便我方能装上28日前后到达此地的直达轮。

Unit 6 Letter of Credit（信用证）

续表

出口商	收到	信用证		Thank you very much for your L/C covering your order No. 100. 感谢你方对第 100 号订单开来的信用证。
出口商	收到	信用证		We have received with thanks your L/C No. 6344 established against the S/C No. NH864. 收到你方对第 NH864 号确认书开立的第 6344 号信用证，谢谢。
出口商	要求	信用证	修改	Amount should be increased up to EU € 15,300. 金额应该增至 15 300 欧元。
出口商	要求	信用证	修改	Our S/C stipulates that the commission granted for this transaction is 3%, but we find your L/C demands a commission of 5%, so you are requested to instruct your bank to amend the L/C. 我们的售货确认书规定本次交易允许的佣金是 3%，但是我们发现你们信用证要 5% 的佣金，所以要求你方通知银行修改信用证。
出口商	要求	信用证	修改	Please amend L/C No. 127 as allowing transshipment and partial shipments. 请修改第 127 号信用证，允许转船和分批装运。
出口商	要求	信用证	修改	Please amend the amount of the L/C to read "2% more or less". 请将信用证溢短装条款改为"大约 2%"。
出口商	要求	信用证	修改	Please amend them according to the contract. 请按合同修改这些规定。
出口商	要求	信用证	修改	Please delete from the L/C the clause, "All bank commissions and charges are for beneficiary's account". Such should be paid by the importing party only. 请从信用证中删去此条款："所有银行佣金和费用由受益人支付"，这些费用理应由进口方承担。
出口商	要求	信用证	修改	Quantity should be reduced to 152 cartons. 数量应该减至 152 箱。
出口商	要求	信用证	修改	The amount both in figures and in words should respectively read "…" 大小写金额应分别为"……"
出口商	要求	信用证	修改	The bill of lading should be "…" instead of "…" 提单应为"……"，而不是"……"
出口商	要求	信用证	修改	The name of the beneficiary should read… 受益人应为……
出口商	要求	信用证	修改	The words "12 dozen per carton" are to be replaced by "20 dozen per carton". 每箱装 12 打应改为每箱装 20 打。
出口商	要求	信用证	修改	We send this email to ask you to amend your L/C No. 3429 as follows. 我们发邮件要求你方将第 3429 号信用证修改如下。
出口商	要求	信用证	修改	You are kindly requested to make necessary amendment for the L/C at an early date. 请贵方尽快对信用证做出必要修改。

出口商	要求	信用证	修改	Your L/C stipulates 60 days sight, whereas our contract shows 30 days sight, so you are requested to make necessary amendment to the L/C and email us before 3 July. 你方信用证规定60天期票，而合同规定30天期票。请对信用证作必要修改，并于7月3日前电邮告知我公司。
出口商	要求	信用证	修改	Since there is no direct ship sailing for your port, we would request you to amend your L/C to allow transshipment. 由于没有驶往你港的直达轮，我方要求修改信用证，允许转船。
出口商	要求	信用证	延展	As there is no direct ship available this month, we should like to request you to extend the validity of your L/C No. 2526 to May 31. 由于本月没有直达轮，我方要求延长第2526号信用证的有效期至5月31日。
出口商	要求	信用证	延展	Owing to the delay in opening L/C, shipment cannot be made as contracted and should be postponed to October. 由于开证延误，装运不能按合同进行，要推迟到10月份。
出口商	要求	信用证	延展	Please extend the date of shipment and the validity of your L/C No. BX182 to August 30 and September 10 respectively and arrange the amendment advice to reach us by July 15. 请将你方第BX182号信用证的装船期和有效期分别延展至8月30日和9月10日，修改通知要在7月15日之前到达我方。
出口商	要求	信用证	延展	Please extend the validity of the letter of credit No. 345 to November 15. 请将345号信用证延期至11月15日。
出口商	要求	信用证	延展	Please have the L/C No. 419 extended until June 4 so that we may make shipment without fail. 请将419号信用证延期至6月4日以便我方能安排好装运。
出口商	要求	信用证	延展	Since there is no direct ship sailing for your port, we would request you to amend your L/C to allow transshipment. 由于没有驶往你港的直达轮，我方要求修改信用证，允许转船。
出口商	要求	信用证	延展	The shipment covered by your credit No. 856 has been ready for quite some time, but the amendment advice has not yet arrived and now an extension of 15 days is required. 856号信用证项下货物已备好多时，但是修改函还未收到，现在要求延展15天。
出口商	要求	信用证	延展	We have to request an extension of the date of shipment and validity of the L/C to September 10 and October 10 respectively. 请你方将信用证的装船期与有效期分别延至9月10日和10月10日。
出口商	指出	信用证	差错	The stipulations in your L/C are not in accordance with the contract. 你方信用证的规定与合同不一致。
出口商	指出	信用证	差错	The unit price stated in your L/C is HK$8.98 per piece, whereas the contracted price is HK$8.68. 你方信用证上的单价为每条8.38港元，而合同规定的单价是9.88港元。

出口商	指出	信用证	差错	We have received your L/C calling for an insurance amount for 150% of the invoice value instead of 110% as stipulated in our S/C. 你方信用证已收到,证上规定的保险额是发票值的150%,而不是我们合同上规定的110%。
出口商	指出	信用证	差错	We regret to say that we have found some discrepancies after examining it carefully. 在仔细检查后,我方很遗憾的发现有些不符之处。
出口商	指出	信用证	差错	Your L/C No. 430 calls for shipment in two equal monthly lots while S/C No. 876 stipulates shipment in a single lot to be made not later than May 2, Please amend accordingly. 第430号信用证规定两批装运,每月一次,每次数量相等,而876号合同规定5月2日前一次装运,请对信用证作相应修改。

2. 进口商

进口商	拒绝	信用证	延展	We are willing to do whatever we can to cooperate with you, but the users are in urgent need of the contracted goods. We regret to say that it is beyond our ability to meet your request to extend the above L/C. 尽管我方很想与贵方尽力合作,但是我方的客户急需此货。我们很遗憾不能满足贵方延展信用证的要求。
进口商	通知	信用证	开立	An irrevocable L/C covering this order for US$5,000 in your favor was opened available until May 15. 以你方为受益人、金额为5 000美元的有关这笔订货的不可撤销信用证业已开出,有效期至5月15日止。
进口商	通知	信用证	开立	Today we have opened an irrevocable L/C in the amount of 35,000 USD covering our Order No. 410 with the Bank of China, Guangzhou. 410号订单项下货物,今天已通过广州的中国银行开立了不可撤销的信用证,金额为35 000美元。
进口商	通知	信用证	开立	We are pleased to inform that we have established a commercial letter of credit in your favor for the contracted amount through Tokyo Bank. 很高兴通知你方,我们已通过东京银行开立了以你方为受益人的相当于合同金额的商业信用证。
进口商	通知	信用证	开立	We have already established the relative L/C to cover our purchase. 我们已经开立了支付我方购货有关的信用证。
进口商	通知	信用证	开立	We have made arrangements with the Commonwealth Bank Australia, Melbourne, to open a credit in your favor. The credit is valid until December 20, 2015. 我们已经安排墨尔本的澳大利亚联邦银行开立以你方为受益人的信用证,有效期至2015年12月20日。

进口商	通知	信用证	开立	We have today established through Tokyo Bank an irrevocable documentary L/C in your favor for the amount of $52,000 covering 1,000 sets of TV. 现通知你方，今天我们已通过东京银行开出以你方为受益人的1 000台电视机的不可撤销信用证，总金额为52 000美元。
进口商	同意	信用证	延展	As requested in your email of April 10, we have instructed our bank to extend the L/C No. 1025 up to October 31. 根据你方4月10日邮件，我们已通知我方银行将1025号信用证延展至10月31日。
进口商	同意	信用证	延展	In compliance with your request, we have already instructed our bank to extend by cable the date of shipment and validity of our L/C to August 10 and 30 respectively. 按你方要求，我们已通知我方银行将信用证的装船期和有效期分别延展至8月10日和8月30日并电传你方。
进口商	同意	信用证	延展	We shall be willing to allow you the extension of 30 days upon your request, and earnestly hope that it will help you out of your present predicament. 只要你们提出，我们愿给你30天的展期，并真诚希望这将有助于你摆脱当前困境。

Unit 7
Packing（包装）

Part Ⅰ. Objectives（目标）

After completing this unit, you will be able to

1. become familiar with the typical English terms and sentence patterns used in emails and messages relating to packing;

2. know the essential components of the emails relating to packing;

3. read and write English emails and messages to discuss packing with your customers.

Part Ⅱ. How to Express（该怎么说）

1. Introducing Packing（出口商说明包装）

A：我是出口商，需要向进口商说明产品的包装方式，我该怎么说呢？

B：你可以这样说：

1）花生用双层麻袋包装。

2）钢笔12支装一盒，200盒装一木箱。

3）我方出口的茶叶通常用盒子包装，24盒装一托盘，10个托盘装一整集装箱。

A：那么，我用英语该怎么说呢？

B：到"常用语句集"去看看，你先找到同类的句型，然后采用截取、替换、拼接的办法稍做加工，你需要的句子就有了。

A：嘿！瞧瞧，我的英语还不错吧！

2. Raising Packing Requirements（进口商提出包装要求）

A：我是进口商，需要向出口商提出对货物的包装要求，我该怎么说呢？

B：你可以这样说：

1）所有箱子必须内衬防水纸。

2）木箱须用钉子钉牢并用整条的铁箍加固。

3）货物的包装必须足够牢固，以最大程度经受途中的粗暴搬运。

A：那么，我用英语该怎么说呢？

B：到"常用语句集"去看看，你先找到同类的句型，然后采用截取、替换、拼接的办法稍做加工，你需要的句子就有了。

A：嘿！瞧瞧，我的英语还不错吧！

3. Mark Instruction（进口商提出唛头和标志语刷制要求）

A：我是进口商，我需要向出口商说明产品外包装上的标记，我该怎么说呢？

B：你可以这样说：

1）请在每个包装上标注收货人的姓名和地址。

2）请在外包装上标注"小心轻放"。

3）请在包上标注我公司的名称缩写"SCC"，放在三角形里面。

A：那么，我用英语该怎么说呢？

B：到"常用语句集"去看看，你先找到同类的句型，然后采用截取、替换、拼接的办法稍做加工，你需要的句子就有了。

A：嘿！瞧瞧，我的英语还不错吧！

Part Ⅲ. Case（案例）

1. Raising Packing Requirements（进口商提出包装要求）

Meggie 是美国 Peace Trading Co., Ltd.的业务员，负责采购儿童玩具。经过询价、报价、还价等磋商环节，Meggie 向中国连云港华洋玩具有限公司下订单订购 4 000 辆优质电动玩具车（choice-quality Battery-driven Toy Cars）。对于包装，Meggie 提出己方的要求。具体包装方式为：每辆玩具车都用聚乙烯袋（polythene wrappers）装好，放入有泡沫塑料（foam plastic）软垫（padded with）的纸盒（cardboard box）中，每盒10辆，50盒装一油纸衬里（lined with oil-cloth）的木箱（wooden case）。

发件人（From）	meggie@peacetrading.com
收件人（To）	zhanghua@huayang.com
主题（Subject）	About Packing
附件（Attachment）	

Dear Mr. Zhang Hua,

With reference to our recent exchange of emails and faxes, we would like to confirm our order for 4,000 of your choice-quality Battery-driven Toy Cars.

As to the packing of our ordered goods, we suggest they should be wrapped in polythene wrappers and packed in cardboard boxes padded with foam plastic, ten toy cars each, 50 boxes to a wooden case lined with oil-cloth. We believe such packing will reduce any possible damage in transit to a minimum.

We trust that you will give careful consideration to our proposal.

Yours sincerely,

Meggie Green

Sentence Patterns Applied（语句归纳）
- 进口商表达订购的愿望；
- 进口商提出要求，对包装方式提出要求；
- 进口商劝导接受。

2. Introducing Customary Packing （出口商说明包装惯例）

连云港华洋玩具有限公司业务员张华收到了美方 Peace Trading Co., Ltd.的订购和包装要求。按照自己包装惯例，华洋公司的电动玩具车的外包装采用标准纸板箱（carton），而不是进口商所要求的木箱。对此，张华以退为进，首先表示华洋公司总是把客户的利益放心上（have our client's interest in mind），承诺可以按照对方的要求进行包装，然后耐心介绍己方的包装惯例及其好处，试图说服对方接受己方的包装惯例。张华在邮件中说，华洋公司十分注重产品包装，在交易中由于包装不善而造成产品受损的情况极其少见。玩具车包装已经进行了改良，标准纸板箱有聚乙烯布衬里（lined with polythene sheet），并用塑料包装带（plastic strap）全面捆好，使内装货物在运输途中不因潮气或颠簸（jolting）、碰撞（collision）而受损。这样包装的好处是，使用纸箱能降低包装成本（packing cost），减轻货物重量（cargo weight）并可节省运费（freight charge）。

发件人（From）	zhanghua@huayang.com
收件人（To）	Meggie@peacetrading.com
主题（Subject）	Packing of Battery-driven Toy Cars

Dear Ms. Green,

We thank you for your email confirming your order for 4,000 choice-quality Battery-driven Toy Cars together with your proposal of the packing of the goods.

As regards the outer packing, we could use wooden cases if you think better. We always have our client's interest in mind.

But, our improved outer packing with cartons for toy cars has been widely accepted by our regular clients. Up till now, there has not been a single complaint from any of them since our adoption of this form of packing. Each of the toy cars is to be wrapped in polythene wrappers and packed in a cardboard box lined with polythene sheet, and 50 boxes to a carton reinforced by plastic strap to protect the contents from moisture or any possible damage from jolting and collision in transit, and suitable for long distance ocean transportation.

Furthermore, by using carton, the packing cost, and cargo weight can be reduced and freight charge can be saved accordingly. If you insist on wooden cases for outer packing, we would strictly follow your instruction. Only that the extra charges should be borne by you.

> If you could accept the above suggestion on packing, we shall pack the goods in cartons as we have recommended.
>
> Yours sincerely,
>
> Zhang Hua

Sentence Patterns Applied（语句归纳）
- 出口商收到订购，收到包装要求，致谢；
- 出口商接受包装要求；
- 出口商说明包装惯例，说明包装方式，评价包装；
- 出口商申明额外包装费用，申明额外费用的承担方；
- 出口商劝导接受包装惯例。

3. Accepting Packing Method（进口商接受包装方式）

美方 Meggie 收到中方张华的邮件后，立刻做出了回复，确认接受对方的包装惯例。

现在，你是 Meggie，你需要回复邮件。

Sentence Patterns for Reference（参考语句）
- 进口商收到包装惯例，致谢，接受包装惯例；
- 进口商说明（重申）包装方式；
- 进口商期盼。

发件人（From）	
收件人（To）	
主题（Subject）	

4. Mark Instructions（进口商提出刷唛要求）

进出口双方就货物包装达成一致后，进口商对货物外包装上的唛头和标志语的印制提出了要求。业务员 Meggie 发邮件给张华要求按照以下方式刷制：把 Peace Trading Co., Ltd.的首字母缩写（initial）"PTC"放在三角形里面印制在外包装上，下方标注目的港名称，此外，外包装上还需印上"请勿踩踏"这类标志语。

发件人（From）	Meggie@peacetrading.com
收件人（To）	zhanghua@huayang.com
主题（Subject）	Marking on Outer Packing
附件（Attachment）	

Dear Mr. Zhang,

About our order No. 213 for 4,000 choice-quality Battery-driven Toy Cars, we wish to add our requirements for the outer packing.

Please mark our initials "PTC" in a triangle, under which the port of destination should be stenciled. In addition, indicative marks like DO NOT STEP ON should also be stenciled.

We thank you for your close cooperation and look forward to your speedy reply.

Yours sincerely,

Meggie Green

Sentence Patterns Applied（语句归纳）
- ➢ 进口商要求包装；
- ➢ 进口商要求唛头刷制，要求标志语刷制；
- ➢ 进口商事先感谢（劝导接受请求），期盼回复。

5. Agreeing with Marking Requirements （出口商接受刷唛要求）

出口方华洋公司收到刷唛要求后，马上做出回复表示同意按照对方要求刷制唛头。现在，你是张华，你需要回复邮件给 Meggie Green。

Sentence Patterns for Reference（参考语句）
- ➢ 出口商收到刷唛要求；
- ➢ 出口商承诺按要求刷唛，说明（重申）唛头、标志语；
- ➢ 出口商承诺货物完好抵达。

发件人（From）	
收件人（To）	
主题（Subject）	

....

....

....

....

....

....

....

....

....

Part Ⅳ. Writing Directions（写作指导）

出口商介绍包装

包装说明是出口商向进口商介绍货物的包装，说明该类货物的包装习惯。内容包括：

- ➢ 提及相关订单、信用证项下的货物；
- ➢ 介绍货物的习惯包装；
- ➢ 说明如此包装的原因；
- ➢ 说明外包装上的印刷标记；
- ➢ 承诺包装效果；
- ➢ 鼓励、劝导对方接受；
- ➢ 期盼回复。

进口商要求更改包装

当进口商不同意出口商的包装方式时，可以提出己方的包装方式。更改包装需要说明理由，要注意语气。内容有：

- ➢ 提及出口商的包装；
- ➢ 告知不能接受；
- ➢ 陈述不能接受的原因；
- ➢ 说明新的包装方式；
- ➢ 说明印刷标记；
- ➢ 劝导对方接受；
- ➢ 期盼回复。

进口商提出包装要求

当然，进口商也可以率先提出包装要求，内容包括：

- ➢ 提及相关订单、信用证项下的货物；
- ➢ 提出具体的包装要求；
- ➢ 说明如此包装的原因；
- ➢ 说明外包装上的印刷标记；
- ➢ 劝导对方接受；
- ➢ 期盼回复。

如果按照进口商的包装方式将会产生额外的包装费用时，出口商还需要回复，必须明确额外费用的承担方。

Part V. Terms and Sentence Frames
（术语与句型）

1. Terms（术语）

包装容器
bag 袋
carton 纸板箱
case 箱子
box 盒
crate 板条箱
drum 铁皮圆桶
cask 木桶
keg 小圆桶
bale 包
parcel 小包，包裹
can 罐
tin 听
carboy 大玻璃瓶
bundle 捆
container 集装箱
pallet 货盘
sack 麻袋
gunny bag 麻袋
poly bag 塑料袋
chest 茶箱
barrel 鼓形桶
hogshead 大啤酒桶
cylinder 钢桶
bomb 钢桶
bottle 瓶
jar 瓮
basket 篓
paper bag 纸袋
straw bag 草袋

fiber board case 纤维板箱
veneer case 胶合板箱
plywood case 胶合板箱
polyethylene bag 聚乙烯袋
jute bag 麻袋
wooden case 木箱
wooden box 木箱

包装种类

inner packing 内包装
outer packing 外包装
selling packing 销售包装
sales packing 销售包装
transportation packing 运输包装
large packing 大包装
small packing 小包装
immediate packing 直接包装
neutral packing 中性包装
customary packing 习惯包装

包装规格

dimension 尺寸、规格
volume 体积、容积
cubic meter 立方米
square meter 平方米
gross weight 毛重
net weight 净重
tare weight 皮重

唛头图形

circle 圆形
triangle 三角形
oval 椭圆形
square 正方形
downward triangle 倒三角形
rectangle 长方形
diamond 菱形

heart 心形

2. Sentence Frames（句型）

包装方式
to be packed in… 包装在……
to have something packed in… 将某物装入……
to be lined with… 内衬……
to be secured or reinforced by… 用……加固

印刷标记
to mark… 标上……
to be marked with… （被）刷上……，标上……
to have the marking of… 标上……，有……标记
to be stenciled with… 被印上……
to be printed with… 被印上……
to indicate… 显示……，标出……

包装要求
to stand rough handling during transit 承受途中的粗暴搬运
to endure heavy pressure 承受重压
to withstand … 承受……
to put up with… 承受……
to be suitable for long-distance ocean transportation 适合于长距离海洋运输
to be fit for… 适合于……

易于受损
to be susceptible to breakage 易于破损
to be susceptible to damage by moisture 易于潮损
to be susceptible to damage by heat 易于热损
to be susceptible to damage by rust 易于锈损

货物状况
in sound condition 状况良好
in perfect condition 状况良好
in good condition 状况良好
in a damaged condition 损坏状态
in a moldy condition 受潮状态

Part VI. Follow Me （跟我写）

Raising Packing Requirements（进口商提出包装要求）

电子邮件模板

Dear Mr. /Ms. （对方的姓）,

  We refer to our order No. （我方订单的编号） for （我方所订购的货物名称及数量） to be shipped during （货物将要装运的时间段）. As the goods are （货物的特性）, we advise to pack the goods according to our instructions to prevent damage in transit.

  Please pack the goods （小包装内的数量） in a （小包装的名称）, （小包装的件数） in a （中包装的名称）, and （中包装的件数） in a （大包装的名称）. The （小包装的名称） are to be padded with （内衬材料的名称）. Apart from this, we hope the inner packing will be （对内包装的要求） while the outer packing （对外包装的要求）.

  We hope our goods will arrive in perfect condition.

  Yours sincerely,

  （署名）

贸易背景

  买方刘文学女士向卖方 Tony Green 先生提出了包装要求：每 6 件装 1 盒（box），每 10 盒装 1 箱（carton），每 2 箱装 1 木箱（wooden case）；小包装要内衬泡沫塑料（foamed plastics）；内包装（inner packing）要引人注目以便有利于销售（attractive and helpful to be sales），而外包装（outer packing）要结实，能经得住粗暴搬运和海运（strong enough to withstand rough handling and the sea transportation）。

  刘女士所订购的是 200 箱（cardboard carton）啤酒杯（beer glass），极易碎（highly fragile），订单号是 6054，合同装运期是五月份。

  现在，刘女士要写邮件提出包装要求。

仿照模板套写

Part VII. Practical Writing （实训写作）

1. Match the words and phrases with their Chinese meanings.

inner packing   中性包装
outer packing   承受重压
neutral packing   内包装
customary packing   净重
net weight   内衬
be lined with   易于破损
be suitable for ocean transportation   状况良好
in perfect condition   习惯包装
be susceptible to breakage   适合于海洋运输
endure heavy pressure   外包装

2. Read the following email and list the sentence patterns applied.

Thank you for your email of Feb.1, 2015 informing us of your usual packing for coffee beans.

We have approached our clients about packing, but our clients insist that the coffee bean should be packed in cartons and these cartons must be fit for ocean transportation. As for the strapping used for binding the cartons, plastic strapping is recommended it is light and strong.

If the above is acceptable to you, please reply as soon as possible. We sincerely hope that we can start a concrete transaction to our mutual benefit.

3. Complete each of the following sentences according to its model given.

1) On the outer packing, please mark the wording, "Handle with Care".
On the outer packing, (标注"勿用吊钩") _____.

2) We trust that you will give special care to the packing in order to avoid damage in transit.
We trust that you will give special care to the packing (以免运输途中受到潮损) _____.

3) Warning marks should be marked on the outer packing.
(指示性标志) _____ should be marked on the outer packing.

4) The cartons should be strong enough to withstand roughest handling during transit.
The cartons should be (足够牢固能承受重压) _____.

5) Cases must be lined with waterproof paper.
Cases must(内衬结实的防潮纸) _____.

6) The packing and marking shall be at seller's option..
The packing and marking (由买方决定) _____.

7) Please mark and number the package according to our instruction.
Please mark and number the package (根据所给的图样) _____.

8) Please see to it that the name of country and trade mark shall appear on each package.
Please see to it that (收货人的姓名和地址) _____ _____ shall appear on each package.

9) The outer packing should be stenciled with "DO NOT STOW ON DECK".
The outer packing (刷有我公司的首字母缩写和订单号) _____.

10) Our usual packing for dyed poplin(染色府绸) is in bales lined with waterproof paper, each containing 200 yards in single color.
Our usual packing for peanuts(用麻袋包装,麻袋内衬防水纸,每袋装25千克)
_____
_____.

4. Complete the following email with words and phrases given in the box.

| 1) to | 2) Transit | 3) each |
| 4) packed | 5) protect | |

Thank you for your fax of May 15 together with the sample shirt.

Attached is our order No. GH-173 placed at the price of $41 per dozen CFR London for 20,000 dozen of Men's Shirts.

For this first transaction between us, we would like to make it clear in advance that all the shirts are to be _____ in poly-bags of one piece _____, 20 dozen _____ a carton lined with water-proof paper.

Please see to it that the cartons used are strong enough to _____ the goods from any possible damage in _____.

We hope the above requirements can be met exactly and await your early shipment.

Part VIII. Linkage（知识链接）

指示性标志（indicative mark）

TOP 上部

BOTTOM 下部

THIS SIDE UP 此端向上

OPEN THIS END 此端开启

OPEN HERE 从此开启

SLING HERE 此处吊索

HANDLE WITH CARE 小心轻放

WITH CARE 小心搬运

FRAGILE 易碎物品

KEEP UPRIGHT 切勿倒置

NOT TO BE LAID FLAT 请勿平放

DO NOT DROP 请勿下扔

DO NOT STEP ON 请勿踩踏

USE NO HOOK, NO HOOK 请勿用钩

STOW LEVEL 注意平放

KEEP FLAT 注意平放

KEEP AWAY FROM HEAT 请勿受热

KEEP AWAY FROM MOISTURE 切勿受潮

KEEP DRY 保持干燥

KEEP COLD 冷藏

KEEP OUT OF THE SUN 避免日光直射
NO SMOKING 严禁烟火
GUARD AGAINST DAMP 禁止潮湿
GLASSWARE – WITH CARE 玻璃器皿——当心
KEEP COOL 低温存放
LIFT HERE 在此起吊
DO NOT STOW ON DECK 禁放甲板上
WAREHOUSE STACK LIMIT（4 PIECES）仓库堆码极限（4件）

警告性标志（warning mark）
POISON – WITH CARE, POISONOUS 小心有毒
ACID – WITH CARE 酸——小心
RADIOACTIVE 放射性物品
CORROSIVE 腐蚀性物品
INFLAMMABLE 易燃品
PERISHABLE 易腐物品
DANGEROUS 危险品
HAZARDOUS 危险品
FRAGILE，HANDLE WITH CARE 易碎物品，小心轻放

Part IX. Glossary of Common Sentences（常用语句集）

1. 出口商

出口商	承诺	包装	改进	We have taken effective measures to improve the packing of the goods so that such damage will not happen again. 我们已经采取了有效的措施改进货物的包装。所以，这样的损坏事件不会再发生。
出口商	承诺	包装	改进	Your opinions on packing will be passed on to our manufactures. 你们对包装的意见将转达给厂商。
出口商	介绍	包装	方式	All bags have an inner waterproof lining. 所有包裹都有防水里衬。
出口商	介绍	包装	方式	Each carton is lined with a polythene sheet and secured by overall strapping, thus protecting the contents from dampness and possible damage through rough handling. 每一纸板箱衬以塑料纸，全箱用铁箍加固，以防货物受潮以及因粗暴搬运可能引起的损坏。

续表

出口商	介绍	包装	方式	Each case is lined with foam plastics in order to protect the goods against press. 箱子里垫有泡沫塑料以免货物受压。
出口商	介绍	包装	方式	Each pair of socks is packed in a polybag and 12 pairs to a box. 每双袜子装一塑料袋,12 双装一盒。
出口商	介绍	包装	方式	Men's Shirts are packed in wooden cases of 10 dozen each. 男式衬衣用木箱装,每箱 10 打。
出口商	介绍	包装	方式	Our cotton prints are packed in cases lined with draft paper and waterproof paper, each consisting of 30 pieces in one design with 5 color ways equally assorted. 我们印花布系用木箱包装,内衬牛皮纸和防潮纸。每箱 30 匹,一花 5 色,平均搭配。
出口商	介绍	包装	方式	Peanuts are packed in double gunny bags. 花生用双层麻袋包装。
出口商	介绍	包装	方式	Pens are packed 12 pieces to a box and 200 boxes to a wooden case. 钢笔 12 只装一盒,200 盒装一木箱。
出口商	介绍	包装	方式	Ten bottles are put into a box and 100 boxes into a carton. 10 支装入一小盒,100 盒装入一个纸箱。
出口商	介绍	包装	方式	The canned goods are to be packed in cartons with double straps. 罐装货物在纸箱里,外面加两道箍。
出口商	介绍	包装	方式	The goods are packed in iron drums, 190kgs net each. 货物用铁桶装,每桶净重 190 千克。
出口商	介绍	包装	方式	The wheat is to be packed in new gunny bags of 100kgs and each bag weighs about 1.5kgs. 小麦用新麻袋包装,每袋装 100 千克,袋重 1.5 千克。
出口商	介绍	包装	惯例	According to our usual practice, the table lamp should be packed in international standard box. 按照我方一般惯例,台灯应该用国际标准纸盒包装。
出口商	介绍	包装	惯例	Our tea for export is customarily packed in boxes, 24 boxes on a pallet, and 10 pallets to an FCL container. 我方出口的茶叶通常用盒子包装,24 盒装一托盘,10 个托盘装一整集装箱。
出口商	介绍	包装	惯例	Our usual packing for dyed poplin is in bales lined with waterproof paper, each containing 600 yards in single color. 我公司的印染府绸通常用布包包装;布包内衬防水纸;每一布包内装有同色的 600 码府绸。
出口商	介绍	包装唛头	方式	The packing and marking shall be at the seller's discretion. 包装和唛头由卖方决定。
出口商	拒绝	包装	要求	Much to our regret, we cannot comply with your special request for packing. 非常抱歉,我方无法依从你方对有关包装的特殊要求。
出口商	评价	包装	效果	I'm sure the new packing will be acceptable to your clients. 我相信新包装定会使您的客户满意。

续表

出口商	评价	包装	效果	Our packing is standardized in a manner which has proved successful in many export shipment. 我们的包装已经标准化，在多次出口装运中已证明是成功的。
出口商	评价	包装	效果	Our packing will be on a par with that of Germany. 我们的包装可以与德国同行相比美。
出口商	评价	包装	效果	The design of packaging has our own style. 这种包装设计有我们自己独特的风格。
出口商	申明	包装	费用	As a rule, the buyer ought to bear the charges of packaging. 通常，包装费用应由买方负担。
出口商	申明	包装	费用	Normally, packing charge is included in the contract price. 一般说来，合同价格中已经包括了包装费用。
出口商	申明	包装	费用	Packing charge is about 3% of the total cost of the goods. 包装费用占货物总值的3%。
出口商	申明	包装	费用	We can meet your requirements to have goods packed in wooden cases; however, you have to bear the extra packing charge. 我们可以满足你方将货物装入木箱的要求，但你方必须承担额外的费用。
出口商	申明	包装	费用	We must insist on charging for packing, since all our prices are quoted exclusive of packing. 我们必须坚持收取包装费，因为我方的一切报价都不包括包装费。
出口商	同意	包装	要求	We agree to line the container with waterproof material so that the goods can be protected against moisture. 我们同意用防水材料做容器里衬，以免货物受潮。
出口商	同意	包装	要求	We've informed the manufacturer to have them packed as per your instruction. 我们已经通知厂商按你们的要求包装。

2. 进口商

进口商	协商	包装	材料	Garments packed in wooden cases are susceptible to damage by moisture. 服装装在木箱子里容易受到潮损。
进口商	协商	包装	材料	I'm afraid the cardboard boxes are not strong enough for ocean transportation. 我担心纸箱对于远洋运输来说不够结实。
进口商	询问	包装		I'd like to know something about the packing in your factory. 我想了解一下你们工厂的包装情况。
进口商	要求	包装	材料	All the cases must be lined with waterproof paper. 所有箱子必须内衬防水纸。
进口商	要求	包装	材料	As this article is fragile, please case it in durable packaging. 这种物品易碎，请以耐用包装来装箱。
进口商	要求	包装	材料	Cases must have an inner lining of stout, damp-resisting paper. 木箱必须内衬结实的防潮纸。

续表

进口商	要求	包装	材料	The goods must be packed in fivefold strong paper bags as stipulated in the contract. 货物应按合同规定用五层厚牢固纸袋包装。
进口商	要求	包装	材料	We advocate using smaller containers to pack the goods. 我们主张用小容器包装这批货物。
进口商	要求	包装	方式	Cases must be nailed and reinforced by overall metal strapping. 木箱须用钉子钉牢并用整条的铁箍加固。
进口商	要求	包装	方式	Packing in sturdy wooden cases is essential. Cases must be nailed, battened and secured by overall metal strapping. 必须用坚实的木箱包装，装箱必须用铁钉钉好，用木板钉住，用一根铁皮钉牢。
进口商	要求	包装	方式	The goods are to be packed in strong export cases, securely strapped. 货物应该用坚固的出口木箱包装，并且牢牢加箍。
进口商	要求	包装	方式	The piece goods are to be wrapped in craft paper, and then packed in wooden cases. 布匹在装入木箱以前要用牛皮纸包好。
进口商	要求	包装	方式	You must reinforce the packing with metal straps. 你们必须用铁箍加固包装。
进口商	要求	包装	改进	We can only accept your offer if you improve packing of your goods. 你方如能改善货物的包装，我方将接受报价。
进口商	要求	包装	改进	We would appreciate it if you could improve your packing to avoid any damage of the goods. 我方很感激如果贵方能改进包装以避免货物破损。
进口商	要求	包装	效果	Packing should be suitable for transport by sea. 包装要适合于海运。
进口商	要求	包装	效果	Please be assured that the packaging is strong enough to withstand rough handling. 请确保包装牢固，足以承受粗糙搬运。
进口商	要求	包装	效果	Special packing measures should be taken to protect the goods from dampness, rain, leaking, pilferage and other damages. 必须采取特别的包装措施来保护货物不受潮、雨淋、渗漏、偷盗和其他损害。
进口商	要求	包装	效果	The key points of packing lie in protecting the goods from moisture. 包装的关键是防潮。
进口商	要求	包装	效果	The outer packing should be strong enough for transportation. As to the inner packing, it must be attractive and helpful to the sales. 外包装应当坚实牢固，适于运输，至于内包装必须能吸引人，且有助于销售。

续表

进口商	要求	包装	效果	The package for export goods should be strong enough to withstand roughest handling during transit. 出口货物的包装必须足够牢固，以经受途中最粗暴的搬运。
进口商	要求	包装	效果	The packaging should be modern and distinctive. 其包装应该是现代的、独特的。
进口商	要求	包装	效果	They should be carefully packed in reinforced carton boxes. 货物应以加固纸箱仔细包装。
进口商	要求	包装	效果	We ask you to see to it that all the goods are well packed so as to avoid damage in transit. 特提请你方注意，所有货物都应妥善包装，以免运输途中损坏。
进口商	要求	包装	效果	We trust that you will give special care to the packing in order to avoid damage in transit. 相信贵公司会特别注意包装，以免运输途中受损。
进口商	要求	包装	效果	We want the garments to be packed for window display. 我们要求服装的包装便于橱窗陈列。
进口商	要求	包装	效果	You should make sure that the cartons could be strong enough to stand rough handling. 您要确保箱子结实，足以承受粗鲁装卸。
进口商	要求	包装	效果	Your packing must be strong, easy to handle and seaworthy. 贵方注意，包装必须牢固、易于搬运且适合远洋运输。
进口商	指示	包装	方式	Please pack one TV set to a cardboard box, 4 sets to a wooden cases suitable for export. 请把每台电视机装一纸板箱，每4台装一适合于出口的木箱。
进口商	指示	包装	方式	Please pack the goods according to our instructions. 请按照我方的指示包装货物。
进口商	指示	包装 唛头	方式 刷制	Every 100 dozen should be packed in a wooden case marked TM and numbered from No. 1 upward. 每100打装一箱，刷上唛头TM，从第一号开始往上循序编号。
进口商	指示	包装 唛头	方式 刷制	The full details regarding packing and marking must be strictly observed. 有关包装和唛头的详细规定，都要严格执行。
进口商	指示	标志	刷制	Every package should have the marking "fragile". 每个包装上应标上"易碎"字样。
进口商	指示	标志	刷制	For the sake of precaution, indicative marks like NOT TO BE STOWED BELOW OTHER CARGO, USE NO HOOKS, etc. should be shown, too. 为了以防万一，指示性标志，如，"勿置于其他货物下面""勿用吊钩"等也应该刷上。
进口商	指示	标志	刷制	On the outer packing, please mark wording "Handle with Care". 在外包装上请标明"小心轻放"字样。
进口商	指示	标志	刷制	Please indicate the name and address of the consignee on each package. 请在每个包装上标出收货人的姓名和地址。

				续表
进口商	指示	标志	刷制	Please make sure you mark the shipment with "CAREFUL HANDLING". 请不要忘记在货物上标明"小心轻放"。
进口商	指示	标志	刷制	Please mark the bales with our initials SCC. 请在包上标注我公司名称缩写 SCC。
进口商	指示	标志	刷制	The batch number should be marked clearly on every container. 每个箱上应清楚地标上批号。
进口商	指示	标志	刷制	Warning marks should also be marked on the outer packing. 警告性标志也应刷在外包装上。
进口商	指示	唛头	刷制	Cases must be numbered from 1 to 50. The word "FRAGILE" stenciled clearly in normal size on four sides of the container. 箱子外部按顺序从 1 到 50 编号,"FRAGILE"字样按常规大小醒目地写在箱子的四面。
进口商	指示	唛头	刷制	Goods are to be marked with our initials in a diamond (circle, triangle, etc.). 货物应标上我方缩写名称,外加菱形(圆形、三角形等)。
进口商	指示	唛头	刷制	Please make sure that all cases are clearly marked and numbered as specified in our order. 请务必做到下列所有的箱子都按我们订单上所明确规定的那样清楚地刷上唛头,编上号。
进口商	指示	唛头	刷制	Please mark and number of the package according to our instruction. 请按照我们的指示制作唛头和标箱号。
进口商	指示	唛头	刷制	Please mark the cases (boxes, bags, casks) as per the drawing given. 请按所给的图案在箱(盒、装、桶)上刷唛头。
进口商	指示	唛头	刷制	Please state the packing marks on each case. 请在每个箱子上刷上唛头。

Unit 8

Shipment（装运）

Part I. Objectives（目标）

After completing this unit, you will be able to:

1. write an email or a message to talk with your business customers on the topic of shipment such as shipping instructions, shipping advice, amendments to shipping clause, urging shipment, postponing shipment, etc.;

2. know the essential components of the above emails;

3. become familiar with the typical English terms and sentence patterns used in mails and messages about shipment.

Part II. How to Express（该怎么说）

1. Shipping Instruction（进口商发出装运指示）

A：我是进口方，与出口方已经签订进出口合同，现在到了装运货物的阶段。我要给对方指定装运货轮、日期，我该怎么说呢？

B：你可以这样说：

1）请尽力用"和平"号轮装运我方货物，该轮预订于5月8日抵汉堡。

2）请将货物装星期五起航的"大连"号，而不是像上周通知你们的装"船长"号。

3）请将第T566号合同下的第一批货装"长风"号轮，并安排于5月10日左右起航。

A：那么，我用英语该怎么说呢？

B：到"常用语句集"去看看，你先找到同类的句型，然后采用截取、替换、拼接的办法稍做加工，你需要的句子就有了。

A：嘿！瞧瞧，我的英语还不错吧！

2. Amending Shipment（出口商更改装运）

A：我是出口方，由于延误、订不到舱位等原因，需要更改装运，我该怎么说呢？
B：你可以这样说：
1）我们无法订到开往汉堡的直达轮舱位。
2）本月无直达船，我们只能在香港转船。
3）由于船期延误，我方只能在下月初装运。
A：那么，我用英语该怎么说呢？
B：到"常用语句集"去看看，你先找到同类的句型，然后采用截取、替换、拼接的办法稍做加工，你需要的句子就有了。
A：嘿！瞧瞧，我的英语还不错吧！

3. Urging Shipment（进口商催促装运）

A：我是进口方，需要催促出口商装运，我该怎么说呢？
B：你可以这样说：
1）直至今日我们还未收到你方有关货物装运情况的消息。
2）为了能让我们的客户在销售季节开始的时候赶上市场的大量需求，请速装运不得延误。
3）如果你们不能在本月底前装运我们的订货，我们就不得不取消订单了。
A：那么，我用英语该怎么说呢？
B：到"常用语句集"去看看，你先找到同类的句型，然后采用截取、替换、拼接的办法稍做加工，你需要的句子就有了。
A：嘿！瞧瞧，我的英语还不错吧！

4. Asking for Postponing Shipment （出口商请求延迟装运）

A：我是出口方，现在无法按照预定的期限装运货物，需要请求对方允许延迟装运，我该怎么说呢？

B：你可以这样说：

1）由于制造商遇到不可预见的困难，我方不能在本月底前装船。

2）因为向美国出口服装新配额的限制，我们不得不延期装运你们第339号订单项下的3000件男西服。

3）虽然我方已尽最大努力，却因为舱位不足而无法保证按时装运。

A：那么，我用英语该怎么说呢？

B：到"常用语句集"去看看，你先找到同类的句型，然后采用截取、替换、拼接的办法稍做加工，你需要的句子就有了。

A：嘿！瞧瞧，我的英语还不错吧！

5. Shipping Advice （出口商发出装船通知）

A：我是出口方，货物已经装船，现在需要通知对方，我该怎么说呢？

B：你可以这样说：

1）兹通知，第3122号销售确认书项下的货物今日由"东风"号轮从宁波运往新加坡。

2）我们高兴地告知你们，756号订单之货物已于今日装上"和平"号轮，该轮将于明日驶往你方港口。

3）你们的100台洗衣机已装"船长"号，该轮将于11月5日驶往温哥华。预计到达时间是12月9日。

A：那么，我用英语该怎么说呢？

B：到"常用语句集"去看看，你先找到同类的句型，然后采用截取、替换、拼接的办法稍做加工，你需要的句子就有了。

A：嘿！瞧瞧，我的英语还不错吧！

Part Ⅲ. Case（案例）

1. Shipping Instruction（进口商发出装运指示）

德国 Sanders & Lowe Co., Ltd.于 2015 年 2 月 15 日向宁波丰连贸易有限公司（Ningbo Fenglian Trading Co., Ltd.）订购了 3 000 件男士衬衣，双方签订了合同，约定于 2015 年 4 月 15 日前装运。3 月 1 日，德方业务员 John Smith 发来邮件，通知宁波丰连公司业务员王欣相关信用证已经开立，指示将货物装上 4 月 8 日前后从宁波港起航的"东风号"货轮。

发件人（From）	John@Sanderslowe.com
收件人（To）	wangxin @ nbfenglian.cn
主题（Subject）	shipping instructions
附件（Attachment）	

Dear Mr. Wang,

We are glad to inform you that L/C No. 734 under S/C No.CV2741, amounting to €17,400 has been opened this morning with the Deutsche Bank. Upon receipt of the same, please arrange shipment of the goods booked by us without delay.

We are informed by the local shipping company that s/s "Dongfeng" is due to sail from your city to Hamburg on or about the 8th April and, if possible, please try your best to ship by that steamer. Your co-operation in this respect will be highly appreciated.

We await your shipping advice.

Best regards,

John Smith

Sentence Patterns Applied（语句归纳）
- 进口商通知信用证已开立，进口商提出装运要求；
- 进口商指示装运货轮，劝导；
- 进口商期盼装运通知。

2. Acknowledging Receipt of Shipping Advice（出口商收到装运指示）

宁波丰连贸易有限公司收到了 John Smith 装运指示，业务员王欣需要回复邮件，表示同意按照对方的指示进行装运。

现在，你是业务员王欣，请你回复邮件。

Sentence Patterns for Reference（参考语句）
- 出口商收到信用证开立的通知，致谢；
- 出口商承诺（按装运要求）装运，说明装运（复述装运要求），承诺寄送装运通知；
- 出口商期盼（更多）订单。

Hints（提示）

当贸易一方同意对方的要求并承诺照办时，信文语句通常采用重复对方原句的方式。通过这种重复，发件人表明自己完全领会了对方的要求，将会全面遵照运作，希望对方放心。

发件人（From）	
收件人（To）	
主题（Subject）	
附件（Attachment）	

3. Urging shipment（进口商催促装运）

装运期临近了，而 Sanders & Lowe Co., Ltd.仍没有收到宁波丰连贸易有限公司关于 3 000 件男士衬衣的装运消息，于是，业务员 John Smith 发邮件催促装船，提醒在合同规定的时间内交货。

发件人（From）	John@Sanderslowe.com
收件人（To）	wangxin@nbfenglian.cn
主题（Subject）	Urging Shipment under S/C No. CV2741
附件（Attachment）	

Dear Mr. Wang,

We are very anxious to know about the shipment of our order for 3,000 pieces of Men's shirts.

According to the terms of S/C No. CV2741, the shipment is to be effected by April 15th, 2015. However, up to now we have not received from you any information concerning the shipment.

As the selling season is rapidly approaching, we are in urgent need of the goods. Please arrange shipment as soon as possible, thus allowing the goods to catch the brisk demand at the start of the season.

Please make efforts to get the goods dispatched within the time contracted. We hope you will let us have your shipping advice at once.

Best regards,

John Smith

Sentence Patterns Applied（语句归纳）

- 进口商询问装运；
- 进口商说明（提醒）装运期限，抱怨未收到装运通知；
- 进口商说明催促理由，催促装运；
- 进口商限定装运期限（合同期），期盼装船通知。

4. Sending Shipping Advice（出口商发送装船通知）

宁波丰连贸易有限公司于 4 月 12 日将货物交中外运集装箱运输有限公司宁波港装船，取得了 GD067134 号提单（B/L）。货物装船后，王欣即给 John Smith 发装船通知，告知对方已将总价值为 17 400 欧元的 3 000 件男士衬衣装在 120 个纸箱（Carton）内，装上 Dongfeng V.203 号货轮，唛头（Marks）为 CV2741/HAMBURG/GERMANY/NOS.1-120，毛重（Gross Weight）为 1 200kgs，总体积（Measurement）为 19.60CBM，启运港为宁波，卸货港为德国汉堡。另外，还附件寄送了提单副本一份。

现在，你是王欣，你发邮件通知对方装船事宜。为了清晰简便，你可以采用列表的方式说明各项信息。

Sentence Patterns for Reference（参考语句）

- 出口商通知货物已装运，列出各项细节；
- 出口商说明品名、数量、金额、船名、提单号、起运日期、装运港、卸货港、唛头、毛重和总体积；
- 出口商附件寄送提单副本；
- 成交祝愿。

发件人（From）	
收件人（To）	
主题（Subject）	

B/L （提单）

Shipper NINGBO FENGLIAN TRADING CO., LTD. NO. 381 ZHANGSHAN ROAD NINGBO, CHINA		B/L No. GD067134 CARRIER 中远集装箱运输有限公司 COSCO CONTAINER LINES Port-to-Port or Combined Transport
Consignee TO ORDER		**BILL OF LADING**
Notify party SANDERS & LOWE CO., LTD. NO. 304 FILAMENT STREET HAMBURG, GERMANY		**RECEIVED** the goods in apparent good order and condition as specified below unless otherwise stated herein. The Carrier, in accordance with the provisions contained in this document, 1) undertakes to perform or to procure the performance of the entire transport from the place at which the goods are taken in charge to the place designated for delivery in this document, and 2) assumes liability as prescribed in this document for such transport. One of the Bills of Lading must be surrendered duly indorsed in exchange for the goods or delivery order.
Pre-carriage by	Place of Receipt	
Ocean Vessel Voy. No. DONGFENG V.203	Port of loading NINGBO, CHINA	
Port of Discharge HAMBURG, GERMANY	Place of delivery	

Marks&Nos. ContainerNo.	No.& kind of pkgs	Description of goods	Gross weight	Measurement
CV2741 HAMBURG GERMANY NOS. 1-120 1X20'FCL, CY / CY CN.: APLU156758 SN.: 853410	120CTNS	MEN'S SHIRTS	1200.00KGS	19.60CBM
Total No. of container or other pkgs or units (in words)		SAY ONE HUNDRED AND TWENTY CARTONS ONLY		

Freight & charges FREIGHT PREPAID	Revenue Tons	Rate	Per	Prepaid	Collect
Ex rate	Prepaid at	Payable at	Place and date of issue: NINGBO, 12 APR., 2015		
	Total prepaid	No. of B(s)/L THREE	Signed by	COSCO CONTAINER LINES NINGBO BRANCH	
Laden on board the Vessel: Date: 12 APR., 2015 By: C.C.L.NINGBO 李成			*As agent for the carrier named above*	李成	

Part Ⅳ. Writing Directions（写作指导）

涉及装运的话题比较多，包括装运方式、装运时间、货轮航次、是否允许分批装运、转运等。从进口商的角度来说，有装运指示、催促装运等，从出口商的角度有请求修改装运条款、要求延迟装运、装船通知等。

装运指示
装运指示是进口商对出口商提出的装运要求，内容包括：
➢ 提及相关的合同、订单、信用证项下的货物；
➢ 指明装运时间，指定目的港、货轮航次等；

- 说明货物包装要求、运输标志等；
- 劝导早日装运。

催促装运

如果交货期已经临近时，进口商就得催促出口商尽快装运，其内容有：
- 询问相关货物的装运情况；
- 提醒装运期临近；
- 催促尽快装运，或限定一个期限；
- 说明原因；
- 说明延迟装运所带来的损失；
- 期盼回复。

请求推迟装运

如果由于缺货或其他难以预料的原因，出口商不能按时装运货物时必须请求推迟装运，内容包括：
- 对相关货物不能按时装运表达遗憾，并请求谅解；
- 请求推迟的原因；
- 提出修改装运日期；
- 劝导合作。

装船通知

完成装运之后，出口商要及时通知进口商。
- 提及相关信件或合同项下的货物；
- 告知装运情况、船名舱位、起运日期、抵达日期等；
- 寄送装运单据；
- 回顾愉快的合作过程；
- 期望更多合作。

货物装运要涉及合同号、品名、数量、包装、船名、航次、净重、毛重、预计到达日期等内容，所以，信件撰写要谨慎，数据要准确。

Part V. Terms and Sentence Frames
（术语与句型）

1. Terms（术语）

船

steamship（缩写 S.S., s.s., S/S, s/s）轮船

steamer 轮船
tanker 油轮
lighter 驳船
regular shipping liner 班轮
voyage charter 定程租船
time charter 定期租船
charter 租船
the chartered ship 租船

提单

Bill of Lading（缩写 B/L）提单
Ocean Bill of Lading 海运提单
Sea Waybill 海运单
Air Waybill 航空运单
Rail Waybill 铁路运单
Combined Transport B/L 联运提单
On Board B/L =Shipped B/L 已装船提单
Received Shipment B/L 备运提单、收货待运提单
Direct B/L 直达提单
Transshipment B/L 转船提单
Multimodal Transport B/L （MT B/L） 多式联运提单
Through B/L 联运提单
Clean B/L 清洁提单
Unclean B/L 不清洁提单
Straight B/L 记名提单
Order B/L 指示提单
Blank B/L =Open B/L 不记名提单
Long Form B/L 全式提单
Short Form B/L 简式提单
Freight Prepaid B/L 运费预付提单
Freight Collect B/L 运费到付提单
On Deck B/L 舱面提单
Anti-Dated B/L 倒签提单
Advanced B/L 预借提单
Stale B/L 过期提单

装运单据

shipping documents 装船单据
original B\L 正本提单

cargo receipt 陆运收据
commercial invoice 商业发票
packing list 装箱单
certificate of origin 原产地证
GSP certificate of origin FORM A 普惠制产地证
certificate of quality 品质证
insurance policy 保险单

装运

shipper 发货人
consignor 托运人
consignee 收货人
shipment 装运、装船
shipping instruction 装运指示
shipping advice 装船通知
shipping space 舱位
date of shipment 装船日期
delivery 交货
time of delivery 交货时间
shipping marks 唛头
immediate shipment 立即装运
prompt shipment 即期装运
partial shipment 分批装运
part shipment 分批装运
transshipment 转运
estimated time of departure (ETD) 预计离港时间
estimated time of arrival (ETA) 预计抵达时间

运费

freight prepaid 运费预付
freight paid 运费已付
freight collect 运费到付
optional charges 选港费

2. Sentence Frames（句型）

装运

to effect shipment 装运
to advance shipment 提前装运
to urge shipment 催促装运

to be ready for shipment　备妥待运
to book shipping space　订舱位
to ship goods by S.S....　由……轮装运货物
to take delivery of goods　提货
to delay shipment　延迟装运
to delay delivery　延迟交货
to delay the execution of order for... because of ...　因为……原因，延期执行对……的订货

装船期

shipment during January　一月份装船
January shipment　一月份装船
shipment not later than Jan. 31st　一月底装船
shipment on or before Jan. 31st.　一月底装船

分批装运、转运

to make a partial shipment　分批装运
shipment in two lots　分两批装船
shipment in two equal lots　平均分两批装船
in three equal monthly shipments　分三个月，每月平均装运
partial shipment not allowed /not permitted /unacceptable　不允许分批装船
shipments within 30 days after receipt of L/C　收到信用证后 30 天内装运
to be transshipped at...　在……转船
transshipment not allowed　不允许转船

运费承担

optional charges to be borne by the buyers　选港费由买方负担
optional charges for buyers' account　选港费由买方负担

装船通知

to advise sb.　通知某人
to inform sb.　通知某人
to notify sb.　通知某人

Part Ⅵ. Follow Me　（跟我写）

1. Replying to Urging Shipment（出口商回复装运催促）

电子邮件模板
Dear Mr./Ms.（对方的姓），

We have already received your email of （对方催促装运邮件的日期）. We feel sorry for the shipment delay, which was caused by （我方装运延迟的原因）. It is our fault not letting you know the cause in time.

In addition, because of （另一个装运延迟的原因）, After communication with related officials, we now have settled the shipment time.

The shipment of （将要装运的货物名称与数量） under S/C No. （合同编号） will be arranged to go forth on board s.s. （货轮号）. The ship will sail from （装运港名） on or about （起航日期）. We will email you immediately when the ship sets off.

Thanks for your understanding and cooperation.

Yours sincerely,

（署名）

贸易背景

King 先生于 2 月 25 日向出口方张伟伟先生发邮件催促尽快装运，称：253 号销售合同项下的 30 吨胡麻籽（30 tons Linseeds）已经临近装运期，然而没有收到任何装运信息。

张伟伟方面的情况是：一是由于货物原产地供货意外延迟（late arrival of the goods from the place of origin），二是由于恶劣天气（terrible weather），港口（harbor）封冻不通航（icebound and not navigable）。现在将由"建安"轮装运，于 3 月 5 日前后从天津出港。

张伟伟需要写邮件回复 King 先生。

仿照模板套写

2. Asking for Shipping Amendment （出口商要求更改装运）

电子邮件模板

Dear Mr./Ms._（对方的姓）_,

We have received your email of _（对方邮件的日期）_ and also your L/C No. _（信用证的编号）_ covering our Contract No. _（合同编号）_ for _（对方订购的产品名称）_, Article No. _（产品的货号）_ in our illustrated catalogue.

As to the latest date for shipment, we regret to inform you that _（对方指定的装运日期）_ is too tight, as _（来不及装运的理由）_. It is impossible for us to get the goods ready before _（对方指定的装运日期）_.

We shall appreciate it if you amend the latest date for shipment to read "_（我方要求的装运日期）_", which is the same as the contract terms.

Meanwhile, please extend the expiry date of the L/C until _（信用证有效期延展至日期）_ to leave us enough time for presenting the documents to the bank for negotiation.

Thank you for your cooperation in advance and look forward to your amendment advice.

Yours sincerely,
_（署名）_

贸易背景

德国一家公司向中国山东一家贸易公司订购了一批货号（Article No.）为 01 的衬衣（shirt），双方签订了编号为 406 的销售合同，合同上最迟装运期为 2016 年 2 月 25 日。随后，中方公司业务员王波收到了德方 Den Smith 先生 2016 年 1 月 10 的电子邮件和编号为 DC-125 的信用证。信用证指定的最迟装运期为 2016 年 2 月 15 日。

中方公司认为对方限定的装运期太紧，因为 2 月上旬（in the beginning of February）是中国的春节（the Spring Festival），有 7 天的假期（a seven-day holiday），2 月 15 日前来不及备好货物装运。现在，业务员王波需要回复邮件要求修改最迟装运期，改为 2016 年 2 月 25 日。同时，王波还要求德方将信用证有效期延展至 2016 年 3 月 15 日，好让中方有足够的时间向银行提交装运单据结算。

仿照模板套写

Part Ⅶ. Practical Writing （实训写作）

1. Match the words and phrases with their Chinese meanings.

Steamer	转运
partial shipment	推迟装运
transshipment	轮船
freight prepaid	运费预付
Combined Transport B/L	订舱位
book shipping space	装运
postpone shipment	催促装运
send shipping advice	分批装运
effect shipment	联运提单
urge shipment	发装船通知

2. Complete each of the following sentences according to its model given.

1）Please try your best to ship our goods by S.S. "Peace" which is due to arrive at Hamburg on May 8.

Please （请尽最大努力于5月9日前装运我方的货物）_____.

2）Please advise us by fax as soon as the B/L is issued.

Please advise us by fax as soon as（货装上船）_____.

3）We are unable to book space of a direct steamer sailing to Hamburg.

We are unable to book space of a direct steamer （从上海出发发往你方港口）_____.

4）In spite of our effort, we find it impossible to make shipment as agreed due to the unusual shortage of shipping space.

We are sorry we（不可能按我们之前达成的那样在12月装运货物）_____
_____due to the strike in our factory.

5）In compliance with the terms of the contract, copies of the shipping documents were sent to you immediately after the goods were shipped.

（根据信用证中的有关条款）_____
_____we are sending the following copies of shipping documents covering this shipment.

6）We have shipped the goods by S.S. Dongfeng which is due to sail for your port on or about July 5.

（我们已将你方订购的货物装上"五月花"号轮）_____
_____ which sails for your port tomorrow.

7）Because of the recent fire in the factory, we cannot make shipment as arranged before.

（因受台风影响）_____, we find it impossible to effect shipment before the end of this month.

8）We have to point out that any delay in shipment will be detrimental to our future business.

We must stress that any delay in shipping the order will（使我们和客户陷入麻烦）
_____.

9）As soon as the relevant L/C is received, we shall book the shipping space.

As soon as the shipment is made, we will（向你方发送装运通）_____.

10）We shall be compelled to cancel this order if we cannot receive the goods by the end of this month.

（我们只能另寻供货商了）_____if you cannot ship our order this week.

3. Complete the following mail of shipping instruction with words and phrases given in the box.

1）copies	2）Possession	3）documents
4）dispatched	5）satisfaction	

We are pleased to inform you that the 5,000 dozen silk pajamas under your L/C No. KP234 have now been _____ via "Victory" from Ningbo, due to arrive at Hamburg on August 11, 2015.

_____ of the shipping _____ were sent to you by courier service, ensuring that you can take _____ of the goods on their arrival at your designated port.

We hope this shipment will reach you in time and turn out to your entire_____.

4. Complete the following mail with words and phrases given in the box.

| 1) advice | 2) co-operation | 3) sail |
| 4) port | 5) steamer | |

We are informed by the local shipping company that s/s "Browick" is due to _____ from your city to our _____ on or about the 10th September and, if possible, please try your best to ship by that _____. Your close _____ in this respect will be highly appreciated.

Should this trial order prove satisfactory to our customers, we can assure you that repeat orders with larger quantities will be placed.

We await your shipping _____.

Part Ⅷ. Linkage（知识链接）

装运条件

装运条件是买卖合同中的一项重要条款，包括装运时间（Time of Shipment）、装运港/地（Port / Place of Loading）、目的港/地（Port / Place of Destination）、运输方式（Transport Modes）、装卸时间、装运单据（shipping Documents）等。

海洋运输

海洋运输是对外贸易中最主要的运输方式之一。海洋运输主要有班轮运输（Liner Transport）和租船运输（Charter Transport）两种。装运是卖方履行交货义务的行为。就国际贸易而言，装运大多数由远洋轮来承担，即不定期货船或定期班轮。不定期货船是没有固定航线或航行日程的一种货船，经常往返于需要舱位的港口之间。而定期班轮则是在特定港口之间有确定的常规起航和到达日程的一种货船。

当出口商在接到进口商寄来的装运指示及相关信用证之后，就应该马上准备下列装运事宜。

1）向船运公司租订舱位。

2）向海关进行出口申报。

3）等待船运公司签发的装运单。

4）收到装运单后开始装船：装运前买方将装运要求以书面形式通知卖方，说明装船方式、包装规定和唛头。这份书面通知即称为装运指示（Shipping Instruction）。

5）装运结束后凭装运单换取承运货轮大副签发的收据。卖方于货物装船后，向买方或其指定的收货人及时发出装运通知(Shipping Advice)。

6）起航之前，再换取正式的海运提单（Bill of Lading）。

装运通知一旦发出，即意味着合同的实现。

海运提单

海运提单是装运的重要单证，具有物权凭证的特点。因此可以通过背书、甚至无需背书即可以转让提单，从而将货物的所有权让出。近年来国际贸易为了加快交货速度，经常采用航空运输，但航空运输的运单不是物权凭证。

Part IX. Glossary of Common Sentences
（常用语句集）

1. 出口商

出口商	承诺	舱位	预订	As soon as your L/C reaches us, we shall book the first available steamer for you. 一收到你方的信用证，我们就在能赶上的第一艘货轮上为你方预订舱位。
出口商	承诺	交货	期限	Preparations for shipment are well under way and we will dispatch the lot without fail by the end of June. 交货准备工作正在进行之中，我们在6月底前一定发货，不会延误。
出口商	承诺	交货	期限	We are doing everything we can to ensure that your order is shipped without further delay. 我们已经尽了最大努力保证您所订货物的装运不会再有任何延误。
出口商	承诺	交货	期限	We can assure you of prompt shipment. 我们可以保证快速装运。
出口商	承诺	交货	期限	We can assure you that shipment will be made no later than the end of August. 我们可以向你保证交货期不会迟于8月底。
出口商	承诺	交货	期限	We will do our best to dispatch the shipment. 我们将尽力迅速装运。
出口商	承诺	交货	期限	You may rest assured that we will make shipment without delay on receipt of your letter of credit. 贵方可放心，一收到信用证，我方立刻安排装运。
出口商	承诺	装运	通知	As soon as shipping space is booked, we shall advise you of the name of the ship. 舱位一订好，我们就会将船名通知你方。
出口商	承诺	装运	通知	As soon as the shipment is made, we will send you our shipping advice containing all the particulars of the shipment. 装运一旦完成，我们会马上给你方寄去包括所有装运信息的装运通知。
出口商	承诺	装运		The goods ordered are all what we have in stock, and therefore, you may fully rely upon our delivery by the first boat "Peking" leaving Tianjin on Wednesday next. 所订之货均系现货，请尽管放心，可以装在下周三驶离天津的第一艘船"北京号"运出。

续表

出口商	承诺	装运		We will try our utmost to ship your goods by S.S. "Peace" which is due to arrive at Hamburg on May 8. 我方会尽力将你方订货上"和平号"货轮，并与5月8日抵达汉堡。
出口商	寄送	装运	单据	Enclosed please find one set of the shipping documents covering this consignment, which comprises: the commercial invoice, bill of lading, packing list, and certificate of origin and insurance certificate. 现附上这批货物的装运单据一套，包括商业发票、提单、装箱单、原产地证和保险凭证等。
出口商	寄送	装运	单据	In compliance with the terms of the contract, a full set of duplicate documents were sent to you today by FedEx after the goods were shipped. 按照合同条款，在货物装船后全套单据今天通过FedEx快递寄给了你方。
出口商	寄送	装运	单据	The Commercial Invoice and Insurance Policy, together with clean on board ocean Bill of Lading have been sent through the National Bank. 商业发票、保险单和清洁已装船，海运提单已交国家银行转送。
出口商	寄送	装运	单据	The originals of the shipping documents are being sent to you through the Bank of China. 装运单据正本正通过中国银行寄送你方。
出口商	寄送	装运	单据	Under the terms of the relative L/C, we are sending the following shipping documents covering this shipment. 根据信用证中的有关条款，我们给你们寄上这批货物的如下单据。
出口商	请求	装运	延期	As the components of our products have been held up in Hong Kong, we are sorry we are unable to ship your order in December we promised. 由于我们产品的部件被滞留在香港，非常遗憾我们不能像答应你们的那样在12月发运你们的货物。
出口商	请求	装运	延期	Due to the recent fire in the factory, all stocks were destroyed. In this case, we cannot make shipment as previously arranged. 由于最近工厂发生火灾烧毁了全部库存，我们不能按原安排交货。
出口商	请求	装运	延期	In spite of our effort, we find it impossible to secure space for the shipment owing to the unusual shortage of shipping space. 虽然我公司已尽最大努力，却因为船位不足而无法保证交期。
出口商	请求	装运	延期	Owing to the delay in opening L/C, shipment cannot be made as contracted and should be postponed to October. 由于开证延误，装运不能按合同进行，要推迟到10月份。
出口商	请求	装运	延期	Owing to unforeseen difficulties encountered by our manufacturers, we find it impossible to effect shipment before the end of this month. 由于制造商遇到不可预见的困难，我方不能在本月底前装船。

续表

出口商	请求	装运	延期	Please accept our apology for the delay which has been caused by the unavailability of shipping space from Bombay to London. 因为未能取得从孟买到伦敦的货位而造成的延误，我方深表歉意。
出口商	请求	装运	延期	The earthquake has caused some delay in the shipment of a number of our orders, and we regret that yours is also held up. 地震使我们延期发运一些货，很遗憾你们的货物也被耽搁了。
出口商	请求	装运	延期	We are aware that your goods are long overdue, but the production was suspended for several weeks because of typhoon. 我们意识到你们的货物早就过期了，但是台风使我们停产几周。
出口商	请求	装运	延期	We very much regret to inform you that we have to delay the shipment of your Order No. 339 for 3 000 men's suits because of the new quota restrictions on the export of garments to the United States. 非常遗憾地告知你们，因为向美国出口服装新配额的限制，我们不得不延期装运你们第339号3 000件男西服的订单。
出口商	拒绝	交货	提前	We are so sorry to inform that we can't advance the time of delivery. 我们非常抱歉地通知您，我们不能把交货期提前。
出口商	启运	祝愿		Thank you again for this trial order and we sincerely hope it will lead to further business. 再次感谢贵方此次试购，我们真诚希望这将促进我们进一步交易。
出口商	启运	祝愿		We have been very pleased to serve you and look forward to your future order. 我们很高兴为你方服务，期待着你方进一步订货。
出口商	启运	祝愿		We hope that our products will be satisfactory to you and that you will let us have the chance of serving you again. 希望我方产品令你们满意，今后再来惠顾。
出口商	启运	祝愿		We hope that you will be completely satisfied with your purchase. 希望我们的产品能让您称心如意。
出口商	启运	祝愿		We sincerely hope that our first transaction together will be the beginning of a long and pleasant business association. 我们真诚希望我们的第一宗交易是长期愉快合作往来的开端。
出口商	启运	祝愿		We trust that this trial order may lead to more important transactions. 相信这次试订购将会增加我们日后更重要的贸易往来。
出口商	说明	运输	费用	All transport transshipment charges will be included in the C.I.F. Price. 所有的转运费用都包括在到岸价里面了。
出口商	说明	运输	费用	We offer free shipping on all orders of 200 euro or more. 所有200欧元及以上的订单我们都将免费寄送。

续表

出口商	说明	装运	费用	If not, dead freight and demurrage should be on your account. 否则空舱费、滞期费将由贵方负担。
出口商	说明	装运	风险	So far as I know, there are risks of pilferage or damage to the goods during transshipment in Hong Kong. 据我所知,在香港转船期间有货物被盗或损坏的风险。
出口商	说明	装运	风险	We have been able to transship S.E. Asian-bound cargoes from rail to ship at Hong Kong without mishap. 我们在香港转船去东南亚的货物途中未曾遇到过麻烦。
出口商	说明	装运	舱位	The goods you ordered will be shipped under deck. 你们订购的货物将装在舱内。
出口商	说明	装运	舱位	The steels are to be shipped on deck. 钢材将被装在甲板上。
出口商	说明	装运	分批	Shipment is to be made during May to July in three equal lots. 在5月至7月间货物分三次平均装运。
出口商	说明	装运	分批	Shipment will be made in two equal lots, the first lot in September, and the second lot one month later. 分两批等量装运,首批9月份,第二批在一个月后装运。
出口商	说明	装运	分批	The goods are to be shipped in three lots of 20 tons each on separate bills of lading. 货物分三批装运,每批20吨,提单分开。
出口商	请求	装运	转运	We have to make transshipment because there is no suitable loading port in the producing country. 因为在生产国找不到合适的装港,我们不得不转船。
出口商	说明	装运	转运	The cargo on S.S. "Xingfu" will be transshipped into S.S. "Shengli" at Guangzhou. "幸福号"轮的货物将在广州转船至"胜利号"轮上。
出口商	通知	舱位	已订	Regarding the goods under S/C No. 456, we have booked space on S.S. "Easter" due to arrive in London on June 8. 在合同号456项下的货物,我们已在"复活号"货轮上订舱,该轮将于6月8日抵达伦敦。
出口商	通知	舱位	已订	We are pleased to inform you that we have booked shipping space for our order No. 1268 of grain on SS. "Shengli" at Guangzhou. 欣告你方,我方已为第1268号订单上的谷物在广州的"胜利"号货轮上订好舱位。
出口商	通知	舱位	已订	We have booked the shipping space on S.S. "Prince". 我们已订妥"王子号"货轮的舱位。
出口商	通知	货物	待运	We have packed and are ready for shipment. 我方已包装好,正待装船。
出口商	通知	货物	待运	Your order is already finished, and we will deliver them in accordance with your instructions. 贵方订单所订货物已生产完毕,我方将按你方指示装运。

出口商	通知	货物	已运	Please be informed that the shipment of the cargo, your purchase order No. 123, was sent yesterday, airway bill No. 123. 特此通知这批货物（你方订单号码是 No. 123）昨天已装运，航空货物的提单号码是 No. 123。
出口商	通知	货物	已运	The furs ordered have been dispatched per air freight. 所订的裘皮已由空运发出。
出口商	通知	货物	装船	According to the terms of Contract No. 318, shipment has been effected by the 20th Jan. 按 318 号合同条款，货物已于 1 月 20 日前装运。
出口商	通知	货物	装船	As per your email of February 16th, we have today delivered the goods under your order No. 345 by S.S. "Hawaii" to Honolulu. 按照贵方 2 月 16 日邮件指示，我方已于今日将 345 订单项下的货物装"夏威夷号"运往火努鲁鲁。
出口商	通知	货物	装船	The cargo has been shipped on board s.s. "DongFeng". 货已装上"东风"号轮船。
出口商	通知	货物	装船	We are pleased to inform you that the goods under S/C No. 3125 went forward per m/v "Washington" of the Pacific Line on May 7. 兹通知第 3125 号售货确认书项下货物已于 5 月 7 日装太平洋航运公司"华盛顿"号轮。
出口商	通知	货物	装船	We wish to inform you that we have shipped the goods by "Shanghai" according to your instructions of August 5. 现通知贵公司，我方已按照您 8 月 5 日的指示将货物装上"上海号"。
出口商	通知	装运		We are glad to inform you that your consignment of 100 sets of Little Swan Washing Machines has been loaded on S.S. "Captain", which is due to sail for Vancouver on November 5. The estimated time of departure is 13:20 and the estimated time of arrival is on December 9. 我们高兴地告知你们，你们的 100 台小天鹅洗衣机已装"船长"号，该轮将于 11 月 5 日驶往温哥华。预计离港时间是 13:20，预计到达时间是 12 月 9 日。
出口商	通知	装运		We have the pleasure in notifying you that the goods under your Order No. 897 have been dispatched by S.S. "Wilson" sailing on May 8 for Liverpool. 兹通知贵方，订单 897 项下的货物已于装"威尔逊"货轮，将 5 月 8 日开往利物浦。
出口商	通知	装运		We have the pleasure of informing you that the goods under Contract No. ABC123 have been shipped today by "East Wind" from port A to port B. 我们高兴地告知你们编号为 ABC123 合同项下的货物今天由"东风"轮从 A 港运往 B 港。
出口商	通知	装运		We take pleasure in advising you that we have today shipped the goods under your Order No. 756 on board S/S "Peace" which sails for your port tomorrow. 我们高兴地通知你方，756 号订单之货物已于今日装上"和平"号轮，该轮将于明日驶往你方港口。

续表

出口商	协商	装运		We can make prompt shipment only if we are able to secure the necessary space. 我们只有订到舱位，才能快速装运。
出口商	协商	装运		If we ship by air, in five working days you can have the products. 如果空运的话，在5个工作日内你就能够拿到货。
出口商	协商	装运		It makes no difference to us, wherever you ship——Shantou or Zhuhai. 无论你们从哪里装货——汕头或是珠海，对我们来说没有什么不同。
出口商	协商	装运		Our experience tells us, it's better to designate Tanggu as the loading port. 我们的经验表明，在塘沽装货比较合适。
出口商	协商	装运		There are more sailings at Shanghai, so we have chosen it as the loading port. 因上海的船次多，我们把这里定为装货港。
出口商	协商	装运		We prefer to designate Yantai as the loading port, for it's near the production plant. 我们希望把烟台定为装货港，因为它离货物的产地要近一些。

2. 进口商

进口商	催促	交货	委婉	I would appreciate it if you could expedite delivery of this shipment. 如果您能加快货物的装运我将不胜感激。
进口商	催促	交货	委婉	We shall appreciate it if you can effect shipment without any delay, thus enabling our customers to meet peak demand at the beginning of the season. 为了满足我们的客户，使货物赶上旺季初的需求高峰，请速装运，切勿延误，不胜感激。
进口商	催促	交货	委婉	We trust you will make all necessary arrangements to deliver the goods in time. 我们相信，你们将做好一切必需的安排，按时交货。
进口商	催促	交货	委婉	We will highly appreciate if you can manage to hasten the delivery. 如果你们能加快装运我们将十分感激。
进口商	催促	交货	严厉	I am afraid that if you are unable to deliver within this month, we shall have no choice but to cancel our order and purchase elsewhere. 如果你们不能在本月内交货，我们别无选择，只得取消订单，考虑从别处购买。
进口商	催促	交货	严厉	If you fail to deliver the goods within the specified time, we shall have to cancel the order. 如果你们不能在规定的时间内交货，我们将取消订货。
进口商	催促	交货	严厉	We are sorry to say unless the goods reach us before the end of this month, we shall be forced to refuse them, as they will be of no use beyond this season. 抱歉，除非货物在本月底之前到达我方，否则我们将拒收货物，因为过季后它们就没用了。

续表

进口商	催促	交货	严厉	Your delay has caused us considerable difficulties and we must ask you to do your utmost to dispatch the overdue goods without any further delay. 你们延期交货已经给我们造成了很大的困难，我们必须要求你们尽最大努力加速装运，不得再有延误。
进口商	催促	交货		As our users are in urgent need of the consignment, please get the goods dispatched within the stipulated time. 由于我方客户急需这批货物，请你方在规定的时间内发运。
进口商	催促	交货		As the season is rapidly approaching, our customers are badly in need of the goods. 由于销售季节马上来临，我们的客户将急需货物。
进口商	催促	交货		Please speed up the dispatch of the first lot of the goods as we are in urgent need of them. 由于我们急需货物请速发运第一批货。
进口商	催促	交货		Please speed up the order. If delivery cannot be made before May 5, we will have to cancel the order and turn to other suppliers. 请加快交货。如5月5日前不能交货，我们不得不撤销订单，向其他供货商购买。
进口商	催促	交货		Since the order No. C209 is urgently in demand, we have to ask you to speed up shipment. 由于急需第C209号订单项下的货物，我们提请你们加快装船速度。
进口商	催促	交货		We must have the goods here in September for reshipment. 货物必须9月份到达此地以便再转运。
进口商	催促	装运	严厉	We have to point out any delay in shipment will be detrimental to our future business. 我们必须指出装运上的任何延误都会有损于我们今后的业务。
进口商	催促	装运	严厉	In case you fail to effect delivery in April, we will have to lodge a claim against you and reserve the right to cancel the contract. 如你们不能在4月份交货，我们将不得不向你方提出索赔并保留取消该项合同的权利。
进口商	催促	装运		Since there is no possibility of L/C extension, you must see to it that shipment is made within the validity of L/C. 由于信用证无展期可能，所以你方务必在信用证有效期内装船。
进口商	催促	装运		We are highly concerned about late shipment. 我们非常担心货物会迟交。
进口商	叮嘱	舱位	预订	Please book the necessary shipping space in advance to insure timely dispatch of the goods ordered. 请提前订好舱位以便及时发货。
进口商	叮嘱	舱位	预订	Please see to it that shipping space should be booked immediately on arrival of covering L/C. 请务必在我方信用证抵达你方时，立即预订船舱。

进口商	叮嘱	装运	通知	Kindly let us have your timely advice of the shipment by email stating the name of vessel so that we may have it insured at this end. 请及时发邮件告知我方载货船名，以便我们能在此地投保。
进口商	叮嘱	装运	通知	Please advise us 30 days before the month of shipment of the contract number, name of commodity, quantity, port of loading and the time when the goods reach the port of loading. 请在交货月份前30天，请将合同号、货名、数量、装运港以及货物到达装运港的时间通知我公司。
进口商	拒绝	交货	延期	Your delivery date is unacceptable for us. Would you please make prompt delivery, since we are in urgent need of this order? 我方无法接受你们的发货期，请立即发货，我们急需这批订货。
进口商	拒绝	装运	延期	It has to be stressed that shipment must be made within the prescribed time limit, as a further extension will not be considered. 我方不得不强调说明，装船必须在规定的期限内进行，不会再考虑任何延期问题。
进口商	拒绝	装运	延期	Our customers are pressing us for immediate shipment and therefore it is impossible for us to extend the shipment to the time you indicated. 我们的客户在催促我们立即装运，因此不可能将船期延至你们提出的时间。
进口商	同意	装运	延期	We agree to postpone the time of shipment for a month. 我方同意推迟船期一个月。
进口商	限定	交货	期限	It's urgent to ship the goods before October or we won't be ready for the season. 10月份以前必须装船，否则，我们便不能赶上销售旺季。
进口商	限定	交货	期限	This order must be fulfilled within five weeks; otherwise we will have to cancel the order. 此订单须在5周内交货，否则我方将不得不撤销此次订单。
进口商	限定	交货	期限	We shall have to turn to other suppliers if we cannot receive the goods this week. 如果本周不能收到货物的话，我们就只得另寻供货商了。
进口商	限定	交货	期限	You must have the goods shipped before August; otherwise, we cannot catch the season. 必须在8月前交货，否则赶不上季节。
进口商	询问	交货	期限	Please indicate approximate time of shipment from receipt of order. 请告知在接到订单后的估计交货时间。
进口商	询问	交货	期限	Please let us know how long it will take for delivery. 请告知多长时间才能交货。
进口商	询问	交货	期限	When quoting, please state terms of payment and time of delivery. 报价时，请说明付款方式和交货时间。

进口商	指示	装运	货轮	Please arrange to dispatch the goods by the first available steamer. 请将货物装第一艘可订到舱位的轮船。
进口商	指示	装运	货轮	Please see to it that the goods are shipped per PEACE sailing on or about October 15th. 请确保货物由10月15日前后起航的"和平轮"装运。
进口商	指示	装运	货轮	Please ship the first lot under Contract No. 123 by S/S "Long March" schedule to sail on or about May 2nd. 请将123号合同下的第一批货装"长征"号轮，该轮将于5月2日左右起航。
进口商	指示	装运	货轮	Please ship the goods by S.S. "Dalian" sailing on Friday instead of S.S. "Captain" as we informed you last week. 请将货物装星期五起航的"大连"号，而不是像上周通知你们的装"船长"号。
进口商	指示	装运	货轮	Please try your utmost to ship our goods by S.S. "Peace" which is due to arrive at Hamburg on 8 May, and confirm by return that the goods will be ready in time. 请尽力用"和平"号轮装运我方货物，该轮预计于5月8日抵汉堡。请回复确认货物将按时备妥。
进口商	指示	装运	暂缓	Please hold shipment till you get our instruction. 请在我们通知之前暂停装货。
进口商	指示	装运		According to the contract stipulations, the aforesaid goods should be shipped in three lots in May, June and August. 按合同所定，上述货物应在5月、6月、8月分三批装运。
进口商	指示	装运		Please make shipment in three equal installments beginning from March. 货物从3月份起分三批等量运来。

Unit 9

Insurance (保险)

Part Ⅰ. Objectives (目标)

After completing this unit, you will be able to:

1. enter into a discussion of insurance with your business customers through English emails or messages;

2. acquaint yourself with the components, sentence patterns, special terms that are commonly used in emails and texts relating to insurance.

Part Ⅱ. How to Express (该怎么说)

1. Introducing Insurance Practice (出口商介绍保险惯例)

A：我是卖方，我需要向买方说明我方通常的保险惯例，我该怎么说呢？
B：你可以这样说：
1）按 CIF 价出售的货物，我们一般投保水渍险。
2）对按 CIF 价出售的货物，我们一般向中国人民保险公司投保。
3）按照我们的惯例，我们只按发票金额110%投保基本险。
A：那么，我用英语该怎么说呢？
B：到"常用语句集"去看看，你先找到同类的句型，然后采用截取、替换、拼接的办法稍做加工，你需要的句子就有了。
A：嘿！瞧瞧，我的英语还不错吧！

----

2. Making Demand on Insurance（提出投保要求）

A：我是买方，我所订购的货物将被装运，我要提出投保要求，我该怎么说呢？

B：你可以这样说：

1）请将货物投保战争险。

2）请注意上述货物保险必须按发票价的150%投保一切险。

3）恳请贵方为我们这批货物安排投保一切险。

A：那么，我用英语该怎么说呢？

B：到"常用语句集"去看看，你先找到同类的句型，然后采用截取、替换、拼接的办法稍做加工，你需要的句子就有了。

A：嘿！瞧瞧，我的英语还不错吧！

3. Notifying of Insurance Effected（出口商通知已投保）

A：我是卖方，我方为出口货物已办理了保险，现在需要通知买方，我该怎么说呢？

B：你可以这样说：

1）我们已代你方投保。

2）我们已将货物投保平安险和破碎险。

3）我方已将你方第214号订单下的货物按发票价另加30%投保至目的港。

A：那么，我用英语该怎么说呢？

B：到"常用语句集"去看看，你先找到同类的句型，然后采用截取、替换、拼接的办法稍做加工，你需要的句子就有了。

A：嘿！瞧瞧，我的英语还不错吧！

Part III. Case（案例）

1. Accepting Order（出口商接受订单）

出口方江西清远瓷器有限公司（Jiangxi Qingyuan Chinaware Co., Ltd.）刚刚收到 Tivol Products PLC 订购 100 箱瓷器（Chinese Porcelain）的一笔订单，对方要求特别关注包装。

以下是江西清远瓷器有限公司业务员王伟回复给进口方采购经理 Chila Trooborg 的邮件。邮件同意接受订单，并附件寄送了销售确认书，承诺将特别关注包装，使之经得住运输途中的野蛮搬运。

发件人（From）	Wangwei@Qingyuanchinaware.com
收件人（To）	Chila@TVL.com
主题（Subject）	Accepting the order
附件（Attachment）	S/C No. 100316

Dear Mr. Trooborg,

Thank you for your email of March 14, confirming your ordering 100 cartons of Chinese Porcelain.

We are pleased to accept your order and, attached is our S/C No. 100316. Please trust that we will take special care of the packing which will stand up to the rough handling in transit.

After receiving the relevant L/C, we will arrange the production right away. And we will make delivery within its validity.

We are waiting for your L/C.

Yours sincerely,

Wang Wei

Sentence Patterns Applied（语句归纳）
- ➢ 出口商收到订单，致谢；
- ➢ 出口商接受订单，附件寄送销售确认书，承诺包装（效果）；

- 出口商要求开立信用证，承诺（如期）装运；
- 出口商期盼信用证。

2. Enquiring for the Usual Insurance Practice（进口商咨询投保事宜）

Tivoli Products PLC 采购经理 Chila Trooborg 收到了王伟的销售确认书。Chila Trooborg 马上回复对方，表示将及时开立信用证，同时询问在 CIF 方式下的投保惯例（usual insurance practice），要求说明。

现在，你是 Chila Trooborg，请你按照上面的背景回复邮件。

Sentence Patterns for Reference（参考语句）
- 进口商收到销售确认书；
- 进口商承诺开立信用证，询问保险惯例；
- 进口商表达长期合作的愿望；
- 进口商期盼回复。

发件人（From）	
收件人（To）	
主题（Subject）	

3. Introducing Usual Insurance Practice（出口商说明保险惯例）

王伟收到了 Chila Trooborg 询问保险惯例的邮件。江西清远瓷器有限公司在 CIF 方式下的投保惯例一般是向中国人民保险公司（the People's Insurance Company of China，PICC）投保水渍险（W. P. A.）。如果对方要投保额外的险别（additional risk），出口方也可以代办，但额外的保费（extra premium）由进口方承担。保额一般按发票金额（invoice value，invoice price）的110%投保，保险加成要提高的话，额外的保费由进口方承担。

下面是王伟说明保险惯例的邮件。

发件人（From）	Wangwei@Qingyuanchinaware.com
收件人（To）	Chila@TVL.com
主题（Subject）	Our Insurance Practice
附件（Attachment）	

Dear Mr. Trooborg,

In comply with your enquiring about the insurance under S/C No. 100316, we wish to give you our insurance practice as follows:

For transactions on CIF basis, we usually cover W. P. A. with PICC. Of course, we can insure the shipment against any additional risks if you require, and the extra premium is to be borne by you. In such circumstance, we will send you the premium receipt issued by the underwriter.

Usually, the amount is 110% of the total invoice value. However, if a higher percentage is required, you, the buyer, have to pay the extra premium.

We hope the above information will be all that you wish to know.

We are looking forward to your reply.

Yours sincerely,

Wang Wei

Sentence Patterns Applied（语句归纳）

➢ 出口商介绍保险惯例；

➢ 出口商说明保险公司，说明保险险别，申明额外保费承担方，承诺寄送保费收据；
➢ 出口商说明保额，申明额外保费承担方；
➢ 出口商介绍完毕，祝愿；
➢ 出口商期盼回复。

An Application Form for Insurance （投保单）

<table>
<tr><td colspan="4" align="center">中国人民财产保险
The People's Insurance (Property) Company of China, Ltd.NINGBO Branch
进出口货物运输保险投保单
Application Form for I/E Marine Cargo Transportation Insurance</td></tr>
<tr><td colspan="4">被保险人
Assured's Name</td></tr>
<tr><td>发票号码（出口用）或合同号码（进口用）
Invoice No. or Contract No.</td><td>包装数量
Quantity</td><td>保险货物项目
Description of Goods</td><td>保险金额
Amount Insured</td></tr>
<tr><td colspan="4">总保险金额：
Total Amount Insured: --
装载运输工具_____ 航次、航班或车号_____ 开航日期_____
Per Conveyance　　　　　　　　　Voy. No.　　　　　Slg. Date
自_____至_____ 转运地_____ 赔款地_____
From　　　To　　　　　W/T at　　　　　Claim Payable at</td></tr>
<tr><td colspan="4">承保险别：
Condition & / or
Special Coverage

　　　　　　　　　投保人签章及公司名称、电话、地址：
　　　　　　　　　Applicant's Signature and Co.'s Name, Add. And Tel. No.</td></tr>
<tr><td colspan="4">备注：　　　　　　　　投保日期：
Remarks　　　　　　　　Date</td></tr>
</table>

4. Making Demand on Insurance（进口商提出投保要求）

Chila Trooborg 收到了江西清远瓷器有限公司在 CIF 方式下的投保惯例。在同意按照投保惯例进行投保之外，Chila Trooborg 要求另外加保破碎险（breakage），额外保费由己方承担（for our account）。邮件如下：

发件人（From）	Chila@TVL.com
收件人（To）	Wangwei@Qingyuanchinaware.com
主题（Subject）	Additional Coverage

Dear Mr. Wang,

Thank you for your detailed information of your usual insurance practice.

However, since the goods are fragile, we would like to ask you to cover the goods against breakage as well for our account, other insurance terms as per your usual insurance practice.

We are looking forward to your speedy response.

Yours sincerely,

Chila Trooborg

Sentence Patterns Applied（语句归纳）
- 进口商收到保险惯例，致谢；
- 进口商要求投保（破碎险）险别，同意承担额外保费，同意接受保险惯例；
- 进口商期盼回复。

5. Notifying of Insurance Effected（出口商通知已投保）

江西清远瓷器有限公司收到对方增加破碎险的要求后，回复表示同意办理。后经双方进一步磋商，签了销售合同，开立了信用证等。

现在，王伟为 100 箱瓷器向中国人民保险公司投保了水渍险和破碎险，保额为 USD550,000，其中破碎险的保费结账单（debit note）与保单（policy）一起将在本月底前寄达对方。另外，这批货物将装上"东风号"（East Wind）货轮于下月底前起航。

现在，你是王伟，你向 Tivoli Products PLC 的 Chila Trooborg 先生回复邮件，说明保险事宜。

Sentence Patterns for Reference（参考语句）
- 出口商通知已投保，说明保险公司、险别、保额；

- ➢ 出口商承诺将寄送保单、结账单；
- ➢ 出口商说明告知装运事宜。

发件人（From）	
收件人（To）	
主题（Subject）	

Part Ⅳ. Writing Directions（写作指导）

关于保险，有出口商说明投保惯例和通知已投保，也有进口商咨询保险、要求代办保险、更改保险条款等。

说明货物投保惯例

出口商说明货物投保惯例的信函一般包括如下内容：
- ➢ 提及相关合同或信用证项下的货物；
- ➢ 说明货物投保的保险公司、险别、保额等；
- ➢ 澄清相关保险条款；
- ➢ 期盼回复。

如果进口商事先已经提出投保额外的险别或提高保险加成，那么，出口商必须澄清额外保费的承担。

咨询保险事宜

进口商向出口商咨询保险事宜的信函无需太长。结构如下：
- ➢ 提及相关合同、信用证项下的货物；
- ➢ 询问投保事宜；
- ➢ 期盼回复。

委托代办保险

进口商委托出口商代办保险的情况出现在 CFR、FOB 等方式下，其内容如下：
- ➢ 提及相关合同或信用证项下的货物；
- ➢ 请求代办保险；
- ➢ 说明投保的保险公司、险别、保额等；
- ➢ 说明保费偿付方式；
- ➢ 期盼回复，或期望收到保单。

此类信函的特点：内容明确，语言简洁，语气友好。

Part V. Terms and Sentence Frames （术语与句型）

1. Terms（术语）

基本险

Free of Particular Average（简称 F.P.A.）平安险
With Particular Average（简称 W.P.A.）水渍险
All Risks 综合险，一切险

一般附加险

Clash and Breakage Risks 碰损、破碎险
Rust Risk 生锈险
Hook Damage Risk 钩损险
Packing Breakage Risk 包装破裂险
Intermixture and Contamination Risks 污染险
Shortage Risk 短量险
Theft, Pilferage and Nondelivery（简称 T.P.N.D.）盗窃提货不着险
Fresh Water Rain Damage Risks 淡水雨淋险
Leakage Risk 渗漏险
Odor Risk 串味险

Sweating and Heating Risks 受潮受热险

特殊附加险

Failure to Deliver Risk 交货不到险

Import Duty Risk 进口关税险

On Deck Risk 舱面险

Rejection Risk 拒收险

Aflatoxin Risk 黄曲霉素险

Seller's Contingent Risk 卖方利益险

Fire Risk Extension Clause for Storage of Cargo at Destination of Hong Kong, Including Kowloon or Macao 出口货物到港九或澳门存仓火险责任扩展条款

Strike Risk 罢工险

Ocean Marine Cargo War Risk 海运战争险

其他险别

Total Loss Only 全损险

Risk of Deterioration 变质险

Risk of Inherent Vice 内在缺陷险

Risk of Normal Loss（又称 Natural Loss）途耗，或自然损耗险

Air Transportation Cargo War Risk 航空运输战争险

Overland Transportation War Risk 陆上运输战争险

Strike, Riot and Civil Commotion 罢工，暴动，民变险

Risk of Mould 发霉险

保单

insurance policy 保单

insurance certificate 保险凭证

open policy 预约保单

general open policy 预约总保单

floating policy 流动保单

voyage policy 航程保单

marine insurance policy 海上水险单

specific policy 单独保单，船名确定保单（以别于船名未确定的流动保单）

time policy 定期保单

transferable policy 可转让保单

基本保险术语

perils of the sea 海上风险

extraneous risks 外来风险
total loss 全损
actual total loss 实际全损
constructive total loss 推定全损
absolute total loss 绝对全损
partial loss 部分损失
general average 共同海损
particular average 单独海损

保险条款

China Insurance Clauses 中国保险条款
Institute Cargo Clauses 协会货物条款

其他

insurance premium 保险费
insurance coverage 保险范围
insurance amount 保险额
insurance agent 保险代理人
insurance claim 保险索赔

2. Sentence Frames（句型）

保险办理

to insure W.P.A.（F.P.A.）投保水渍险（平安险）

to insure …against… 投保……险（注：在表示"投保……险别"时，在险别前要加 against，但是在 W.P.A. 和 F.P.A.前不加 against）

to cover…against… 投保……险
to insure …for… 按……金额投保……险
to insure… with … 向……投保……险
to arrange insurance 投保
to effect insurance 投保
to cover insurance 投保
to take out insurance 投保
to provide cover against… 投保……
to cover All Risks and War Risk for sb. 为某人投保一切险和战争险

保费承担

for your account 由你方承担
at buyer's cost 由买方承担

to be borne by you 由你方承担

保额

for 110% of invoice value 按发票金额110%投保
for 10% above the invoice value 按发票金额110%投保
at invoice value plus 10% 按发票金额110%投保

保险赔偿

to submit an insurance claim 提出保险索赔
to entertain your insurance claim 受理你方所提出的保险索赔
to compensate for the loss sustained 赔偿遭受的损失
to compensate you for the losses 赔偿你方损失

Part Ⅵ. Follow Me （跟我写）

1. Entrusting with Insurance （进口商委托代办保险）

电子邮件模板

Dear Mr. /Ms. （对方的姓），

Our order （我方订单的编号） covering （我方所订购的货物名称及数量） was placed on a CFR basis. As we now desire to have the shipment insured at your end, we shall be much pleased if you will kindly arrange to insure the same on our behalf against （所要投保的险别） at invoice value plus （发票金额外加的比率）, i.e. （投保的总额）.

We shall of course refund the premium to you upon receipt of your debit note or, if you like, you may draw on us at sight for the same.

We sincerely hope that our request will meet with your approval.

Yours sincerely,

（署名）

贸易背景

Jack Steve 先生所在的公司向马小飞先生所在的公司订购了400箱（carton）洗碗机（dish washer），订单号是873，是按照CFR（成本加运费）成交的。现在，Jack Steve 需要发邮件请求马小飞代办保险，按发票金额外加5%，即总额3 400美元投保综合险。

仿照模板套写

----

2. Accepting to Arrange Insurance （出口商同意代办保险）

电子邮件模板

Dear Mr. /Ms. ＿＿（对方的姓）＿＿,

  This is to acknowledge receipt of your requesting us to effect insurance on your order No. ＿＿（对方订单的编号）＿＿ concerning ＿＿（对方所订购的货物名称及数量）＿＿.

  We are pleased to confirm starting to cover the above shipment with ＿＿（保险公司名称）＿＿ against ＿＿（所投保的险别）＿＿ for ＿＿（投保的总额）＿＿. The policy is being prepared accordingly and will be forwarded to your by ＿＿（将要寄送的时间）＿＿ together with our debit note for the premium.

  For your information, this parcel will be shipped on s/s ＿＿（货轮号）＿＿, sailing on or about ＿＿（起航的日期）＿＿.

Yours sincerely,

＿＿（署名）＿＿

贸易背景

  马小飞先生所在的公司受进口商 Jack Steve 的委托并同意为其代办保险。所投保的货物是 400 箱洗碗机，其订单编号是 873。马小飞按发票金额外加 5%，即总额 3 400 美元，着手向中国人民保险公司（PICC）投保一切险，预计本周末前可将保险单（policy）与保险费（premium）的结账单（debit note）一并寄给对方。

  现在，马小飞需要向 Jack Steve 发邮件，顺便告知对方该批货物将装"长江"号（Changjiang）货轮于 4 月 4 日前后起航。

仿照模板套写

_____
_____
_____
_____
_____
_____
_____
_____
_____
_____
_____

Part VII. Practical Writing （实训写作）

1. Match the words and phrases with their Chinese meanings.

insurance policy	投保……险
insurance premium	投保平安险
insurance amount	水渍险
All Risks	投保
W.P.A.	保险费
for your account	保单
at invoice value plus 10%	一切险
insure F. P. A.	按发票金额 110%
effect insurance	保险额
cover…against…	由你方承担

2. Read the following email and list the sentence patterns applied.

We have received your email of January of 23, asking us to insure the goods for an amount of 130% of the invoice value.

Although it is our usual practice to take out insurance for 110% of invoice value, we are prepared to comply with your request for getting cover for 130% of the invoice value. But the extra premium will be for your account.

We are looking forward to your reply.

....
....
....

3. Complete each of the following sentences according to its model given.

1）You are requested to insure the goods.

You are requested (对货物投保一切险)_____.

2）Please arrange to take out insurance for us.

Please arrange (对该批货物投保一切险)_____.

3）Please cover the goods against War Risk.

Please (将货物投保水渍险和破碎险)_____.

4）Insurance is to be covered for 110% of the invoice value.

Insurance is (按发票金额110%向中国人民保险公司投保一切险) _____.

5）We usually insure W. P. A. on CIF sales.

We usually (对按CIF价出售的货物向中国人民保险公司投保水渍险)_____.

6）Please note that we don't cover Breakage.

Please note that (除非买方要求，我们不投保特殊附加险)_____.

7）Extra premium is at buyer's cost.

Extra premium (由买方支付，如需增加其他险别的话)_____.

8）We have insured the goods.

We (已将你方第235号订单下的货物按发票价另加30%投保至内陆城市)_____.

9）An insurance claim should be submitted to the insurance company.

An insurance claim (应在货物到达目的港30天内提交保险公司)_____.

10）The insurance is subject to a franchise of 5%.

The insurance (仍有5%的免赔率，即使已投保额外的破碎险)_____.

4. Complete the following email with words and phrases given in the box.

1) at your end	2) on our behalf	3) draw on us
4) refund	5) premium	

Referring to the Order No. X145 for 1,000 sets of Changhong Brand color TV, you can see that this order was placed on CFR basis.

Now we would like to have the shipment insured _____. We shall be grateful if you kindly arrange to cover the goods _____ against All Risks for 110% of the invoice value, i.e. USD 680, 000.

As to the _____, we will _____ it to you upon receipt of your debit note（结账单）, or you may _____ at sight for the same.

We are looking forward to your early reply.

5. Complete the following email with words and phrases given in the box.

1) on the basis of CIF	2) with	3) effect insurance
4) follow this practice	5) for the buyer's account	

Thank you for your order No. 3459 for 2000 cartons of our tinned sardines（沙丁鱼罐头）on the basis of CFR.

We are now emailing to remind you that most of our clients are placing their orders with us _____. This will save their time and simplify procedures（简化程序）. We would like to suggest that you _____.

For orders on CIF basis, we usually _____ against All Risks and War Risk for 110% of the invoice value _____ the People's Insurance Company of China. If broader coverage is required, the extra premium is _____.

We hope you will accept our suggestion and your early reply will be greatly appreciated.

Part Ⅷ. Linkage（知识链接）

国内外部分知名保险公司

The Min An Insurance Co., Ltd. (Hong Kong) 中国香港民安保险有限公司
American International Assurance Co., Ltd. (AIA) 美国友邦保险有限公司
American International Underwriters Corporation (AIU) 美国国际保险公司
Tokyo Marine & Nichido Fire Insurance Co., Ltd. 东京海上火灾保险株式会社
Winterthur Insurance (Asia) Ltd. 丰泰保险（亚洲）有限公司

Royal and Sun Alliance Insurance PLC 皇家太阳联合保险公司
Federal Insurance Company 美国联邦保险股份有限公司
Mitsui Sumitomo Insurance Co., Ltd. 三井住友海上火灾保险公司
Samsung Fire And Marine Insurance Co., Ltd. 三星火灾海上保险有限公司
Bank of China Group Insurance Co., Ltd. 中银集团保险有限公司
Sompo Japan Insurance Inc. 日本财产保险公司
Munich Reinsurance Company 慕尼黑再保险公司

中国人民保险公司

中国人民保险集团股份有限公司（People's Insurance Company Of China, PICC），简称中国人保，是一家综合性保险（金融）公司，世界五百强之一，是目前世界上最大的保险公司之一，注册资本为 306 亿元人民币，在全球保险业中属于实力非常雄厚的公司。目前旗下拥有人保财险、人保资产、人保健康、人保寿险、人保投资、华闻控股、人保资本、人保香港、中盛国际、中人经纪、中元经纪和人保物业等十余家专业子公司，中国人保还持有中诚信托 32.35% 的股权。

中国人民保险集团股份有限公司总部在北京，成立于 1949 年，2013 年营业额为 306 亿人民币元，世界排名 256 位。

中国人民保险公司网址：www.picc.com.cn

安盛集团

法国安盛集团（AXA）是全球最大保险集团之一，亦是全球第三大国际资产管理集团。安盛集团首家公司于 1816 年在法国成立，通过多项收购及合并活动，安盛已成为全球首屈一指的保险集团，业务网络覆盖全球五大洲逾 50 个国家及地区，全球职员及保险代理人约 11 万名。安盛的主要业务为保险及资产管理。

截止到 2009 年年底，法国安盛集团拥有：70 000 000 客户遍布世界各地 60 多个国家，110 347 名工作人员。2009 年收入 1 245 亿欧元，管理资产 10 640 亿欧元，净收入 35.6 亿欧元。

安盛集团网址：http://www.axa.com.hk

德国安联集团

德国安联保险集团于 1890 年在德国柏林成立，总部设于德国巴伐利亚州首府慕尼黑市，截至 2012 年，安联保险集团全世界约有 18 万名员工。安联集团作为全球金融行业的巨头，在财富杂志世界 500 强排名当中长期位居前列，2008～2012 年安联集团分别位居世界 500 强第 22、20、20、27 和 28 位。此外，2010 年安联的净利润在欧洲最大的三家保险商当中（法国安盛、意大利忠利、德国安联）位居第一。

安联集团网址：https://www.allianz.com

Part IX. Glossary of Common Sentences
（常用语句集）

1. 出口商

出口商	承诺	保险	代办	We shall arrange insurance on your behalf. 我们将代表你方办理保险。
出口商	承诺	保险	代办	We will effect insurance on your behalf. 我们愿代你方投保。
出口商	承诺	投保	险别	We'll have the goods covered against Free from Particular Average. 我方将为货物投保平安险。
出口商	承诺	投保	险别	Upon receipt of your approval, we will effect insurance for the captioned goods without any delay. 一得到你方批准，我方会立即对标题商品办理保险。
出口商	承诺	投保	险别	We shall cover All Risks and War Risk for you. 我们将为你方投保一切险和战争险。
出口商	介绍	保险	惯例	According to our usual practice, unless the buyers require it, we usually do not cover these special additional risks. 如果买方没有特殊要求，按照惯例，我们通常不投保特殊附加险。
出口商	介绍	保险	惯例	Generally we cover insurance W.P.A and against War Risk in the absence of definite instructions from our clients. 在未收到我方客户的明确指示时，我们通常投保水渍险和战争险。
出口商	介绍	保险	惯例	Our usual practice is to insure shipments for the invoice value plus 10%. 本公司一贯按照发票金额增加10%投保。
出口商	介绍	保险	惯例	We generally insure W.P.A. on CIF sales. 按CIF价出售的货物，我们一般投保水渍险。
出口商	介绍	保险	惯例	We shall insure the goods for 110% of the invoice value. 我们将按发票金额110%投保此货物。
出口商	介绍	保险	惯例	We usually effect insurance against All Risks and War Risk for the invoice value plus 10% on the goods sold on CIF basis. 对于按CIF条款成交的货物，我们通常按发票金额加10%，对货物投保一切险和战争险。
出口商	介绍	保险	惯例	We usually insure with the People's Insurance Company of China for the goods sold on CIF basis. 我们一般对按CIF价出售的货物向中国人民保险公司投保。
出口商	介绍	投保	险别	The goods are to be insured F.P.A. 这批货物将投保平安险。
出口商	介绍承诺	投保	险别	Insurance is to be covered against All Risks and War Risk. 保险将投保一切险和战争险。

续表

出口商	介绍申明	保险	惯例费用	Insurance on the goods shall be covered by us for 110% of the CIF value, and any extra premium for additional coverage, if required, shall be borne by the buyers. 将由我方按照到岸价的发票金额110%办理该货的保险，如果需要，额外增加保险的费用将由买方承担。
出口商	申明	保险	费用	If coverage against other risks is required, such as breakage, leakage, T.P.N.D, hook and contamination damages, the extra premium involved would be for the buyer's account. 如果要加保其它险别，例如破碎险、渗漏险、盗窃遗失险、钩损和污染险等，所产生的额外保险费由买方负担。
出口商	申明	保险	费用	If you desire us to insure against a special risk, an extra premium will have to be charged. 如果你方想要我方投保其他特殊的险别，则须支付额外的费用。
出口商	申明	保险	费用	Since the premium varies with the insurance coverage, extra premium is at buyer's cost. 保险费随保险险别而定，如需增加其他险别，额外保险费由买方支付。
出口商	申明	保险	费用	This kind of additional risk is coverable at a premium of 2%. 这种附加险的保险费为2%。
出口商	申明	保险	费用	We paid the total premium of $1,300. 我们付了总共1300美元的保险费。
出口商	申明	保险	费用	We shall insure W.P.A at your cost. 我们将投保水渍险，费用由你方负担。
出口商	申明	保险	条款	An insurance claim should be submitted to the insurance company or its agents within 30 days after the arrival of the consignment at the port of destination. 保险索赔应在货物到达目的港30天内提交保险公司或其代理商。
出口商	申明	保险	条款	If any damage to the goods occurs, a claim may be filed with the insurance agent at your end, who will undertake to compensate for the loss sustained. 货物如发生损坏，可向贵地的保险代理提出索赔，他们将赔偿你方遭受的损失。
出口商	申明	保险	条款	Insurers here will not underwrite this risk. 此间保险商不承担这种险。
出口商	申明	保险	条款	It is general practice that the insurance is to be covered in the same currency as in the letter of credit. 按惯例，投保币种应和信用证规定的币种一样。
出口商	申明	保险	条款	Should any damage be incurred you may approach the insurance agents at your end and submit an insurance claim supported by a survey report. 如果货物发生损坏，你方可凭检验报告与你处保险代理联系并提出保险索赔。
出口商	通知	保险	已办	We have covered the goods against... 我们已为货物投保了……险。
出口商	通知	保险	已办	We have covered the goods WPA as required by you. 按照你方要求我们给货物投保水渍险。

续表

出口商	通知	保险	已办	We have insured the goods F.P.A. and against All Risks. 我们已将货物投保平安险和一切险。
出口商	同意申明	投保保险	要求费用	We accept your request for insurance to be covered up to the inland city, but the extra premium should be for your account. 我方可接受你要求，将货物投保延至内陆城市，但额外保费须由你方负责。
出口商	同意申明	投保保险	要求费用	We shall cover the goods against War Risk, and the extra premium involved will be for buyer's account. 我们可以对货物投保战争险，但由此产生的额外保费由买方支付。
出口商	协商	保险	险别	We think FPA gives enough protection to all our shipments to your area. 我们认为平安险对于我们发到贵地区的货物已足够了。

2. 进口商

进口商	申明	保险	条款	As our order was placed on a CIF basis, the insurance is to be arranged by you. 由于我方是按 CIF 价订货的，应由你方投保。
进口商	申明	保险	条款	In accordance with the contract No. 3456, you are requested to insure the goods against All Risks at invoice value plus 20%. 根据 3456 号合同，你方须对货物投保一切险，保额为发票金额的 120%。
进口商	委托	保险	代办	Please insure F.P.A. at your end. 请在你处投保平安险。
进口商	委托	保险	代办	Please insure the goods at our cost against damage in transport. 请对货物在运输中的损失投保，费用由我方承担。
进口商	委托	保险	代办	We leave the insurance arrangements to you but we wish to have the goods covered against All Risks. 保险事宜交由你方安排，但希望为该货物投保一切险。
进口商	委托	保险	代办	Will you please arrange to take out all risks insurance for us on the consignment radio receivers from our warehouse to Bombay. 我方有一批收音机，需要从仓库运往孟买，恳请贵方为我们安排投保一切险。
进口商	协商	保险	条款	We are not satisfied with the items of insurance listed in your quotation of 20th. We are wondering whether you can reconsider. 我方对于你方 20 日发来的报价中的保险事项不甚满意。我方想知道你方能否对其重新考虑。
进口商	协商	保险	险别	W.P.A. coverage is too narrow for a shipment of this nature. Please extend the coverage to include T.P.N.D. 针对这种性质的货物只保水渍险是不够的，请加保偷盗提货不着险。
进口商	要求	保险	保额	Insurance is to be covered at invoice value plus 10%. 保险按发票金额 110%投保。

Unit 9 Insurance（保险）

				续表
进口商	要求	保险	保额	Insurance is to be covered for 110% of invoice value. 保险按发票金额110%投保。
进口商	要求	保险	保额	We desire to have the goods insured for 110% of the invoice value. 我们希望按照发票金额的110%对货物办理保险。
进口商	要求	保险	保额	We wish you to insure the goods for the invoice value plus 10%. 我们希望你方按发票金额加10%投保。
进口商	要求	保险	险别	Our customer requests that the shipment be insured against pilferage. 我们的客户要求货物必须投保偷窃险。
进口商	要求	保险	险别	Please cover the goods against War Risk. 请将货物投保战争险。
进口商	要求	保险	险别	We would like to cover the risk of breakage for this lot of goods. 我们想为这批货投保破碎险。
进口商	要求	保险	险别	We must cover Risk of Breakage. 我们必须投保破碎险。
进口商	要求	保险	险别 保额	Pleased see to it that shipment is covered for 150% of invoice value against All Risks. 请注意上述货物保险必须按发票的150%投保综合险。
进口商	要求	保险	险别 保额	Please insure the shipment for RMB 5 000 against All Risks. 请给这批货物保5 000元人民币的综合险。

Unit 10

Complaints and Claims
（投诉与索赔）

Part Ⅰ. Objectives（目标）

After completing this unit, you will be able to

1. read and write English emails and messages to make a complaint or lodge a claim against your business clients when you suffer a loss;

2. read and write English emails and messages to settle a complaint or a claim;

3. become familiar with the typical English terms and sentence patterns commonly used in business emails and messages above.

Part Ⅱ. How to Express（该怎么说）

1. Making a Complaint（进口商投诉）

A：我是买方，收到货物后发现存在一些问题，我要与卖方进行交涉，我该怎么说呢？

B：你可以这样说：

1）559 号合同项下货物质量与合同不符。

2）在打开 45 号箱后，我们发现箱里装的不是我们所订的货。

3）很遗憾，我们只收到 97 箱绿茶，短缺 3 箱。

A：那么，我用英语该怎么说呢？

B：到"常用语句集"去看看，你先找到同类的句型，然后采用截取、替换、拼接的办法稍做加工，你需要的句子就有了。

A：嘿！瞧瞧，我的英语还不错吧！

2. Dealing with Complaints （出口商处理投诉）

A：我是出口商，收到了进口商的投诉。经查，差错在我一方，我要处置投诉，我该怎么说？

B：你可以这样说：

1）我们已经了安排正确的货物，并将立即发往你处。

2）经调查此事，我们发现由于包装时箱号搞错而确实出现差错。

3）我方理解你方的不便和烦恼，并会尽力处理此事，使你方满意。

A：那么，我用英语该怎么说呢？

B：到"常用语句集"去看看，你先找到同类的句型，然后采用截取、替换、拼接的办法稍做加工，你需要的句子就有了。

A：嘿！瞧瞧，我的英语还不错吧！

3. Lodging a Claim （进口商索赔）

A：我是买方，由于卖方的差错给我方造成了损失，现需要索赔，我该怎么说呢？

B：你可以这样说：

1）我们要求你方替换受损货物，并给我5%的折扣来补偿我方损失。

2）很遗憾通知你方，第3号和第4号箱子坏了，损失由你方赔偿。

3）因你方发货短缺500千克，我方不得不提出索赔。

A：那么，我用英语该怎么说呢？

B：到"常用语句集"去看看，你先找到同类的句型，然后采用截取、替换、拼接的办法稍做加工，你需要的句子就有了。

A：嘿！瞧瞧，我的英语还不错吧！

4. Settling Claim（出口商理赔）

A：我是卖方，经调查发现由于我方的过错给买方造成了损失，现同意赔付，我该怎么说呢？

B：你可以这样说：
1）很抱歉将这些有瑕疵的设备寄给了你方，我们今天已将12台替代品寄往你处。
2）我们将汇给你方4 600美元以弥补损失。
3）由于货物已由公证人检验过，我们打算接受你方对于500千克短重的索赔。

A：那么，我用英语该怎么说呢？

B：到"常用语句集"去看看，你先找到同类的句型，然后采用截取、替换、拼接的办法稍做加工，你需要的句子就有了。

A：嘿！瞧瞧，我的英语还不错吧！

5. Rejecting Claims（出口商拒绝赔付）

A：我是卖方，现收到买方的索赔。经调查，发现对方的索赔要求不当，应予以拒绝，我该怎么说呢？

B：你可以这样说：
1）你方所提供的证明不充分，因此我方不能考虑你方的索赔要求。
2）我们很抱歉难以接受你们的索赔，因为损坏是在途中发生的。
3）由于此批货已办理保险，你可以将此事提交保险公司或其在你地的代理人处理。

A：那么，我用英语该怎么说呢？

B：到"常用语句集"去看看，你先找到同类的句型，然后采用截取、替换、拼接的办法稍做加工，你需要的句子就有了。

A：嘿！瞧瞧，我的英语还不错吧！

Part III. Case（案例）

1. Complaining of Wrong Delivery （进口商投诉货物错发）

2015年5月美国纽约哈德森有限公司（Harderson Co., Ltd.）的销售经理Geoff Pullar向浙江华丽针织袜业有限公司（Zhejiang Huali Kniting Socks Co., Ltd.）订购了1 000打羊毛男袜。7月20日货物抵达目的港，但是Geoff Pullar检查后发现箱内装的是1 000打女式莱尔线袜（women's lisle stockings），并非他们所订的货物。所以他发邮件给浙江华丽针织袜业有限公司的销售经理王平，投诉货物错发，并要求立即换货。

发件人(From)	geoff@harderson.com
收件人(To)	WP@huali-socks.com
主题（Subject）	Wrong dispatch of our Order No. F2432
附件（Attachment）	Order No. F2432

Dear Mr. Wang,

We are writing to complain about the shipment of our Order No. F2432 for 1 000 dozen men's woolen stockings received this morning. These were ordered on May 20, 2015 and confirmed by fax on May 21 (attached copy). However, upon opening the boxes, we found that they contained 1 000 dozen women's lisle ones.

We have to ask you to arrange for the dispatch of replacement at once as we need the stockings we ordered to complete deliveries to our new customers.

Meanwhile, we are holding the mentioned stockings at your disposal. Please let us know what to do with it.

Best regards,

Geoff Pullar

Harderson Co., Ltd.

Sentence Patterns Applied（语句归纳）
- 进口商抱怨订单货物错发；
- 进口商催促（重新）发货；
- 进口商申明错发货物保管的费用承担，询问对错发货物的处理意见。

2. Dealing with Wrong Delivery（出口商处置货物错发）

浙江华丽针织袜业有限公司的销售经理王平收到了 Geoff Pullar 的投诉，他调查发现，由于包装时把订单编号弄混了，把 Geoff 和另一个客户的货调换后出现了错发。现在，王平已经安排正确的货物发出，相关手续办好后将马上发给对方，不日将抵达对方所在地，请求对方将错发的货物退换。

现在，你是销售经理王平，你需要回复邮件处置货物错发。

Sentence Patterns for Reference（参考语句）
- 出口商收到投诉，表达遗憾；
- 出口商解释造成差错的缘由，致歉；
- 出口商要求退回货物（理赔），装运替代货物（理赔），寄送单据；
- 出口商致歉，期望继续合作。

发件人（From）	
收件人（To）	
主题（Subject）	

3. Making a Claim（进口商索赔）

2015 年 3 月，上海恒昌贸易有限公司（Shanghai Hengchang Trade Co., Ltd.）的业务经理孙虹与美国纽约哈德森有限公司（Harderson Co., Ltd.）签订了第 564 号购销合同，向对方订购 10 公吨小麦粉（wheat flour）。6 月 15 日，货物抵达目的港，在检查货物时发现有 50 袋包装破损。随后安排检验，发现损失面粉 1 000 千克，损失是由于包装袋不合标准引致。孙虹随后发电邮给哈德森公司的销售经理 Geoff Pullar，向对方提出索赔，并附上第 TS6478 号检验报告（Survey Report）。索赔包括：损失 1 000 千克小麦粉折价 483 美元，检验费 70 美元，合计 553 美元。

现在你是孙虹，请你发邮件索赔。

Sentence Patterns for Reference（参考语句）
- 进口商收到货物；
- 进口商抱怨包装破损，货物受损；
- 进口商抱怨货物短量，说明受损原因（抱怨包装劣质），申明责任方；
- 进口商索赔；
- 进口商附寄检验报告，期盼回复。

发件人（From）	
收件人（To）	
主题（Subject）	
附件（Attachment）	

4. Accepting Claim（出口商同意理赔）

Geoff 收到孙虹的电邮和检验报告后，即刻进行了调查，核查发现短重确实是由于 50 袋小麦粉没有按照合同规定的 5 层耐用纸袋包装，使得部分货物包装在运输途中破损。

Geoff 向孙虹回复电邮，告知核查结果，为己方的过错道歉，并表示同意支付索赔 553 美元。

发件人（From）	geoff@harderson.com
收件人（To）	sunhong@hengchang.com
主题（Subject）	Claim for 1,000 kgs short weight of wheat flour

Dear Ms. Sun,

With reference to your claim for short delivery of 1 000 kgs of wheat flour, we wish to express our deep regret over the incident.

After a check-up by our staff, it was found that part of the consignment was not packed in 5-ply strong paper bags as specified in the contract, thus resulting in the breakage during transit, for which we tender our apologies.

We are most concerned to maintain our long-standing trading relationship. We, therefore, will make payment for US$553.00, the amount of the claim, into your account with the Bank of China, upon receipt of your agreement.

We trust that this unfortunate error will not affect our future relations.

Best regards,

Geoff Pullar

Sentence Patterns Applied（语句归纳）
- 出口商收到索赔邮件，表达遗憾；
- 出口商答复索赔，解释缘由（承担责任），道歉；
- 出口商表达良好愿望，珍视关系，理赔。

Part Ⅳ. Writing Directions（写作指导）

国际贸易中，当一方认为对方未能全部或部分履行合同，通常就提出抱怨或索赔。抱怨就是向对方提意见、申诉或投诉，索赔就是要求赔偿损失。

此类信函需要讲究策略和技巧，要掌握好语气和措辞。一方面抱怨、投诉不能拖延，反映问题要依据事实，尽量清楚具体；另一方面，必须克制情绪，切忌态度粗暴、得理不饶人。抱怨和索赔的目的是为了得到对方更好的服务和合理的赔偿，而不是为了指责对方，更不是攻击个人。

在接到抱怨与索赔后，应该尽快回复，即使一时不能做出答复，也要解释问题正在调查。如果问题的确是由于己方的过错引起，应立即承认并道歉，并承诺解决措施。如果抱怨、索赔不合理，应该礼貌地指出，不使对方难堪。不论对方的抱怨与索赔多么微不足道，应该一律谨慎对待，认真回复。

这类信函的特点：开门见山，描述清楚，态度明确，有礼有节。

抱怨

抱怨包括以下内容：
- 提出抱怨，表达遗憾；
- 陈述事实，说明出现的差错；
- 要求予以解释；
- 提及由此而造成的不便；
- 询问对方的处理措施，或提出己方的纠正建议；
- 期盼回复。

回复抱怨

回复应该包括：
- 对来信表示感谢；
- 对给对方造成不便表示歉意；
- 说明造成差错的缘由；
- 说明将采取的措施；
- 期待进一步合作。

索赔

索赔一般包括以下要点：
- 告知相关订单项下的货物出现差错；
- 描述详细情形；
- 提供证明、鉴定报告等；
- 提出具体的索赔要求；
- 要求对方采取相应措施，如换货、维修、退款或赔偿；
- 期盼回复。

回复索赔

回复索赔要点如下：
- 对出现差错表示歉意；
- 承诺采取纠正措施；
- 说明差错的缘由；
- 对以后做出保证；
- 期待以后的合作。

Part V. Terms and Sentence Frames
（术语与句型）

1. Terms（术语）

各种索赔

a claim arising from a breach of the contract 违约所引起的赔偿要求

a claim arising from a defect of the goods 货物瑕疵所引起的索赔

a claim arising on a bill of lading 有关提单引起的索赔

a claim based on lack of conformity of the goods 货物不符产生的索赔

a claim based on physical loss damage 货物灭失所产生的索赔

a claim for compensation of damages 损害赔偿的诉权

a claim for contribution in general average 要求分摊共同海损

a claim for damage 由于损坏的索赔

a claim for financial loss 关于经济损失的诉权

a claim for general average 分摊共同海损的诉权

a claim for short delivery 由于短交的索赔

a claim for inferior quality 由于品质低劣的索赔

抱怨索赔缘由

short delivery 短交
short shipment 短运
short weight 短重
inferior quality 质量低劣
inherent vice 内在缺陷
conglomeration 结块
fermentation 发酵
leakage 渗漏
blown cans 膨听（罐头）
rust stains 锈斑
vermin bitten 虫咬
water stain 水渍

检验报告

Survey Report on Examination of Damage or Shortage 检验残损证明书
Survey Report on Inspection of Tank Hold 船舱鉴定证明书
Survey Report on Quality 品质鉴定证明书
Survey Report on Weight 重量鉴定证明书
Certificate of Inspection 检验证书

常见检验机构

CCIC 中国进出口商品检验总公司
CIQ 中华人民共和国出入境检验检疫局
FDA 美国食品药物管理局
SGS 瑞士日内瓦通用鉴定公司
OMIC 日本海外货物检验株式会社
UL 美国保险人实验室
Lloyd's Surveyor 英国劳合氏公证行
B.V 法国船级社

2. Sentence Frames（句型）

抱怨

to make a complaint with … about sth. 因某事向……抱怨
to lodge a complaint with … about sth. 因某事向……抱怨
to lay a complaint with … about sth. 因某事向……抱怨
to file a complaint with … about sth. 因某事向……抱怨

to complain to sb. of (about) sth. 向某人抱怨

提出索赔

to claim US$10,000 索赔美元 1 万元

to claim a compensation of US$10,000 要求赔偿美元 1 万元

to claim US$10,000 for damage 因损坏赔偿美元 1 万元

to claim US$10,000 on the goods 对该货索赔美元 1 万元

to claim US$10,000 from the underwriters 向保险公司索赔美元 1 万元

to claim on/upon us for inferior quality 因质次向我方提出索赔

to lodge / raise / file / put in / make / issue / lay / register / render / enter/ bring up / set up a claim against / with /on / upon sb. for sth. 因为某种原因向某人提出索赔

to reserve the right to claim 保留索赔权

to waive a claim 放弃索赔

to withdraw a claim 撤回索赔

to relinquish a claim 撤回索赔

理赔

to accept a claim 同意索赔

to admit a claim 同意索赔

to entertain a claim 受理索赔

to settle a claim 解决索赔，理赔

to dismiss a claim 驳回索赔

to reject a claim 驳回索赔

Part VI. Follow Me （跟我写）

Making a Claim(进口商为包装破损索赔)

电子邮件模板

Dear Mr./Ms._（对方的姓）_,

We regret having to inform you that _（货物的数量与名称）_ covered by our Order No. _（订单号）_ and shipped per s/s _（货轮号）_ arrived in such an unsatisfactory condition that we cannot but lodge a claim against you.

It was found upon examination that nearly _（受损货物的箱数）_ of the packages had been broken, obviously attributed to improper packing. Our only recourse (追索，要求赔偿), in consequence, was to have them repacked before delivering to our customers, which inevitably resulted in extra expenses amounting to _（我方我重新包装所支付的费_

用）. We expect compensation from you for this.

We are attaching one copy of Inspection Certificate No. ＿（检验证书的编号）＿ together with our Statement of Claims.

Please give our claim your most favorable consideration and let us have your settlement at an early date.

Best regards,

（署名）

贸易背景

Smith 先生向张晨先生所在的公司订购了 3 000 套衬衣（3,000 shirts），订单号为 6013。4 月 20 日货物经"和平号"（Peace）货轮运抵目的港后，经检查发现货物的包装十分糟糕，以致将近 20%的包装(20% of the packages)破损。检验部门出具了编号为 BD2009 的检验证书。Smith 重新包装了破损的货物，为此花费 650 美元。

于是，Smith 先生把检验证书和索赔声明发给张晨，要求偿付 650 美元的额外支出。

仿照模板套写

Part Ⅶ. Practical Writing （实训写作）

1. Match the words and phrases with their Chinese meanings.

claim   投诉
short delivery   质量低劣

CIQ	商检局
Complaint	索赔
settle a claim	提出索赔
lodge a claim	短交
make a complaint	检验报告
inferior quality	检验证书
survey report	理赔
inspection certificate	进行投诉

2. Read the following email and list its main points.

Thank you for your mail of 15 May referring to the consignment of cotton goods sent to you per S.S. Ocean Emperor. We regret to note your complaint.

We have investigated the matter thoroughly. As far as we can ascertain, the goods were in first class condition when they left here. The bill of lading is evidence for this. It is obvious that the damage you complain of must have taken place during transit. It follows, therefore, that we cannot be held responsible for the damage.

We therefore advise you to make a claim on the shipping company, Emperor Line, who should be held responsible. We are grateful that you have brought the matter to our attention. If you wish, we would be happy to take issue with the shipping company on your behalf.

We look forward to resolving this matter as soon as possible.

----

3. Complete each of the following sentences according to its model given.

1）After re-inspection, we found that the quality of the goods was not in conformity with the contract.

After re-inspection, we found that the quality of the goods (与样品不符)_____ _____.

2）We are sorry to learn that the quality of your goods is not up to the agreed specifications.

Your goods are (达不到标准) _____ commonly accepted.

3）Your last shipment is so disappointing that we have to lodge a complaint against you.

The delivered goods are in such bad condition that we have to (向你方投诉)_____.

4) On unwrapping the cases, we found the goods partly soaked by rain.

On examining the goods, we found (有7箱破损) _____.

5) Please send the goods we need to replace those damaged during transit.

Please send the right goods to replace (发错的货物)_____.

6) We lodge a claim with you for a short delivery of 50 pieces.

We make a claim with you for (短重50千克)_____.

7) We raise a claim amounting to US$600 plus inspection charge.

(我们提出索赔金额为450美元)_____ for the loss.

8) We confirm having received your remittance of US$780 in settlement of our claim.

We are offering you a discount of 10% (作为理赔) _____.

9) The evidence provided by you is not sufficient, so we cannot entertain your claim.

The cases were(完好无损)_____, so we find it difficult to accept your claim.

10) We are not responsible for the loss resulted from the rough handling during transit.

We are（对损坏不负责）_____ which happened during transit.

4. Complete the following mail of complaint with words and phrases given in the box.

| 1) match | 2) Supply | 3) replace |
| 4) quality | 5) resolve | |

Dear Sirs,

Our order No.CM365 of 6 July for upholstery materials has now been delivered.

We have examined the shipment carefully and, to our great disappointment, find that they are not of the _____ we ordered.

The materials do not _____ the samples you sent us. The quality of some of them is so poor that we feel that a mistake has been made in making up the order.

The goods do not match the requirements of our company. We have, therefore, no choice but to ask you to take the materials back and _____ them with materials of the quality we ordered.

We are very keen to _____ this matter amicably. If you can replace the materials, we are prepared to allow the agreed delivery time to run from the date you confirm that you can _____ the correct materials.

We look forward to your early reply.

Best regards,

5. Complete the following mail of dealing with a complaint with words and phrases given in the box.

1）contents	2）Contain	3）order
4）documents	5）inconvenience	

Dear Sirs,

Thank you for your letter of Mar. 12 referring to your Order No.252. We are glad to hear that the consignment was delivered promptly.

We regret, however, that case No.46 did not _____ the goods you ordered. We have investigated the matter and find that we did make a mistake in putting the _____ together.

We have arranged for the correct goods to be dispatched to you at once. The relevant _____ will be mailed to you as soon as they are ready.

Please keep case No.46 and its _____ until called for by our agents who have been informed of the situation.

We apologize for the _____ caused by our error.

Best regard,

（署名）

Part Ⅷ. Linkage（知识链接）

中国检验认证（集团）有限公司

中国检验认证(集团)有限公司（China Certification & Inspection (Group) Co., Ltd., CCIC）是经国务院批准成立，在国家工商总局登记注册，以"检验、鉴定、认证、测试"为主业的跨国检验认证机构。

该公司与全球许多国家和地区的检验认证机构建立良好的合作关系，如：国际知名的 UL（美国安全检测试验所）、CSA（加拿大标准协会）、TUV（德国莱茵技术监护顾问有限公司）、ITS（天祥公证行）、JET（日本电气安全环境研究所）等。

国家质量监督检验检疫总局

国家质量监督检验检疫总局(General Administration of Quality Supervision, Inspection and Quarantine of the People's Republic of China, 缩写为 AQSIQ)，是国务院主管全国质量、计量、出入境商品检验、出入境卫生检疫、出入境动植物检疫和认证认可、标准化等工作，并行使行政执法职能的直属机构。

Part IX. Glossary of Common Sentences
（常用语句集）

1. 出口商

出口商	抱怨	付款	延误	Unfortunately, we have not yet received payment for your order of August 10th. 遗憾的是，我们至今仍未收到您 8 月 10 日所下订单的货款。
出口商	抱怨	信用证	延误	If your L/C fails to reach us by the end of July, we will be forced to cancel your order. 如果信用证不能在 7 月底前抵达，我方将不得不取消你方订单。
出口商	抱怨	信用证	延误	We regret that we could not ship the goods by a May vessel only because of the delay of your L/C. Please attend to this matter with all speed. 十分遗憾，由于你方信用证耽误，我们不能在 5 月份装船。请快速解决此问题。
出口商	承诺	理赔		We propose to have the goods inspected immediately. If the inspection confirms the accuracy of your estimate, compensation will be allowed at once. 我们请求迅速检查这批货物，如检查确认你方估计准确，我们会马上赔偿。
出口商	答复	抱怨	短量	The alleged shortage might have occurred in the course of transit, and that is a matter over which we can exercise no control. 所提的短缺也许是在运输途中发生的，这是我方无法控制的事情。
出口商	答复	抱怨	延误	We apologize for the delay and hope you will understand that it is due entirely to causes beyond our control. 对于延误我们深表歉意，希望你们了解这完全是我们无法控制的原因造成的。
出口商	答复	抱怨	延误	We are not responsible for the delay. The shipper must be held responsible. 延误的责任不在我方。必须由承运人负责。
出口商	答复	抱怨		I'll try to answer each of your questions one by one. 我会按顺序回答您的每个问题。
出口商	答复	索赔		As the goods have been insured, you may refer the matter to the insurance company or their agents at your end. 由于此批货已办理保险，你可以将此事提交保险公司或其在你地的代理人处理。

				续表
出口商	答复	索赔		As the shipping company is liable for the damage, your claim, in our opinion, should be referred to them for settlement. 由于船运公司对货物的损坏负责，我们的意见是你方应将索赔提交他们处理。
出口商	答复	索赔		I have directed your inquiry to our technical staff. 我已经把你的问题转给我们的技术人员。
出口商	答复	索赔		I'll consult with my boss and give you a reply later. 我要请示我的上司后才能答复您。
出口商	答复	索赔		It is established beyond controversy that the shipping company is responsible for the damage of the goods in transit. 确定无可争议的是，船运公司对货物在运输途中受损负有责任。
出口商	拒绝	理赔		Such color deviation existing between the products and the samples is normal and permissible. Therefore, the claim for compensation is unacceptable. 产品和样品之间的这种色差是正常的也是被允许的。所以，索赔是不能接受的。
出口商	拒绝	理赔		We must repudiate our liability for the claim on account of lack of evidence. 由于缺乏证据，我们拒绝对你方索赔负责。
出口商	拒绝	理赔		We regret that we cannot entertain your claim, as it has nothing to do with us. 很遗憾我们不能接受索赔，因为事情根本与我们无关。
出口商	拒绝	理赔		We regret we cannot entertain your claim, which is without any foundation. 很遗憾我们不能受理你方索赔，它没有任何根据。
出口商	拒绝	理赔		You claim should be supported by sufficient evidence. 贵方索赔须有充分证据。
出口商	理赔	货物	错发	On reviewing the matter, we find a mistake was indeed made in the packing through confusion in numbers. We have arranged for the right goods to be dispatched to you at once. 通过调查此事，我们发现由于在包装时弄混了号码而确实出现了差错。我们已立即重新安排货物发送你方。
出口商	理赔	货物	错发	The misplaced piece may be returned to us per next available transport for our account, but it is preferable if you can dispose of them in your market. 这批弄错的货物将由我方负责，我方会安排第二批可装运的轮船退回我方，但如果能在你们的市场上处理掉该货更好。
出口商	理赔	货物	错发	We have arranged for the replacement goods to be dispatched to you at once in settlement of your claim. 现已安排立即运送替换货物以解决你方索赔要求。
出口商	理赔	货物	不符	Though we find no difference between the shipping sample and the original sample in our hands, we will meet you halfway by offering a discount of 10% in settlement of the dispute. 虽然出货样与手边之原样相同，但我们仍愿意做出让步，减价10%以解决争端。

出口商	理赔	货物	劣质	We are sorry to learn of your complaints about the quality of the goods and are prepared to accept your claim. 我们遗憾地得知你方关于货物质量的意见，并准备接受索赔要求。
出口商	理赔			I propose we compensate you by 3% of the total value plus inspection fee. 我想我们赔偿贵方3%的损失，另外加上商检费。
出口商	理赔			Would you please return the broken items so that we can claim from our insurance company. 请退回破损的货品以便我方能向保险公司索赔。
出口商	致歉	交货	延期	I would like to apologize for the lengthy delay in shipping your order. 我要为交货延迟这么长时间而向您道歉。
出口商	致歉	交货	延期	We apologize for the delay in shipping your order. 我们对交货延误深感抱歉。
出口商	致歉	交货	延期	We are sorry about the inconvenience of the delay. 对延迟交货造成的不便我们很遗憾。
出口商	致歉			I would apologize to your company on behalf of our company. 我愿代表我公司向贵公司道歉。
出口商	致歉			We are sorry for the trouble caused by the error and wish to assure you that much care will be taken in your future orders. 对此次失误我方甚感抱歉，以后的订单我方会多加注意。

2. 进口商

进口商	抱怨	包装	不当	Apparently, it was due to careless packing. 很明显是包装太马虎了。
进口商	抱怨	包装	不当	In our opinion, the damage was caused by improper packing. A machine of this size and weight should be blocked in position inside the export case. 在我们看来，货物破损是由于包装不妥所致。一台这样尺码和重量的机械应该是固定在箱内的。
进口商	抱怨	包装	不当	It was found upon examination that nearly 30% of the packages had been broken, obviously attributed to improper packing. 经检查发现将近30%的包装已破损，很明显是因为包装不当造成的。
进口商	抱怨	包装	不当	The packing inside the case was too loose with the result that there was some shifting of the contents and several cups and plates have been broken. The attached list will give you details. 该货的包装太松，因此里面的货有点移动，几个杯子和碟子已破损。现随寄清单供你方参考。
进口商	抱怨	包装	不当	The result of our investigation showed that the damage was caused in the first place by inadequate packaging, which allowed damages to the packages. 我们调查的结果是，首先是由于包装不合格，才使这些包装箱受损。

进口商	抱怨	包装	不当	We have had the case and its contents examined by the insurance surveyor but, as you will see from the attached copy of this report, he maintains that the damage was probably due to insecure packing and not to any unduly rough handling of the case. 我方让保险检验员检查了箱外以及箱内货物，如附件中的报告单复印件所示，他认为货物的损坏可能是由包装不当引起的，而不是由粗鲁搬运所致。
进口商	抱怨	包装	劣质	The quality of your wine is fine, but its packing is rather poor. Bottles are subjected to breakage and paper boxes are very thin. 你们的酒质量很好，但包装较差，瓶子易碎，纸盒太薄。
进口商	抱怨	包装	劣质	According to the report, the damage was caused by poor packing. 根据报告上的鉴定，破损原因是包装太差。
进口商	抱怨	包装	破损	Several boxes were broken and the contents damaged. 有数箱破损，内装货物受损。
进口商	抱怨	包装	破损	We are sorry to inform you that of the shipment received there are 30 broken bags. 我们很遗憾地告知你们在到达的货物中有 30 个包破损。
进口商	抱怨	包装	破损	We regret to inform you that 20 cartons were damaged and the contents spilled, leading to some losses. 遗憾地通知你方，货物到达时 20 个纸箱破裂，箱内物品撒落导致一定的损失。
进口商	抱怨	货物	错发	On examination we find that the consignment does not correspond with the original sample. 检查后我们发现这批货与原来的样品不一样。
进口商	抱怨	货物	错发	Unfortunately, on opening the case, we found it contained completely different articles, and we can only presume that a mistake was made and the contents of this case were for another order. 不幸的是，在开箱后我们发现，箱里装的是完全不同的货物，我们只能猜想，箱内物品是属于另一订单的。
进口商	抱怨	货物	错发	We are sorry to say you delivered the wrong goods. We ordered Model 124 but you sent us Model 123. 很遗憾你们发错了货。我们订的是 124 型，你们寄来的是 123 型。
进口商	抱怨	货物	错发	What we have received is not what we ordered. 我们收到的货物并不是我们所订购的。
进口商	抱怨	货物	错发	You have evidently sent us the wrong goods, and, as we are in a hurry for the shirts that we order, this error is inconvenient and annoying. 你方肯定发错了货。由于我们急需这批所订的衬衫，这次差错给我方带来了极大的不便和困扰。
进口商	抱怨	货物	错发	You have sent us the wrong goods and we are in urgent need of the goods we ordered. 贵方将货发错，而我方急需所订货物。

续表

进口商	抱怨	货物	短量	According to the surveyor's report, there was a shortage of 300 pounds. 根据检验报告，短缺 300 磅。
进口商	抱怨	货物	短量	Five boxes were missing from the consignment delivered to us today. 今天交给我们的货物缺少 5 箱。
进口商	抱怨	货物	短量	On checking the consignment we have found that one case under B/L No. 311 is missing and the Case No. is 100-97. 经验收，我们发现第 311 号提单项下的一箱货丢失，箱号为 100-97。
进口商	抱怨	货物	短量	There is a difference of 25 tons between the actual loaded weight and the invoice weight. 实际重量和发票重量相差 25 吨。
进口商	抱怨	货物	短量	There is a discrepancy between the packing list of Case No. 53 and your invoice: 3 dozen Tea Sets are correctly entered on the invoice but there were only 2 dozen in the case. 53 号箱的装箱单与你方发票有差异：发票上所签的是 3 打茶具而箱子里只有 2 打。
进口商	抱怨	货物	短量	Upon examination we find that the cases weight is short by 5 to 12 Pounds. 经检查，我们发现货箱短重 5～12 磅。
进口商	抱怨	货物	不符	After re-examination, we found that the quality of the goods was not in conformity with the contract stipulations. 复验后发现，质量与合同规定不符。
进口商	抱怨	货物	不符	After reinspection at the port of destination, the quality of the goods under Contract No. 559 was found not in compliance with the contract stipulation. 在目的地复验后，发现 559 号合同项下货物质量与合同不符。
进口商	抱怨	货物	不符	On examination we have found that the goods do not agree with the original samples. 经过检查我方发现货物与样品的质量不符。
进口商	抱怨	货物	不符	The goods submitted do not correspond with the sample sent. 到货与所送样品不一致。
进口商	抱怨	货物	不符	The products do not match the sample you sent us. 产品与你方所送样品不符。
进口商	抱怨	货物	质量	This consignment is not even up to your own standard. 这批货甚至没有达到你们自己的标准。
进口商	抱怨	货物	质量	Upon examining the goods, we discovered to our surprise that they were altogether inferior in quality to the samples on which we placed the order. 经检查，我们惊讶地发现所有货物的质量与所订的样品完全不符。
进口商	抱怨	货物	质量	We are sorry to learn that the quality of your shipment is not up to the agreed specifications. 我们遗憾地发现你方货物的质量达不到所商定的标准。

续表

进口商	抱怨	货物	质量	We have examined the shipment carefully and to our great disappointment, found that they are not of the quality we ordered. 我们仔细检查了此批货物，令人十分失望的是，发现这批货的质量与我方所订的不符。
进口商	抱怨	货物	花色	We regret to complain that your consignment of cotton goods shipped by s.s. "Taching" is not of the color of the sample piece. 你方由"大庆"号轮所装的棉匹布的颜色与样品布不符，我们对此表示不满。
进口商	抱怨	货物	花色	When unpacking the case, we found the color unsatisfactory. 开箱后，我方发现颜色令人不满意。
进口商	抱怨	货物	受潮	We found two cartons were completely wet. 我们发现有两箱完全受潮。
进口商	抱怨	货物	受损	On examination, we have found that many of the sewing machines are severely damaged, though the cases themselves show no trace of damage. 在检查时，我方发现许多缝纫机损坏严重，可是货箱本身没有损坏的痕迹。
进口商	抱怨	货物	受损	The items in two of the crates were damaged. 两个箱中的商品有损坏。
进口商	抱怨	货物	受损	The ship encountered heavy weather, and 252 cases were damaged by sea water. 货船遇到了恶劣天气，252箱茶叶被海水损坏。
进口商	抱怨	货物	受损	Upon examination, we found that many of the goods were severely damaged, though the case showed no trace of damage. 经过检查，发现许多货物严重破损，尽管箱子未出现任何破损痕迹。
进口商	抱怨	货物	受损	We have examined them one by one, and found that they were all leaking. 我们将货物逐个检查，发现几乎每件都有泄漏。
进口商	抱怨	交货	延期	I have not yet received the computer hardware that I ordered over six weeks ago. 我6周以前订购的电脑硬件至今仍未收到。
进口商	抱怨	交货	延期	In your email of July 8, you assured us that we would receive the goods by July 31. 您在7月8日的邮件中向我们保证过7月31日能收到货物。
进口商	抱怨	交货	延误	Regarding our Order No. 337, we have to point out that you only delivered 1,000 pieces in May, and the shipment of the remaining 1,000 pieces is long overdue. 关于我们337号订单，我们必须指出你方5月只交了1 000件，剩下1000件的装运期早已过期。
进口商	抱怨	交货	延误	This is not the first time delay in delivery has occurred. We are sorry to point out that business cannot be continued like this any longer. 很遗憾这已经不是第一次延迟交货。我们必须指出不能再如此做生意了。

Unit 10　Complaints and Claims　（投诉与索赔）

进口商	抱怨	交货	延误	We are now in a very awkward situation because our customers are very impatient to take delivery of the goods. 我们现在很为难，因为我们的客户急于提货。
进口商	抱怨	交货	延误	We have been dealing with your company for more than three years, during which time we have been satisfied with your delivery. However, you have started to deliver later than agreed lately. On two occasions, we have failed to meet our own deadlines because of your delays. 我们与贵方做生意已有3年多了，我们一直对你们的交货感到满意。但是，你们最近开始迟交货，有两次由于你们延迟交货使得我们没能赶上自己的交货期。
进口商	抱怨	装运	延误	Your shipment delay has put us in a very difficult position, for which we have to make many explanations. 你方的迟装已把我们置于非常困难的境地，为此，我们不得不给我方客户做出许多尴尬的解释。
进口商	抱怨	装运	延误	Your shipment is so late that we have a lot of difficulty in the disposal of the goods. 贵方装运过迟，致使我们难以处理这批货物。
进口商	抱怨		延误	This delay is threatening the loss of our best customers. 这次延误将使我们失去最好的客户。
进口商	抱怨			We are writing this email to complain about Order No. 339 to Mexico. 我方对发往墨西哥的339号订单提出申诉。
进口商	抱怨			We hope that similar cases will not recur. 我们希望类似的事情不要再发生。
进口商	索赔	货物	短量	Buyers have lodged a claim on this shipment for RMB 1 500 for short weight. 由于分量短少，买主对此批货物索赔人民币1 500元。
进口商	索赔	货物	短量	We filed a claim with you for the short weight. 关于短量问题，我们已经向你方提出索赔。
进口商	索赔	货物	短量	We lodge a claim with you for a short delivery of 50 kg. 货物少交了50千克，我们向你们提出索赔。
进口商	索赔	货物	短量	Your shipment of our Order No. 298 was found to be short weighted by 1,000 kgs for which we must file a claim amounting to £987 plus inspection fee. 我方298号订货短重1,000千克，为此我们必须提出索赔，共计987英镑外加检验费。
进口商	索赔	货物	损失	We are therefore, compelled to make a claim against you to compensate us for the loss, $27,500, which we have sustained by the damage to the goods. 因此，我方被迫向贵方提出索赔，来补偿我方由于货物受损而遭受的27 500美元损失。
进口商	索赔	装运	延误	We have to hold you responsible for any loss that may occur to us through the delay. 我们不得不让你方对延期而造成的损失负责。

参考文献

[1] （美）约翰·伍兹. 商务信函：2500 成功沟通范例. 王楚明译. 上海：上海人民出版社，2002.
[2] MAYMARK 语言学习工作室. 英文商用 E-mail 强化对策. 西安：世界图书出版公司西安分公司，2007.
[3] 王美玲. 商务英语函电. 北京：中国商务出版社，2007.
[4] 葛欣，王欢. 英文 E-mail 写作 100 主题. 北京：外文出版社，2008.
[5] 李爽. 国际商务函电. 北京：清华大学出版社，2008.
[6] 方宁，王维平. 商务英语函电. 北京：机械工业出版社，2008.
[7] 刘嵩，曲丽君. 纺织服装外贸英语函电. 北京：中国纺织出版社，2008.
[8] 徐明莺，李强. 无敌商务英语信函. 大连：大连理工大学出版社，2009.
[9] 王金荣. 贸易函电英文写作案例大全. 北京：中国宇航出版社，2009.
[10] 蔡文芳. 外贸英语函电. 上海：上海交通大学出版社，2009.
[11] LAWPACK. Business Letters & Emails MADE EASY. London：2010.
[12] 罗慕谦. 英文商务书信范例&应用. 上海：华东理工大学出版社，2011.
[13] 胡鉴明. 商务英语函电. 北京：中国商务出版社，2011.
[14] 伊辉春. 外贸英语信函写作. 北京：高等教育出版社，2011.
[15] 刘裕. 巧用外贸邮件拿订单. 北京：中国海关出版社，2013.
[16] 王乃彦. 商务英语函电. 北京：清华大学出版社，2013.
[17] 陆墨珠. 国际商务函电. 北京：中国商务出版社，2013.
[18] 葛萍，周维家. 外贸英语函电. 上海：复旦大学出版社，2014.
[19] 林继玲，莫馥宁. 外贸英语函电. 北京：机械工业出版社，2014.
[20] 兰天. 外贸英语函电. 大连：东北财经大学出版社，2015.
[21] 张慧庭英语研发团队. 英文 E-mail 实用大全. 南京：江苏凤凰科学技术出版社，2015.